The
Pick of Punch

THE PICK OF PUNCH

Selected and Introduced by
Miles Kington

LONDON
The Folio Society
1998

Set in Garamond at The Folio Society
Printed on Balmoral Wove paper by
Butler & Tanner Ltd, Frome and
bound by them in material printed
with a design by Helen Smithson
incorporating Punch cartoons

CONTENTS

5

6

CARTOONS

INTRODUCTION

When I left Oxford in 1963, I only wanted to do one thing: write humour. In my last university days I met another young man who wanted to be a comic writer, called Terry Jones, and together we determined to collaborate on some of the most brilliant comedy scripts ever to hit the BBC. By the time we had written together for a year and had nothing accepted, it began to dawn on us that either the BBC was blind to talent or we were doing something wrong.

It was Terry who worked it out first.

One day he took me aside and said: 'Look, Miles, I think to be honest we are going in different directions. I want to write stuff to be performed, preferably stuff that I can perform myself, whereas I think you just want to write for the printed page. I honestly think we would be better off going our separate ways. Together it's not going to work. In any case, there's a friend of mine just leaving Oxford called Michael Palin who I want to write with . . .'

What Terry was saying (apart from the fact that he wanted to write with Michael Palin) was that I was a humorous writer by bent and he was a comedy writer. He wanted to get up on stage. I wanted to see my words in print. He wanted to see his face on TV. I wanted to see my name at the top of articles. How right he was proved by the fact that half a dozen years later he was one-sixth of *Monty Python's Flying Circus*, while I was one-sixth of the staff of *Punch* magazine. In other words, he was facing firmly into the future and I was facing fearlessly into the past.

Effectively, the pedestal occupied by the humorous writer, and probably by the cartoonist too, has been forcibly repossessed, and they have both been replaced by the comedy writer, and the strip cartoonist and the animator. There is still a place for a humorous columnist like me, as there is for the travelling rug, the open log fire and the individually hand-crafted stink bomb, but I have to recognise that history has passed on by another route, into television and film, and that I am in danger of becoming part of a heritage industry.

Nevetheless, there was a time when the humorist and the cartoonist were the most modern comic performing animals it was possible to conceive, and *Punch* was the repository of the best of them, and if we look back to its golden days we will see both at their best. Not only that, but I was incredibly lucky to be a staff member of *Punch* while it was still within hailing distance of its great days, and after visiting the archives for the purpose of assembling this book, I am not sure that the golden days weren't closer to the present than we generally think.

At any rate, the things that made me laugh out loud were almost all written or drawn within the last fifty years or so, and for the contents of this book I have drawn largely on the years 1950–80. Now, I know this is not conventional wisdom. I know that the golden age of *Punch* cartooning is generally said to centre on Leech and Keene, and later on Phil May and du Maurier, and that the great writers of *Punch* were the A. P. Herberts and E. V. Knoxes and H. F. Ellises from before 1950. Well, yes and no. Yes, they drew and wrote beautifully. No, they don't seem that funny any more.

But then it was always said of *Punch* that it wasn't funny any more. The accepted wisdom in this century is that the dentist's waiting-room was the proper place for it, and even in its heyday it was considered normal to laugh about it. Auberon Waugh used to maintain that even very good and funny writers were bad in *Punch*. *Private Eye* used to send out rejection slips marked 'Why not try *Punch*?' Timothy Shy, in World War II time, used to excuse limp jokes by saying, 'Good enough for *Punch*.' Going back a century, a Victorian editor of *Punch* once said to W. S. Gilbert, 'Do you know, we get hundreds of jokes sent in every week!' 'Really? Then why don't you print some of them?' said Gilbert caustically.

In my experience the only people who were ruder about *Punch* than these outsiders were the staff themselves. We were so conscious of the great cartoons and good things done by *Punch* in the past that it was rather depressing to bring out a weekly issue and realise that nothing in it was nearly so good. It was also depressing to bring out issues in which there were good things and have nobody notice, just because nobody expected *Punch* to do anything new or good. We felt the weight of the millstone of history round our necks. We felt the force of inertia of a somewhat dozy readership. But as much as anything we felt that we had to fight against the editor as well, whoever he might be.

This was especially true of the tenure of William Davis, in the Sixties and Seventies. Davis felt that he had to drag the magazine kicking and screaming into the twentieth century. He wasn't the first. Malcolm Muggeridge had been hired in the Fifties to get rid of the old readers and attract a new set. His brand of modernism had managed to get rid of the old but not attract the new, which had helped *Punch* on to a downward slide in circulation which was never to be halted in the next two or three decades.

In a vain attempt to staunch this, Davis nailed his colours to the cause of being in touch, that is, being topical, being political, being satirical. Nothing wrong with that, except that *Private Eye* and *TW3* were already doing it much better, and *Punch* was the wrong magazine to do it with. There seemed little point in our planting little squibs under the Vietnam War, or Scottish nationalism, or the three-day week, if we were always a week late and didn't add anything to it. Look back through the *Punch* of that era and you will find a lot of dead humour washing around in the shadows, attached to long-forgotten TUC leaders, and car strikes, and now unrecognisable Cabinet ministers. We all know the sensation of opening an ancient volume of *Punch* and wondering exactly why Gladstone *is* getting cross about Bulgaria (or rather, not caring in the least why he is doing it), but you can get exactly the same effect in recent *Punches*. Who is Jack Jones? What was the Cod War . . .?

(There was one week when I was actually acting editor of *Punch* because both editor and deputy, Davis and Alan Coren, were away. I put into that issue things which I liked because I thought they were good and funny, including one of which I am quite proud, because it was the only portion of his autobiography ever penned by Paul Desmond, the saxophonist with Dave Brubeck. It is a very funny piece, and when Davis came back and saw it in *Punch* he exploded. 'I turn my back for a week, and rubbish like this gets in!' I have put the piece by Desmond in this book. There is nothing by Davis.)

So you will not find any topical humour in here. You will not find classic chestnut cartoons of the kind normally found in *Punch* treasuries ('curate's egg', 'I keep thinking it's Wednesday', 'bang went saxpence', etc.) or indeed venerable chunks of prose. What you will find is pieces which have had me creased up with respect or laughter over the last twenty years—pieces by unexpected figures like Anthony Burgess, Barry Humphries and William Boyd, by regulars like E. S. Turner and Basil Boothroyd, and by people who probably don't even remember writing for *Punch*, like Peter Buckman and Andrew Barrow. Or by Alexander Frater, who when he is writing his fantastical dreamlike stories set mostly in the South Seas, is—in my opinion—the funniest man who wrote for *Punch* since the war.

You will also find pieces and cartoons which I came across quite by accident in the *Punch* library, the unexpected shrine to humour which these days sits rather oddly opposite Harrods. To get to the *Punch* library you have to go through the ultra-modern offices of the ultra-modern version of the magazine (still alive at the time of writing) and then pass back a hundred years into the leather-lined library, where the first time I visited it a Japanese scholar was silently scrutinising the private letters of Tom Taylor, the Victorian editor of *Punch* whose main claim to fame was that he wrote the play at which Lincoln was assassinated . . .

Help! I am sinking back into history already, succumbing to the historical spell of *Punch* again. I don't really want to go back down that road. It was lovely to go back again for a while, and I hope you enjoy what I have brought back, but I escaped from *Punch* fifteen years ago, and have lived a comparatively normal life ever since, despite what Terry Jones forecast.

I have not resisted the temptation to include a piece or three of my own. Still, it was nice to find a piece by Terry Jones and Mike Palin which made me roar with laughter, so that has gone in as well. A pity they didn't write more. They could have been very good humorous writers, those two, if they hadn't gone off and wasted all their time making films and going round the world . . .   MILES KINGTON

FOGARTY'S WEDDING

Alexander Frater

Fogarty sat on a bollard by the Grand Canal, cracking humbugs between his teeth and gazing at the pearly palaces and gun-metal skies with apprehension. Venice was mirrored darkly in his patent leather boots—the gilded, sun-dappled piazza of St Mark's, the passing bum-boats and moored steamers—and, for the fourth time since brunch, he mumbled, 'This is the biggest day of my life.'

'Oh, stop saying that,' I said. 'You don't have to convince me.'

'I was talking to a barman last night who said that Venice is a great place for weddings. They've had some pretty wild ones here, apparently. Have you ever heard of a Peruvian timber tycoon known, I think, as the Stinkwood King?'

'No,' I said.

'He loved animals,' said Fogarty, 'and flew a selection from his private zoo across to add a bit of colour to the reception. The barman said that several escaped. Apparently two gorillas pinched a gondola and set off for Yugoslavia, rowing strongly, and a female warthog burst into Florian's and tried to give suck to the espresso machine.'

'What arrant bloody nonsense,' I said.

Fogarty frowned. He looked at me with a worried gleam in his strange, wine-coloured eyes and said, 'The hotel porter told me this morning he could smell fog. That's all I need. Here I am, marrying a Venetian lady on a goddam duck sanctuary in the middle of the lagoon, and somebody smells fog. Can't we change the venue? There are plenty of spare churches right here in town.'

'Her family has always been married on that island,' I said. 'Anyway, all the guests will be out there waiting.'

Fogarty sighed, and we waited for the two gondolas to come. They hove into view eventually, the first empty, the second carrying a heavy-breasted girl in white lace, clasping a massive bunch of snapdragons, and an elderly lady with blue hair. Fogarty swallowed. 'Got the ring?' he said.

I nodded. The leading gondola drifted into the landing and Fogarty and I ran down the steps and jumped in. 'Well, hi,' called Fogarty to his bride, reaching out across the water for her hand.

'You no touch her, Fogarty,' snapped the girl's mother. 'Not till after the priest finished his business.'

'Yes, signora,' said Fogarty, sitting down in the cushions. He seemed suddenly happy. As we moved off over the lagoon, he beamed across at the girl, making little popping noises with his lips and stretching sensuously till his limbs cracked. They had met some months before when Fogarty was on vacation; he was swimming at the Lido one morning when she had damn near truncated him with her speeding pink water skis. Her name was Immaculata, but she was known as Lulu, and she brought roses and pomegranates to his hospital bedside and accepted his proposal of marriage by letter a few weeks after he returned home. Fogarty and I had flown out for the ceremony the previous evening. We lit cigarettes and lay back, enjoying the salt air and the slapping of the water against the hull. Then, some time later, the gondolier muttered and shook his head. 'What did he say?' said Fogarty.

'I think he says fog is coming,' I said.

He wasn't joking. Fogarty groaned and watched as it swept down on us like smoke, thick, pearly clouds of it rolling in from the Adriatic, smelling of oysters and old wrecks. Soon Venice was ephemeral and half-seen, a pink, marbled moon city hazy through streaming cirrus, and then it was gone. 'Bloody hell,' said Fogarty, looking around for Lulu's craft, some way behind, but it had vanished; our gondolier shipped his oar, wrapped himself in a blanket and sat on the deck, smoking. Fogarty tried to organise community singing. 'It will keep our spirits up,' he said. 'They did it in the war, of course, when they took to the boats. I understand the Admiralty even issued song sheets along with the salt pork and biscuits. "Eskimo Nell", and stuff like that. "Eskimo Nell" was a great favourite of Winston's, you know. He sang it at the Yalta Conference. Stalin took his hat off. He thought it was a hymn.' He turned to the gondolier. 'Allora cantiamo, sport. Arrive derci Roma, or something. Okay?'

'You go sug eggs,' muttered the gondolier.

Fogarty, with his missionary talent for seeing the best in people, said, 'He speaks quite good English,' and glanced at his watch. 'I wonder where they've got to? Lulu!' he called. 'Lulu!' but there was no reply. 'I don't much like this,' he said. 'Right now she's probably drifting helplessly towards the African coast, following the Babylonian tin route with her mum.' He suddenly leant forward and looked at me hard. 'She'll like England, won't she?' he said. 'The dynamism of the cities and the lush green countryside? Besides, we have many shared interests, like our love of winter sports and sparkling wines. Oh, this marriage is going to be a notable success. Isn't it?'

'The gods have always smiled on you, Fogarty,' I said.

He nodded and lay back in the cushions, staying that way until abruptly he sat up and pointed. A high, rust-streaked shape was looming towards us, towering like the side of a cliff and painted with the words, barely perceived, 'MV *Spirit of Thames Ditton*'. 'Hey, she's British!' exclaimed Fogarty. He stared up at it, then said, 'Shall we go aboard? It's at anchor. Perhaps they'd give us coffee, or something. I could do with a cup of something hot.'

'Good idea,' I said. 'We can at least ask,' and I motioned to the gondolier to make fast to the gangway and wait. We climbed the swaying stairs and, when we reached the deck, stood there, calling softly. A woman's voice said, 'Who's that?' and a tall, angular figure in boots and a worsted poncho appeared through the mist. 'Are you the men with the fruit?' she said.

'No, ma'am,' said Fogarty. 'Our gondola is fogbound and we were wondering whether you could possibly let us have a hot drink.' She considered us a moment, then nodded. 'Very well,' she said. 'You'd better come to the galley,' and we followed her along empty decks, past humming ventilators belching warm, egg-and-beans scented breath, and arrived at the vessel's kitchen, a small, dimly lit room hung with butchers' calendars and a picture, torn from a magazine, of a grinning Negress, naked but for pads and a Surrey cap, whacking a ball through the covers at some tribal cricket match.

'Tea or coffee?' said the lady.

'Coffee, please,' we said. She nodded and placed a kettle on the stove. She had cropped blonde hair and a bony, introspective face. 'Are you a passenger?' I asked.

'No,' she said. 'I am the master's wife. I always travel with my husband. He's asleep now. We attended a Mariners' Costume Ball ashore last night and got back rather late.' She sighed. 'He went as King Kong and I as the Statue of Liberty, and it wasn't a very pleasant evening. During the Excuse Me I was forced to smack a little Cunard purser across the chops with my torch. He came as Lassie the Wonder Dog and, under the influence of alcohol, he rather rudely widdled on my plinth. The atmosphere was somewhat chill.'

'I'll bet it was,' murmured Fogarty, with a glazed look.

She nodded. 'I could do with some sleep myself, as a matter of fact. It's been a hell of a trip, this one. We had to transport thirty-five church organs across from New Orleans. The pipes were battened down on deck and all the way over the wind blew steadily, making this awful moaning music night and day. Then we hit a hurricane. Dear God,' she murmured. 'It sounded like Bach stewed to the eyeballs, if you will pardon the expression, and using the keyboard as a trampoline. What wild, insane melodies we heard! It got so bad that a French killer sub crash-dived as we came by. Wooop wooop wooop, wailed its hooter, and it disappeared in an acre of boiling foam. Off the coast a Navy sloop came racing up to investigate the racket. When we reached Gibraltar they sent us a monkey and a tin cup by Admiralty messenger.' She sighed and placed the coffee mugs before us. 'Now tell me,' she said, 'what were you doing out on the lagoon?'

'We were going to my wedding,' said Fogarty.

'Your *wedding*?' She stared at him. 'Well, bless my soul. That takes me back a while.' She laughed. 'Here, I'll give you some advice. Know what my mother said to me before *my* wedding? She said: "Play your partner like a stringed instrument." Isn't that droll? I tried of course, with George, but it was like strumming an old suspension bridge. Know what I mean?'

'Some people are stringed instruments, and some are not,' said Fogarty.

'Exactly.' She nodded.

'I myself am woodwind, I think,' said Fogarty. 'Sort of reedy and haunted. I am a muted sort of person.'

'Oh, George is muted too,' she said. 'No question of that. In fact, if he wasn't so bloody muted he could be commanding a big refrigerated cargo job right now, instead of this scow, speeding prime beef from the Argentine.'

We sat drinking our coffee. Then there was a knock at the door and a Tonk stoker stood there with Lulu, who looked wraith-like and chilled, with beads of mist in her hair. She ran in and seized Fogarty's arm. 'We drifted past this ship,' she said, accusingly, 'and saw your gondola. What are you doing?'

'Having coffee, love,' he said, passing his cup.

'The fog's thicker than ever,' she sighed. 'It could last for days.'

The captain's wife, who had been considering them morosely, suddenly stood up. 'She's right, you know,' she said. 'But I have an idea. If you two are really determined to go ahead with this, why not let George do it? Ships' masters can marry people. He once spliced a Spanish torch singer and her child groom a couple of hundred miles off Nome. Hang on, and I'll call him up.' She unwound a speaking-tube from the wall and blew into it.

'Captain here,' said a nasal voice.

'Climb out of your pit,' said the lady, crisply. 'We have a proposition to put to you.'

'Muriel?' said the captain. 'Muriel, it's time for my egg nog. And will you please lower your voice to a sorta muffled bellow and tell me what's happened to my goddam chest expanders? They've gone. Have you got them?'

'Aw,' she said, with disgust, and replaced the speaking-tube. 'He doesn't make much sense at this hour of the day,' she said, earnestly. 'I'll just pop up and see him. Meanwhile, why don't you just sit here and discuss the matter yourselves. Back in a moment.' She went out the door. We waited till her footsteps had receded then Fogarty, very pale, grabbed his bride and we crept out too. Silently we loped down the deserted decks towards our rocking gondolas, poised and waiting to carry us on across the lagoon.

FINAL NOTICE

Alan Melville

Someone on, of all things, the *Guardian* rang up and said he was
sorry to trouble me but he had a request to make which might
be thought unusual and even somewhat, er, macabre. They were
having, he said, a bit of a spring-clean on their obituary notices,
and would I by any chance consider doing X—naming a well-
known actress with whom I crossed paths, among other things,
in the palmy days of intimate revue. 'Good gracious!' I said. 'Is
she—? . . . I mean, is it, er, *urgent?*'

'Not at all,' said the *Guardian*. 'On the contrary, according to
the latest available reports, the lady in question is in rude health.
But one has to be prepared for any eventuality. *Venienti occurite
morbo.*'

There is really very little one can think of on the spur of the
moment in reply to a crack like *venienti occurite morbo*. Squeams
are not things I go in for in a big way, but I did feel slightly
squeamish about the whole thing. However, I know X as well
as anyone and there are at least a couple of stories about the old
girl which I felt might amuse the reader without actually offend-
ing the next-of-kin. So I agreed to do her, and the *Guardian*
character said at once, 'While you're at it, you wouldn't like to,
er, knock off Y, would you?'—referring this time to an equally
famous actress who from time to time has done her own variations on lines, lyrics, and sketches I have written for her. It
seemed odd to me: here I am, a senior citizen, half-price on
British Rail, bus tokens and all the rest of it, embarking on a
new career as a knocker-off of obits. Still, I thought, if the news
gets around I might do quite well out of it in the way of hospitality: if you want a decent notice on the way out, keep in with
old Al.

I felt terrible writing the things. Using the past tense is the
worst bit; every time I wrote that Miss X *was* something, or that
Miss Y *had been* something else, I felt I was not just being prema-

ture but in an underhand sort of way hastening the end. The *Guardian* character, however, was delighted. 'Just what the doctor ordered,' he said on receipt of the valedictories. 'The personal touch, the occasional shaft of good humour—I'm sure, when the time comes, they'll be greatly appreciated. How about having a go at Z, mmm? I know he's in that serial, but he *is* eighty-four . . .'

It happened, of course. I was walking down the Haymarket and bumped slap-bang into X. Looking, to my relief, in the pink of condition and irritatingly young for her years. (I'd looked her up in *Who's Who* and subtracted five as an old chum.) '*Darling!* . . . ,' she said, smothering me in her simulated. 'I thought you were dead. What are you writing these days—or have you given it all up?' I was so pleased to see her that I invited her to lunch; halfway through the meal, during which she told me her plans for the future, she said, 'Look who's just come in, darling—better ask her to join us: poor soul, she looks *ghastly*.' I have to ask you to take my word for this: it *was* Y. I have rarely eaten a less enjoyable meal. Y kept saying that all she seemed to do nowadays was attend other people's memorial services, and reminding us that we were all—the three of us—contemporaries and, let's face it, living on borrowed time. X kept saying absolute balls, darling, you're as young as you feel, and I've no patience with people who keep on about the Great Reaper and sans eyes, sans teeth, and sans all that jazz. She also suggested a second bottle of Sancerre to drink to the success of the new musical she was doing when she got back from Australia early in 1982. Both girls had a large Armagnac with their coffee; the bill came to £48.70, plus VAT.

I also met Z the other day. He was, correction, is a very famous comedian, but recently he's taken to writing: it's an overcrowded profession. We met at the barber's; he was preening himself after a boyish short back and sides. 'Got to look my best,' he said. 'It's my brother's birthday. He's 100.' He looked at me in what seemed to me an accusing manner. 'Longevity', he said, 'runs riot in our family. Finished that autobiography you said you were writing? Better get on with it, y'know. Time's running short. Well, see you soon—I hope . . .' And off he went,

humming *Silver Threads Among the Gold*, which, considering I was
following him into the barber's chair, I took amiss.

Worrying things, obits. The people most concerned never
read them, and writing them puts years on you. I get this feeling
the *Guardian* has asked Z to do mine.

'*Of course, nowadays we only keep him around for the tourists.*'

WHEN I WAS YOUNG AND IGNORANT

Patrick Barrington

When I was young and ignorant I loved a Miss McDougall,
Our days were spent in happiness, although our means were frugal;
We did not sigh for worldly wealth, for vain and tawdry treasures,
We were a simple country pair with simple country pleasures.
Beneath the village chestnut-tree it was our joy to meet once;
We used to tread the dewy fields with wonder-waking feet once;
We wandered once in leafy lanes and walked in woodlands shady;
But now she's gone to Birmingham to be a Bearded Lady.

I loved her as I loved my life when I was young and tender,
And happily our time was spent, although our means were slender.
We used to pass the golden days in countrified pursuits once;
We walked through simple country bogs in simple country boots
    once.
High hopes of happiness I had, but now my hopes are zero,
Alas! my love has left me now to carve her own career O;
Not all the hopes of her I had are worth a maravedi;
My love has gone to Birmingham to be a Bearded Lady.

My love now dwells in circus halls with clowns and tight-rope
    dancers,
Where dromedaries play bassoons and sea-lions do the lancers;
She moves amongst trick-bicyclists, buffoons and comic waiters,
With elephants and acrobats and prestidigitators.
No longer daily by my side she wanders through the hay now,
The glamour of the public eye has lured her far away now.
Remorseless Fates, my tender hopes how cruelly betrayed ye!
My love has gone to Birmingham to be a Bearded Lady.

When I was young and ignorant I loved a Miss McDougall;
But that was e'er she heard the call of Fame's imperious bugle.
I thought her kind as she was fair, but I was green and calfish;
My love, though brighter than a star, was colder than a starfish.
High hopes of happiness I had when I was young and tender;
But time and tide have falsified my juvenile agenda.
Farewell, my castles in the air! Phantasmal mansions, fade ye!
My love has gone to Birmingham to be a Bearded Lady.

'Good Grief! Her conduct is even more outrageous than last year!'

PROMISES PROMISES

JOHN MORTIMER keeps his word

I have always found a deep inner pessimism and total lack of faith in all promises the best prescription for a happy and contented life. My father, to whom I listened attentively when a child, never, so far as I can recall, promised me anything. He told me that immortality, if it existed, would be exceedingly dull, a case of sitting about for all eternity; a note of horror entered his voice as he described it: in some vast transcendental hotel with no wireless and nothing to do in the evenings.

He also told me that sex had been greatly overrated by the poets and that the best to be expected from time was that it would pass quickly; indeed its rapid flight could be greatly assisted by an endless re-reading of the Sherlock Holmes stories, Shakespeare's sonnets or a daily attack on *The Times* crossword puzzle.

With nothing much to expect so far as 'life' was concerned, my father remained extremely cheerful: and because of him I have never felt that the future has broken any particular promise, although I have come to the cautious opinion that sex, if not all that Algernon Charles Swinburne cracked it up to be, is not quite as ridiculously uncomfortable a process as my father would have had me believe.

When I went to school, promises were made to me, however. If we took care to sleep only on our left sides, avoided dreams, refrained from stuffing foreign objects down the bogs or pinching the soap kept chained to the washbasins, if we knelt beside our beds, shivering in our Clydella pyjamas, to chat to a surely bored Almighty about our triumph in the Cock House Match, we would enter into Eternal Life. I remember my father's description of this state, which I always saw as an indefinitely prolonged wet weekend at the Imperial Hotel, St Leonards, and happily continued to stuff my illicit copy of *Film Fun* down the drain. As the dark clouds gathered over Europe, and over me, we were promised the opportunity of dying for England, which was also a bargain I secretly hoped wouldn't be kept.

If we did particularly well in the History Essay we were promised a game of golf with the Headmaster, followed by a slap-up tea and his playing *The Pirates of Penzance* in its entirety on the pianola. To avoid the fulfilment of this promise it was necessary to pepper the History Essay with a few well-chosen deliberate mistakes. If anyone makes you a promise it's always best to allow them a decent way out, even if you have to get Oliver Cromwell into the Wars of the Roses to do it.

So when I get promised anything I have always found it safest to cultivate advanced disillusion. Making promises yourself is something else again. In those distant mists of childhood, when all our attitudes are formed, I promised Sammy Boxall, son of the chair-leg maker next door, that I would take him to the pantomime in Reading. It was a solemn promise, frequently repeated; but I broke it when Mr Boxall came to my father and explained that he had a gramophone record called *The Laughing Friar* which he played Sammy once a year at Christmas.

Any additional pleasure, he felt, such as the Reading panto, would not only make Sammy discontented with *The Laughing Friar* but would lead him on to giddier and more fatal pleasures until he ended up God knows where ... slumped in some Oxford opium den or clad only in silk stockings dancing the can-can down the High Street at Thame. Convinced by this ludicrous argument I broke my promise, and I have never forgotten Sammy Boxall's howls of disappointment. I have lost touch with him over the years: I believe he is living somewhere near Slough, sunk into middle age, a man with no more experience of pleasure than an annual cracked recording of a monk laughing his head off.

This early trauma, however, has given me a strange terror of breaking promises, especially those made over the telephone when asked, sometime next July, to discuss 'Obscenity and the Permissive Society' with the Young Farmers or 'Modern Trends in British Drama' with the Mothers' Union. Faced with these requests I become insanely like the young lady in *Okla-*

homa and totally unable to say 'no'. One powerful reason for this, of course, is that I have no faith in the existence of next July. Next July, I am sure, I will be arrested for debt and locked up in the Marshalsea, or gone to live in Fiji—so why not afford the Young Farmers the easy satisfaction of a 'yes'? But incredibly next July arrives, apparently in about a week, as I seem to have inherited my father's gift for keeping time nipping along.

It's then that I realise with terrifying clarity that obscenity is something that should be done in the comfort of the home, preferably between consenting adults, and never written to *The Times* about or chatted about on *Nationwide* and certainly not discussed by the Young Farmers who are quite capable of getting on with it by themselves without any help at all from me. It's then that I go through a succession of possible lies, ending with the idea of having simple black-bordered stationery specially printed to convince them of my death.

But Sammy Boxall with *The Laughing Friar* raises his ghostly head. How can I cheat the Young Farmers of their longed-for evening with old homely tales of *Lady Chatterley's Lover* and the statistics of flashing in Copenhagen? How can the Mothers' Union go on bottling plums in painful ignorance of the latest flicker of comedy in the work of Marguerite Duras? So, an idiot slave to promises, I turn up after a couple of hours driving and trying to squint at the map under changing traffic lights, to discover that the Young Farmers have all gone to see *Tamburlaine* at the National and the Mothers' Union think I'm N. F. Simpson.

As a lawyer I have long realised the importance of promising your client nothing. If he asks you what he'll get for a bit of petty larceny the wise barrister goes green and mutters 'death', on the sensible theory that eighteen months in the Scrubs will then seem like a free holiday on the Costa Brava. But another part of my life, the world of the movies, is, of course, built on promises. Promises that the money is on its way from Canada, that Claude Chabrol is interested in directing, that Elizabeth Taylor will play the father. Without such totally insubstantial promises no movie would ever get made. Hollywood and Pinewood are staffed by persons whose simple faith and humble credulity are unequalled since the days of Pope Joan and St Francis of Assisi. My first brush with the movie business no doubt formed my attitude to such promises.

I was sitting in my Chambers looking forward to a legal triumph in an undefended divorce case in about six minutes' time when a Mr Orland Skinner rang up in an impeccable Brooklyn accent, asked if I were the famous author of a short story in the *Evening News* and invited me to write a script about diamond smuggling in Africa. He also asked me to his studio which was not far away; in fact it was just off Ludgate Circus. I went there at once and there did appear to be, in a basement not far from St Paul's, a small underground movie studio, full of lights, make-up girls, camera crews and Mr Orland Skinner himself, his white phone still hot from calling me, sitting behind a huge black and chrome desk begging for my services.

If I would write his movie he promised me not only money, huge sums of money not to be had for even the most complex undefended divorce, but a trip on location in Africa. I was also promised a participation in the profits—and there would be extras, beautiful girls available regardless of creed and colour who, Mr Skinner hinted delicately, were only cast to comfort the writer on lonely evenings by the water-hole. I walked back up Fleet Street in the rain filled with an extraordinary elation; my life had changed. England would see me no more, and if they wanted me for the Undefended, messages would have to be sent out from the Law Courts by tom-tom.

I finished Mr Skinner's script in two months. It was, I thought, nimble and exciting and there were parts for all the beautiful extras he had mentioned. But that year I saw no water-hole, no jungle, no ravishing girls in bush shorts and indeed no more of Mr Orland Skinner either. When I got back to the studio the basement was still there: but what a change was wrought! The cameras, the make-up girls, the black and chrome desk had all vanished. Of Mr Skinner himself there was no sign. The place, whose address I still have graven on my heart, had become a wholesale greengrocer's. There were many boxes of citrus fruits from Israel and a man in a brown apron checking lists. I had to stand aside as a fresh consignment was barrowed in. No, they had been there almost two months and no, they had never heard of a film studio. That, I promise you, is the way with promises. They vanish utterly, and you're lucky to be left with a box of oranges.

'It's a little chilly, so I've put an extra dog on your bed.'

BROUGHT WITH THE WIND

Anthony Burgess

I was walking through St Leonards-on-Sea and I found a ten-shilling note on the pavement. Considering it too trivial a sum to take to the police station to be claimed, I thought the best place for it would be one of those charity-boxes in pubs which, rightly, seek to exploit the philanthropic phase of drunkenness. I entered a public bar and found a game of Shoot in progress. There was, however, no charity-box of any kind, not even one for indigent lovers of Shoot. I joined the game, which was mostly being played by Irish labourers, and used my ten-shilling find as stake-money. As the ten shillings were buckshee I played recklessly and so walked out with three pounds fifteen. The fifteen shillings I placed in the charity-box of another public bar, where no game of Shoot was in progress. The three pounds I took home.

That evening a girl called Myrtle Spurge came to the house with specimens of her Professional Typing (special rate of four bob a thousand words for anything over seventy thousand—an encouragement to novelists to write longer novels). I felt sure that Myrtle Spurge was not a real name. I looked it up in the encyclopaedia and found it had some sort of vegetable meaning, I forget what now. An alternative form was Caper Spurge. The next morning I opened the *Daily Mirror* at the racing page and found that a horse called Caper Spurge was running in the three o'clock at Doncaster. I rang my bookie and put three pounds on to win. The horse, naturally, came in at a hundred to eight. (Check this if you like in Cope's—the November of 1961.)

There was now the question of the Manchester November Handicap. The evening before it was run, there was an old film on ITV, something about war in the desert and the Eighth Army and Lili Marlene. El Alamein. It rang a bell somehow. Yes, there it was in the *Evening Standard*—Dalnamein, ridden by J. Greenaway. I rang my bookie next morning and put on twenty-five pounds to win at twenty-eight to one. I watched the race on television, and it was a very close thing. Dalnamein didn't seem to stand a chance, what with New Warrior, Mossy Face, Pandofell, Sunrise and Sabot fighting it out in the first furlong, with Windy-Edge as one of the backmarkers. It was in the last two furlongs, with Pandofell a length in front, that Dalnamein began to challenge, with Windy-Edge a dangerous contender, and when Dalnamein passed the post he had only beaten Windy-Edge by a neck. Seven hundred pounds, plus, of course, the stake-money.

In the one-thirty at Birmingham on Monday I backed Cobbity each way—twenty pounds at a hundred to nine—and it came in third. In the two o'clock I had thirty pounds each way on Ladignac at thirty-three to one, and it came in second. In the two-thirty I had fifty pounds for a win on Up the Vale, and it came in third. Careful, careful. But in the three o'clock I didn't do too badly. Fifty each way on Winter Wanton and Hydrant and, in that very big field, Winter Wanton came in first at six to one and Hydrant third at eight to one. Things were going much too well now, but—having received a letter from Dublin that morning from a girl I had once been friendly with called Mary O'Connell—I couldn't resist putting fifty on Eire's Flame in the three-thirty (each way, thirty-three to one), and it came in third. T. Brookshaw up. Check all this, I say again, in the *Racegoer's Encyclopaedia.*

There was racing at Worcester the following Wednesday—small stuff and heavy going—but I put two hundred pounds each way on My Mark in the one o'clock, and it came in second at a hundred to seven. It didn't matter much, then, that in the two o'clock Soltown should come in last, with thirty nicker of mine on his back. But I put five hundred on Wire Warrior to win in the three o'clock, and that came in at a hundred to nine.

I won't bore you with the rest of the week's racing, except to say I splashed with a fine carelessness at Sandown Park, Newcastle and Doncaster the following Saturday. I did best at Doncaster, with sizeable packets on Royal Spray in the one o'clock at a hundred to seven, and Nigarda second in the Try Again Hurdle at three o'clock (eleven to two) and, in the same race, Pendle Pearl, third at thirty-three to one. Sabre at Sandown, with a thousand to win, came in at a hundred to nine. Venturesome Warrior—second at thirteen to two—offset handsomely some ill-advised bets in the Medburn Novices' Hurdle at Newcastle. Totting up my gains at the end of the day, I found I had about forty thousand pounds. It was time to be done with racing.

Reginald Horsley, who was at that time starting his own publishing firm (chess-knight as colophon, books of undoubted literary value to be a speciality), was glad to take me in as a partner. Because of a failure properly to organise the advertising and sales sides, the first titles, excellent though they were, fell very flat. The following season, he decided, with my concurrence, to risk everything on the ghosted autobiography of a pop star. This pop star had been much in the press as a consumer of hallucinogenic weeds, a seducer of teenage girl-fans, and a follower of perverted Vedantists. His life-story sold well in the first weeks of publication, but then a minor character in the book—a failed bass-guitarist whose pastimes had been somewhat misrepresented by the ghost-writer—decided to bring a libel action. Settlement out of court, as well as the pulping-up of the whole of the large second impression, cost very dear. Horsley now felt that he was not really cut out for the career of publisher. My forty thousand pounds had sunk without trace.

But I felt little except exhilaration. After all, I had expended minimal energy on accumulating that sum, and the initial capital had been buckshee. Strictly speaking, the whole speculative operation lay in a pocket outside the scope of my normal affairs: it was right that money not rightfully mine should turn out to be fairy gold. I had not worked any the less at my profession of writing, and the rewards of that profession had not been— which might be argued to be impossible—less than before the windfall. There was not one permanent possession the more in my house, and I had consumed, because of the excitement of punting, perhaps five cigarettes a day more than normally. Nothing to grouse at, then. Easy come, easy go.

I was walking through St Leonards-on-Sea and I found a ten-shilling note on the pavement. Somewhat wearily, I envisaged the whole process beginning again—the win at Shoot, the successful punting, the final and inevitable failed speculation at something nobler, like publishing a pop star's memoirs. A man selling newspapers said, 'Cohen sidence, guv. Twice I seen you do that. Near a year ago it was, the other time.' I said: 'That means you too saw the note on the pavement. Why didn't *you* pick it up?' He said: 'Do me a favour. Stealing, that would be. It may have fell from your pocket, but it's still your money, way I see it.'

But how could I be sure he was remembering accurately? How could I be sure that that second ten-shilling note, carelessly dislodged when I took out my handkerchief to wipe my eyes against the fierce St Leonards sea-wind, blown some way along the pavement by that same wind, was really re-enacting the adventure of the first? I would never be able to be sure. All I could do then was to be very angry and inveigh at the stupidity and even criminality of Reginald Horsley. I mean, to be so careless with other people's money: he should have had the manuscript vetted by a lawyer.

I am becoming poorer now, chiefly because I am doing less work, also because I am deliberately dropping odd ten-shilling notes on the streets of St Leonards-on-Sea. When people pick them up, I am impelled to follow them to see what they do with the money. Most are unimaginative: they just pocket the cash and presumably treat it as their own. Once or twice my heart has lifted when I have seen the money taken to a pub, but nothing outside a windfall stout or gin-and-tonic has come from it. It's amazing how blind some people are: several notes of mine have been ignored and windswept out of my view. What I am looking for is a man who will play Shoot and then the horses and be willing to pass on tips. Such men, humanity being on the whole a suspicious breed, are hard to find. Am I going mad? Am I superstitious about windfalls? Am I attaching too much importance to money?

Please send anonymous ten-shilling notes so that I may pursue my enquiries into the nature of luck. You may send them care of this journal.

FRIENDS
OF THE CATHEDRAL

John Betjeman

At the end of our Cathedral
   Where people buy and sell
It says 'Friends of the Cathedral'
   And I'm sure they wish it well.

Perhaps they gave the bookstall
   Of modernistic oak
And the chairs for the assistants
   And the ashtrays for a smoke.

Is it they who range the marigolds
   In pots of art design
About 'The Children's Corner',
   That very sacred shrine?

And do they hang the notices
   Off old crusaders' toes?
And paint the cheeks of effigies
   That curious shade of rose?

Those things that look like wireless sets
   Suspended from each column
Which bellow out the Litany
   Parsonically solemn—

Are they a present from the Friends?
   And if they are, how nice
That aided by their echo
   One can hear the service twice.

The hundred little bits of script
    Each framed in *passe-partout*
And nailed below the monuments,
    A clerical 'Who's Who'—

Are they as well the work of Friends?
    And do they also choose
The chantry chapel curtains
    In dainty tea-shop blues?

The Friends of the Cathedral—
    Are they friendly with the Dean?
And if they do things on their own
    What does their friendship mean?

RODIN'S PARTY GAME

DAME EDNA'S XMAS TELEX

Barry Humphries

As I stood on the confetti-strewn steps of All Hallows Moonee Ponds in the far-off forties beside the man who was later to become Australia's first grateful prostate recipient, I little thought that I would one day be sprawling here in the designer-designed colour co-ordinated saloon of my very own jumbo 45,000 feet up midway between the Seychelles and the Costa Smeralda, voluptuously doing this with my fingers.

I refer, *Punch* readers, to my handy in-purse digital Telex. Not so many moons ago, I needed the pittance with which *Punch* rewards its contributors. How I would strive to make my composition witty and acceptable! But now that an avalanche of fame and fortune has fallen into my Ted Lapidus lap, how the Magli boot is on the other foot! I know it sounds awful but I don't care if this item is funny or not. I'm sorry but I don't. Such is fame and the huge tax-free take-home honorarium of super-stardom.

If my Bahamian accountants could see what I've got my nose into at the moment, they'd have a blue fit.

'For Heaven's sake, Edna,' they'd Telex, 'haven't we told you not to earn *anything*—however trifling—for the next fifteen years?' But trying to staunch my creative flow would be like trying to dam the mighty Murrumbidgee, stop Joan Sutherland singing or Rolf Harris making a fool of himself.

Putting it simplistically, I'm a workaholic.

I'm sorry but I am. To me, every day is a challenge, be it Ash Wednesday, Pancake Day or even Christmas. And now that my kiddies have flown the nest and my husband is more or less permanently institutionalised, I'm taking a long, hard, pragmatic look at the logistics of the Festive Season vis-à-vis the changing parameters of my post Lévi-Straussian lifepath.

So don't expect a card from me this year, possums; I'm re-thinking the Chrissie syndrome.

I'm going out on a limb now. I'm going to Telex a concept to my *Punch* editor that's never been Telexed before. I make no apology for shocking you with a notion that will certainly never have crossed your mind before and has only just this second popped into mine.

Christmas has become a wee bit commercialised.

Immediately I sense that I have alienated some of my readers with this ostensibly tasteless bombshell. But someone had to be the first to say it, possums, and it's better that it comes from me, a caring and compassionate wife and mother, than from Russell Harty, Angela Rippon, or some other hard-hearted glamour-puss of the Media.

I suppose what I'm trying to say is: don't expect a prezzie from me.

It is common knowledge that celebrities and heads of state in my position with more than enough of this world's goods are constantly embarrassed by their loyal subjects pressing upon them an unsolicited surfeit of gimcrack gee-gaws (hark at me!). The box room of Buckingham Palace must be bursting with Brummy goods which my good friend the Sovereign *dare not* put out for her trusty dusty, since Her Majesty, who is arguably further up the entertainment tree than yours truly, has to *hoard* every unwelcome knick-knack in case the eagle-eyed donor pops in for a knighthood and doesn't see it on the mantelpiece.

I know how you all feel. You feel you have to *repay* me. And Christmas is a sort of ritualised opportunity for you to give me back a fraction of what I give you in love and laughter as a world-class entertainer and *monstre sacré*, not to mention *jolie laide*. But you're wrong. I give for the sake of giving, and at every opportunity, driven by the daemon of my Damehood, just like Van Gogh, Zelda Fitzgerald, Sylvia Plath and Cleo Laine. It breaks my heart at this time of year to see disadvantaged little English folk *beggaring* themselves in Harrods and Asprey's to give me some token of their gratitude, which I'm only going to have to pay my Filipino staff to lose as quickly as possible. Heavens alive, as it is—Christmas or no Christmas—I must shove an average of five or six unsolicited digital clocks down my waste disposal unit every week of my life and think nothing of it!

But don't think I've gone all heathen, darlings. Once C of E, always C of E. It's just that my funny old psychic powers tell me that Our Lord didn't go through the mill all those decades ago with Oxford Street uppermost in His mind. Do you think for a second that Dame Nature in Her wisdom wanted lethal lasers in the Bethlehem Bazaar on Saturday morning?

This doesn't mean that my nearest and dearest aren't going to get what my wonderful mother used to call 'a thought'. Hubby Norm, back home in Melbourne in his closely controlled environment (where they spoil him silly), can look out for an exciting variant on an old Yuletide standby.

Straight off the drawing board at Penhaligon's, the perfume people, comes a delightful requisite for the mature cot-case: blanket bath salts. Barbados Lime, Haddock and Cavalry Twill. From £38. At Dunhill, The White House and Macfisheries.

If bridesmaid Madge hasn't got everything that opens and shuts, she's certainly got *something* that opens and shuts, I'm afraid. Such a difficult woman to buy for; I always have to rack my brains. I'd give the creature a tube of popular depilatory cream if she wasn't so obviously in need of a drum of US Army surplus defoliant. You'd really need to break every Geneva Convention in the book to curb Madge's facial undergrowth.

Still, it's an ill wind because they're dusting those fluffy old chops of hers with talc and dolling her up as Mother Christmas for the Australia House Festival of Nine Lessons and Arm Wrestling.

My dearest son Kenny is giving himself to me this Christmas, heaven be praised. He's coming across at last for the big Fifties Art Deco and Contemporary Bygones auction at Chris Elephantine's Bond Street Gallery, hoping to snap up an autographed Barbara Stanwyck poster in a chipped Lalique frame that once nearly belonged to Joe Orton. All the darling wants for Christmas is 'something stunningly naff and camp' but you'd be amazed how uncalled for some of those Hatton Garden types can be when asked nicely to display their range of men's Bakelite jewellery.

As I playfully indite this seasonal Telex from the command module of Wombat One, it strikes me that despite the hoo-ha and twaddle surrounding Christmas Day, this public holiday will at least afford me a respite from the thunderous applause and coarse laughter which attends my nightly stint at London's chockablock Piccadilly Theatre. Fortunate woman that I am! As lesser West End stars struggle at curtain's fall to bus or Tube it to Islington or Barnes, I am whisked by chopper to coral strands or nice resorts. But unlike some flashy theatricals and politicos I could mention, I won't be getting cheap publicity this year by conducting choirs of carolling paupers or ladling wassail to the waifs of Wapping. Beyond giving myself nightly body and soul to the public I'll find time for only one typically generous act.

On Christmas morn you'll find me at the London Clinic visiting the bedsides of those *more* fortunate than myself.

End of message.

DAME EDNA EVERAGE IS A
DIVISION OF THE BARRY
HUMPHRIES GROUP.

'Amazing! You should write a book.'

Inspired by Paul Theroux's latest travels on the
Old Patagonia Express, E. S. TURNER sets out on

THE WORST RAIL JOURNEY
IN THE WORLD

(*The journey begins at Orpingham Green—which is not its real name—situated 15 miles from London.*)

As the train lurches out into the dank suburban wasteland, past the long rows of posters which ask women whether they are pregnant, you suddenly think: 'I've been here before.' These fields of derelict buses, these abandoned factories which once turned out miles of plastic parsley for fishmongers' windows—yes, it is all uneasily familiar. In fact, you saw it yesterday. And the day before.

We are bound for the capital of a once-legendary imperial power. No one knows when we shall get there. Back in the station the chalked messages warned us of absentee guards, faithless drivers, cancellations, diversions, industrial action. Already the sun is half-way up the mucus-yellow sky. Within the grubby coach where we shall spend an eternity in the company of strangers there is an ill-concealed air of menace, as those who light cigarettes are told to put them out again and those who failed to get seats stand on the feet of those who did.

I am one of the luckier ones and to cover my embarrassment I pretend to read the Bible tract that was lying on my seat. 'Babylon the Great, the Mother of Harlots and Abominations of the Earth,' it says. 'I saw the woman drunken with the blood of the saints.' I fold it to use as a marker in Hardy's *The Dynasts*, which I hope to start, and perhaps finish, on the journey.

I keep thinking of the homeless family who were lying sprawled on the platform from which we started, the flotsam of a decayed society, with all their worldly goods in plastic bags. 'My Mum frew me art, dint she?' the mother said to a patient policeman. 'Couldn't stand my Kevin and the boys no more, could she? Now we're sleeping rough in stations, aren't we? Yeah, I bin to the council but they dint want to know. But I'll get bloody Shelter on to them. And bloody *Nationwide*. And the bloody *Evening News*.' Throughout her spirited outburst her Kevin, a portly youth of about seventeen, kept a bored silence, contenting himself with cuffing his offspring, though he seemed too young to have sired more than three of them. What a land of raw human tragedy this is! Yet the children seemed in no way dispirited; their hyperactivity was amazing to behold.

We halt for ten minutes, in sight of a church bearing the whitewashed message: WOGS OUT. It is an exhortation we shall see endlessly repeated on the walls of hospitals and schools.

The air of menace in the coach deepens. Suddenly a pistol is thrust in my ear, there is a sharp report and my brains spatter across the window. Or so it seems. 'Don't *do* that, Wayne,' says a woman's voice. 'The gentleman doesn't like it.' There was a lifetime of nagging in her flat voice. The overfed child, a future white Bokassa, kicks her shins until she stops rebuking him.

The incident reminds me of the wife and son I have left at

home while I voluntarily undertake the Worst Rail Journey in the World. Shall I ever see them again? Shall I be the same man when I return? I fidget uneasily; and one reason why I fidget is that a metal spring in the vandalised seat is piercing me to the quick. When I can no longer stand it I rise and give up my seat to an elderly nun.

'ALL OUT! ALL OUT!' comes the shout from a pale tapeworm of a youth in a railwayman's cap. Why must we get out? Because he says so. Will there be another train today? That is no concern of his. Where are we? Apparently we must learn to read. The desolation, the sense of ultimate despair on this lone platform in the midst of nowhere is terrifying. Something like panic sets in, as famished travellers tug at the drawers of slot machines, which have probably held no chocolate for years. The plight of the very young is pitiful to behold. Some of them have had nothing to eat for thirty minutes. How are they to survive the mounting privations ahead?

The youth like a tapeworm disappears through a door marked PRIVATE, no doubt to rejoin his card school. We never see him again. Reluctantly I allow myself to be drawn into conversation with a neatly-dressed young man who, from his appearance, seems to have undergone some unspeakable ordeal. 'God! I never knew it would be like that!' he keeps saying. When I offer him a sip from my brandy flask he takes a long swig. Eventually the sordid story comes tumbling out. He is an office worker in Cheapside and, egged on by his fellow workers, he applied for 24 hours leave to see his first child being born. His old-fashioned employer told him he was a lewd fellow and that such matters were the concern of midwives only, but he would not listen. Now, at a fearful cost, his eyes have been opened. 'Serves you right,' I say, bitterly regretting the waste of brandy.

The loudspeakers vibrate with the accents of Barbados and Uttar Pradesh. People look at each other blankly. There is a rumour that the train has been ambushed. Across the track just outside the station is one of those sinister concrete bridges from which youthful guerrilla bands hurl prams and traffic bollards at passing trains.

From a waste bin I retrieve a copy of the *Sun*, which is open at the book review page. CAUGHT IN A WEB OF FORBIDDEN LUST runs one headline; PASSION IN THE WILDS runs another. The lady reviewer ends her saucy summaries of the plots with 'This romantic tale will make you feel like seducing your man' and 'Meredith's adventures will put a lot of hot and steamy thoughts into your head.' Truly, in the Republic of Letters there are now job opportunities for all. How Juvenal would have revelled in the contents of a British Rail waste bin!

While I am thus absorbed, the train is shunted out and a new one shunted in. We are not allowed to board until they decide whether to route it by Elmer's End or Potter's Bar, or perhaps they said Potter's End and Elmer's Bar. At length we are ordered aboard and roundly cursed for not moving quickly enough. Once more the nightmare landscape rolls past, its hard edges mercifully softened by the filth on the windows.

'It looks like Sodom and Gomorrah,' says a man in a pin-striped suit. 'It does not,' I snap. 'I have been to Sodom and Gomorrah and I know.' He does not like this. I do not like it either. We are all getting short-tempered.

I read a few chapters of *The Dynasts*. An American tourist who looks like John Foster Dulles asks me in an aggrieved tone why all these travellers are not at their places of work. In America they would have been at their desks for three hours by now. I say nothing. What is there to say?

We are offloaded again, in a station resembling every other station and with scant hopes of further transport. I decide to make a short exploration of the nearby town. Children are riding cycles round the station booking-hall, maintaining that their fathers said they could do so, as the roads are unsafe. A large notice boasts: THERE ARE NO TOILETS IN THIS STATION. Nearby is a betting shop full of postmen, fresh from delaying the second-class mail. News bills proclaim RAIL CHAOS LOOMS and RAIL FARES UP AGAIN. A dog pauses to defile a car priced at £4,999—'This Week's Snip'. The only liveliness is when a willowy youth emerges from a uni-sex hairdresser's to stamp his foot petulantly at the burglar alarm ringing away on the premises above. Otherwise, there is an air of apathy and dejection everywhere. I count four abandoned cars, all with notices on the windscreens saying they will be destroyed if not claimed.

Back to the station, just as a train, all unannounced, pulls in. There is a furious scrimmage for seats by those who still cherish hopes of reaching the capital today. It moves off slowly. And in a brief instant my eye, long starved of beauty, feasts on the sight of a single exquisite tree silhouetted against the sky. It is growing from the gutter of a factory, established in 1931 for the manufacture of patent bottle closures, if I read the faded lettering aright. The whole composition is perfect, with a scarcely bearable poignancy.

Now we are halted in a tunnel. After ten minutes the driver reluctantly switches on the lights, just as I am pouring the last of the brandy down my throat. As we sit and swelter hysteria begins to mount. The windows are jammed shut. A traveller who looks like an ordnance major pokes out a pane with his rolled umbrella, to admit what he fancies will be fresh air. Suddenly everyone begins to break windows—this sort of thing is infectious. Then with a great lurch we are off again and stop in another anonymous station, where we are invaded by an army of Common Market schoolchildren, squealing and jostling as if they were in a cathedral. Because of the broken windows the train is held to be unserviceable and we are all ordered out.

The station waiting-room has a single occupant, a singing white-whiskered Silenus dressed in scarecrow clothing, outrageous and malodorous, with rows of empty bottles beside him and a cap on the floor containing two decoy coins. He is the only happy person I have seen today.

He motions me to join him, but I sit ill-temperedly on the broken bench outside, gazing at a discoloured block of flats. All the cistern overflow pipes are dribbling, the water shining silvery in the weak sun. It is a familiar sight in these parts. No power on earth, it seems, can remedy it. This people is defeated, utterly, by the physical problems of urban living.

At last, the capital, the Mother of Abominations herself! Some say we are entering Waterloo, some say Liverpool Street; only time will show. Again the posters ask women if they are pregnant. There is wild elbowing and pushing as those who have been seated make clear their determination to get off before those who have been standing. What vitality these people display when the showdown comes! I am proud to have journeyed with them, through the last disenchantments of a run-down civilisation doomed, as it must now seem, to speedy oblivion.

Next week:

THE TERRIBLE JOURNEY HOME AGAIN.

RUTHIE

Larry Adler

If it's names you like conjuring with, howsabout Ruth Etting?

Ruth Etting, the purest singer of popular (not pop) songs I ever heard, died last week, aged 82. I recorded with her in 1929—kee-*rist*, that's 49 years ago!—under very unprofessional circumstances.

Ruth was headlining at the Palace in New York and I was on the bill. Despite the hokum about the Palladium, there was nothing like the Palace. To play there was like winning the Nobel Prize and everybody who *did* play there spent time each day standing in front of the theatre showing off before the envious crumb-bums who were 'resting'.

I was on the bill but had no billing, being part of Gus Edwards' Kiddie Revue. Gus, who wrote *School Days*, was famous for discovering talented kiddies and his alumni included Eddie Cantor, George Jessel, Lila Lee, even Walter Winchell who, before becoming a journalistic menace, was a hoofer. Now *I* was a kiddie.

The Palace was two-a-day vaudeville (music-hall to you) and I watched Ruth Etting every show. She would come out, lean against the proscenium arch and just sing. No gimmicks, no mannerisms, a completely relaxed style. She respected her material and never altered a lyric—how many singers can you say *that* about? Her diction was flawless and you could hear every word, clear to the back of the theatre. Remember, in 1929 we didn't yet have stage microphones, and singers (crooners, they were called) like Rudy Vallee, Bing Crosby, Dick Powell and Russ Columbo used cardboard megaphones, like college cheer-leaders. Ruth wasn't a belter like, say, Sophie Tucker or Ethel Merman (*she* was Ethel Zimmerman, then) but she didn't need any help, either. Rogers and Hart wrote 'Ten Cents a Dance' for her.

Ruth was married to the first honest-to-God gangster I'd

ever met. Col. Moe Snyder—the 'Col.' was honorary, from Kentucky, and the state governor threw such titles about like confetti—had a limp, from a gang brawl, and was called The Gimp. Moe the Gimp. Moe carried a gun and once shot a stage-hand for the crime of ogling Ruth. He did two years for that. He scared hell out of me.

The Doris Day film *Love Me or Leave Me* was Ruth Etting's story, and it was pretty accurate. I'll tell you how accurate. The studio paid the Gimp 25 Gs for permission to show him as the louse he was. Gimp took the dough and the studio was safe from suits; James Cagney, as the Gimp, really laid it on but, so help me, he came out *nicer* than Moe.

I was doing the standing-in-front-of-the-Palace bit one day (a waste of time as nobody knew who the hell I was) when Gimp arrived in a black Packard. He signalled to me; and, brother, when the Gimp beckons, you *approach*.

'Hey, kid, c'mere. Ya got da ting witcha?'

'The what?'

'Come *ahn*! Da ting, da doohickey. Da tin sannwich.'

'Oh, the mouth-organ! Yes, I've got it.'

Gimp opened the door, grabbed me by the neck and pulled me in. He drove up Broadway, swearing whenever we were slowed down by trolley-cars.

'Where we going?' I asked.

'Sheddep,' he replied courteously.

He parked on 57th St, we got out and, with Gimp again holding me by the neck, went to the Columbia Recording Studios. Outside Studio 1 a red light was on, meaning they were recording. Gimp walked in anyway, me with him; and Ruth Etting, who had been recording, had to stop.

'Gimp,' she said, 'you saw the red light—you *knew* we were recording.'

'Put dis kid on da rekkid,' said Gimp.

'Gimp, what are you *talking* about? We've got musical arrangements, we've been rehearsing 45 minutes, we were doing a take—we can't just like that add another musician!'

Gimp looked at her and I wouldn't have liked to be on the receiving end of that look.

'Ruthie, you don't hear real good. I said *put—dis—kid—on—da—rekkid.*'

In the studio band they had Joe Venuti (*he* died only a few months ago), Eddie Lang, Lou Alter, Charlie Spivak, Jimmy and Tommy Dorsey, and, of course, they put the kid on da rekkid. Venuti suggested he lay out for eight bars in the 2nd chorus and I, ashamed of myself, appropriated Venuti's solo. The tune was 'If I Could Be With You'.

Later I approached the Gimp.

'Excuse me, sir,' I said, 'how much do I get paid?'

Gimp, as if he hadn't heard me, just lit a cigar. I gulped but repeated what I'd said.

Gimp measured me the way an undertaker would.

'You little bastid,' he said, 'git *ahta* here.'

I could see by the look on Ruth's face that the advice was good. I took it.

When the record came out my name wasn't on it. Not only unpaid, unbilled as well.

Ruth finally broke away from the Gimp and once she did, Gimp was nobody. In the 40s I entered Henrici's Restaurant in Chicago (their slogan: 'No Orchestral Din'), and there was Gimp, alone, unnoticed. I came over.

'Hello, Col. Snyder,' I said, 'I'm Larry Adler.'

His face creased and I thought he might cry. It was an awful moment.

'Hoddia *like* that! Sure, you're da kid wit da doohickey, I remember. Siddown, have a coffee and Danish, it's on me.'

I did, and felt I was the first to have spoken to Gimp in, maybe, weeks.

Ruth Etting never really liked showbiz. Her whole career spanned only twelve years but in that time she starred with Eddie Cantor in Ziegfeld's show *Whoopee* (also with Cantor in the film *Roman Scandals*) and in the Ziegfeld Follies twice. She co-starred with Ed Wynn and Harry Richman.

As I've shown, on her records she only used the best sidemen.

She retired in 1937, still at the top, and she died last week.

PUSSIES GALORE

Jeffrey Bernard

I'm quite seriously worried about going mad. I don't think I could take another really bad winter without cracking at the seams and the long-range weather men say that the athletes among us will soon be skating on the Thames. That thin dividing line that people are so fond of referring to, the one between sanity and insanity, was breached by three of us—in Battersea of all places—the last time we had a surfeit of snow and ice. What happened was that they had to cancel all racing for several weeks. Well, it might not have worried you much, but Caspar the diplomat, Tom the copywriter and myself never let work get in the way of racing in those days and we'd be punting from the first to last race every day.

But I'd better explain about Caspar because this is about him more than about Tom or me. He wasn't really a diplomat but he worked at a foreign embassy as a press officer and to hear him talk you'd think he ran the Middle East. Actually, he was mad before the winter started and he looked it. Unkind people likened him to a petrol pump or a visitor from Mars. He was very short, had an enormous bald head and looked something like a hairless peach on matchsticks. Above all he was a racing fanatic and when I first met him his wife had just left him after he'd told her, in a moment of intoxication and great frankness, that in his considered opinion the great Italian racehorse, Ribot, was far more important than she was. Anyway, there he was living alone in an enormous flat opposite Battersea Park when the snow began to fall. Disaster. All racing cancelled.

For days on end we fidgeted in the pub reliving the glories of our past wins and near misses, nigh desperate for a horse to bet on. Then, in the third week of the great cold spell, Caspar walked into the pub one day and said, 'D'you fancy coming racing tonight?' I pointed out that there wasn't any racing except in Australia and California but he said, 'Yes there is. At my place tonight at seven o'clock.' I asked him what sort of racing. Was it some daft kid's game or card game?

'No,' he said, his eyes shining brightly, 'it's cat racing.' Of course, I knew he was bonkers, but having nothing better to do I duly popped round to his flat at the appointed hour.

Now Caspar had two cats and having been something of a socialist in his early days they went by the names of Keir Hardie and George Lansbury. Keir Hardie was a vicious, black bastard of an animal and Lansbury was a rather neurotic marmalade. When I got to the flat, was led into the kitchen and had the plan explained to me, I knew for certain that Caspar had gone beyond recall. He'd actually laid out a racecourse along the passage from the kitchen to the front door—a good forty feet. And this is what he told me in all seriousness.

'Normally, of course, I'd have arranged a flat race but since we're in the middle of the National Hunt season I've built a hurdle course. There are four flights of hurdles,' and he showed me four sticks at equal intervals along the passage that had dish cloths draped over them, 'and I haven't fed the cats for two days. Now I'm going to place a saucer of tinned salmon by the front door, give them a sniff of it, bring them back to the kitchen and then let them go.'

Well, I was fascinated by cats and man and although I thought he'd gone a bit far in not feeding the wretched things for two days I couldn't resist having half a crown with him on Lansbury at 3–1. At those odds he seemed like good value. We stood in the kitchen and had a drink and, being something of a meticulous stickler as well as lunatic, he actually made me wait until 7.30 p.m. That, he said, was the time of the race. The clock ticked round and we squatted on the floor holding an animal each and then they were 'off'.

Keir Hardie never attempted to jump. He crashed through every hurdle in his desperation to get to the tinned salmon and never once did he appear to be in any danger of falling. George Lansbury was a great disappointment to me. He hit the top of every jump and was beaten by an easy three lengths. Although I realised that any responsible body of medical men, let alone the RSPCA, would have had us committed if they'd witnessed the scene, I have to admit I was hooked. While Hardie and Lansbury attacked the salmon Caspar and I retired to the sitting-room, hereinafter referred to as the Steward's Room, to discuss the next meeting and we arranged it for the following weekend.

Came the Saturday and Caspar had gone even further round the bend. He'd invited the copywriter called Tom who'd brought a tabby with him all the way from Wimbledon and if you know anything about racing you'll know that they don't travel all that way for the fresh air. The tabby was called Samantha—Caspar kept referring to her as a 'filly'—and she had extremely powerful-looking quarters. If she could jump, I thought, she might be a good thing. It was then that Caspar asked Tom and me for a pound each.

'What the hell for?' I asked him.

'Well, all races are run for prize money and owners have to put up the entrance money, don't they?' I agreed to that and then asked him what we were racing for.

'The winner', said Caspar, 'gets a bottle of Sauterne and the second gets twenty Players.'

When we lined them up in the kitchen doorway you could see the poor blighters had been on a diet all right and Keir Hardie was dribbling, he was so hungry. It was more or less the same story all over again. Hardie was never going to be much in the way of a jumper but he was a real speed merchant. He won again, this time by about two lengths, and we reckoned that Samantha and George Lansbury just about dead heated for second place. While they tore into the salmon we had a bit of a conference in the Steward's Room. 'It's going to be a bit boring if Keir Hardie keeps on winning all the time,' I ventured. Caspar nodded in agreement and then a madder than usual look came into his eyes.

'I've got it,' he said and I have to admit that he then came out with the greatest brainwave since the invention of whisky.

'We'll handicap them.'

'And how in the hell d'you propose to do that?' I asked.

'With kitchen scale weights,' he answered and I knew I was in the presence of genius.

We couldn't wait until the next weekend so Caspar and Tom

put their cats on an immediate crash-course diet and we met two nights later. We agreed that if horses get three pounds for a length then cats should get an ounce for a length. Caspar pulled the kitchen scales out of a cupboard—about the only thing his wife had left him—and he then proceeded to fix a three-ounce weight with the aid of some Sellotape on to Keir Hardie's back. He didn't like it and I didn't care much for the dodgy look in Tom's eye as we got them ready for the Off. Samantha was very much on edge and a few years in the racing game have made me easily suspicious. I was even more so when Tom asked us— dead nonchalantly—if either Caspar or I would like to lay him four fivers on her. We declined and I had a quid at threes on Lansbury, who I was convinced was improving with every race.

At eight o'clock they got off to a level if rather loud start. For once Keir Hardie was never in the hunt. Lansbury raised my hopes momentarily at the halfway stage but Samantha won from trap to line. She did more than that. She jumped the saucer of salmon and tried to crash out of the flat through the letter box. You'd have thought Caspar was Lord Derby the way he carried on. He actually pulled a red handkerchief out of his pocket, which I correctly guessed to be cat racing's equivalent of the red flag at the races, denoting a Steward's Enquiry, and we retired to the Steward's Room to debate the debacle. I tumbled what had happened right away. I know bloody writers, even copywriters.

'You doped your cat, didn't you, Tom?' I said, opening his prize of a bottle of Mouton Cadet. 'What *are* you talking about?' he said.

'Come on, you gave it a Dexedrine or some sort of pep pill, didn't you?' Of course, he denied it, but I knew I was right. I also knew, as the evening wore on and as we drank more and more, that my cat racing days were over. Caspar was very nearly due for a straitjacket. He got completely carried away.

Very pompously he put down his empty glass at the end of the evening and turned to Tom and told him, 'I'm sorry to have to tell you, Tom, that I agree with Jeffery and I have no alterna- tive but to inform you that you are "warned off".'

The words echoed in my head as I sat on the tube going

home. The phrase so dreaded by those had up in front of the Jockey Club and now I'd heard it in all seriousness in a Battersea flat. Warned off. Good God, I thought, Caspar really is mad. As I got home, I noticed it was beginning to thaw. What, I wondered, would Caspar do now with Keir Hardie and George Lansbury? Turn them out in a field for the summer, I shouldn't be surprised. Nothing was beyond him. And thereby hangs a sequel.

A few months later—you're not going to believe this but I swear it's true—Caspar moved to St John's Wood and I bumped into him one morning on Primrose Hill as I was returning home from an all-night party. He was standing on top of the hill itself, looking, would you believe, at something through a pair of binoculars.

'What the hell are you doing?' I asked him.

'Cantering Keir Hardie,' he told me. I insinuated that he must be joking but he merely said, 'We could be in for a very dry summer. A drought, in fact. In that case, what with hard going, the fields could cut up. Not many trainers would want to risk horses on that sort of ground.'

To date, Caspar hasn't actually been carried off to the funny farm. I see him from time to time and I'm told he now earns a living writing pornography since he got the sack from his embassy for spending too much time in the betting shop. Mind you, if it ever does come to it again and we do have to race cats this winter I think it might be much better if we did it with an electric mouse.

EXCLUSIVE—FOUR UNPUBLISHED EARLY MASTERPIECES

Now that it's becoming the fashion to dig out the juvenile works of famous writers, MILES KINGTON jumps on the bandwagon with a quartet of previously unknown works of genius

THE CASE OF THE MISSING NAVY
Conan Doyle's first story (age 13)

'What do you make of this, Watson?' said Holmes, throwing a paper dart at me across the room. I unfolded it and saw that it was a letter.

'It has a message of some sort written on it,' I said. 'Gosh! Is this a new case?'

'Read it and find out,' said Holmes, filling his mouth full of the liquorice allsorts which he always stuffed himself with when he was hot on the scent of another villain.

'WATSON IS GETTING TOO BIG FOR HIS BOOTS,' it said. 'WE SHALL GET HIM.'

'Well,' I said, 'I would deduce that it has been written by someone who thinks that I am getting too big for my boots and they are going to get . . .'

At that moment the door burst open and in came Queen Victoria, the Prime Minister, the First Lord of the Admiralty and several crowned heads of Europe. They were all disguised.

'Please sit down . . . Your Majesty,' said Holmes. 'Have an all-sort.'

The Queen gasped.

'You recognised me!'

Holmes smiled.

'I could not help noticing the little marks on your forehead, which can only be caused by a crown. Perhaps you have read my

54

essay on "Marks made by Hats". You are not the Kaiser, therefore . . .'

They all gasped.

'Wow, you certainly have an incredible gift for deduction,' said the Prime Minister. 'But let us get on with the story. We are in great trouble, Mr Holmes. The First Lord of the Admiralty has reported that the British Navy has vanished. If some German spy sneaks on us to the Kaiser, it could mean the end of civilisation as we know it, or at least it could mean the German Navy coming and shooting our holidaymakers.'

'Have *all* the ships gone?' said Holmes to the First Lord of the Admiralty, his keen eyes (Holmes's eyes, I mean) looking out from under his keen eyebrows. 'Even the Zeus class destroyers with twin fourteen-inch turrets?'

'Unfortunately are they all disappeared,' said the First Lord. With one stride, and then another one, Holmes leapt forward and pulled the moustache, beard, spectacles, hat and false nose from his face.

'Gentlemen,' said Holmes. 'Otto von Krempel, the German spy!'

'But how did you know?' I asked Holmes later.

'Jolly easy,' said Holmes. 'Any chap knows that Zeus class destroyers have a sixteen-inch turret, also he spoke in a German accent. I am writing an essay on German accents. They only have one, the Umlaut. I thought of that joke this morning.'

'One thing more.'

'Yes?'

'Who wrote that threatening letter to me?'

'Who do you think?' said Holmes, throwing a cushion at my head.

DEATH AT TEA TIME
Ernest Hemingway's first story (14 years old)

Haley went out into the school yard. The first leaves of autumn were falling and it was chilly. The teacher told Haley to get his coat on or he would freeze to death. Haley went and got his coat. Then he went out into the school yard. It was a school yard much like other school yards, or I suppose so as I have not seen other school yards yet. Even if I had I would say it was much like other school yards as I have just discovered the expression 'much like' and I like it.

'Hello, Haley,' said Andersen.

Andersen was a huge Swede, standing well over five feet. He had blood on his chin where he had tried to shave himself. His shoulders were much like big shoulders.

'Hello, Andersen.'

'I am going hunting in the woods. Are you coming?'

Haley knew what he meant. They were going to look for rabbits. They had never caught one yet and Haley was glad inside himself because they said that when you cornered a rabbit it was much like a mountain lion and tried to bite you, only lower down, about the knees.

When they were in the woods, Andersen stopped and shivered.

'It is a funny feeling, hunting rabbits. It is like the feeling of the thing between a man and a woman.'

'What is the thing between a man and a woman?'

'I am not sure. I thought you knew.'

'No, I do not know. But I thought you knew.'

'No.'

They went on a way further and they watched the leaves fall from the trees and hit the ground, which is the way of leaves when they fall off the trees. Haley shivered and said it was cold. Andersen said nothing. Haley said it again. Andersen said that it was not too cold to hunt rabbits. Haley said he did not mean he was trying to get out of hunting rabbits, he only thought it was cold and that was all he thought.

'Look!' said Andersen. 'A rabbit!'

'Where?' said Haley.

'Over there.'

'I cannot see it.'

'It has gone now. It does not matter. Perhaps it was not a rabbit at all. It is very cold.'

'Shall we go back to school now?' said Haley.

They went back to school and did some more lessons and then Haley went home but he did not tell his parents of what had happened.

DR EVIL

The first James Bond story (Ian Fleming, 14½)

James Bond strode into the hallway of Dr Evil's house, wearing an immaculate school blazer which had been made for him by Jacob Schneider of Lucerne, which I think is in Switzerland, and asked the receptionist to tell Dr Evil that James Bond had come to see him.

'Dr Evil?' she said into the phone. 'There is a boy called Bond to see you.'

'Who is almost 17,' said James.

'Who is only 17,' she said. 'Yes, sir. Will you take the lift to the third floor?'

When Bond left the lift at the third floor he found himself face to face with Dr Evil, a squat, ugly, horrible little man who was uncannily like a certain schoolmaster.

'What can I do for you, Master Bond?' he said, leering.

Bond felt in his pocket casually to check that his 2½lb catapult, made of choice elm wood by a master craftsman in Bond Street, which is a very important street near Piccadilly, was loaded. He only used the very best conkers, imported from his aunt in Ireland, which was better than most aunts who only sent you book tokens.

'I think you know what I have come for,' he said coolly, no, icily. 'You have my replica authentic Japanese destroyer which fires real hara-kiri aeroplanes, which you confiscated for your own devilish ends, sir.'

The face of Dr Evil went pale and he reached for his poison gun, but before he could pull it out Bond had pounced. At lightning speed he fastened the evil man in a half-Nelson, gave him a Chinese burn, did a quick knuckle-crusher and punched him in the nose. Dr Evil sank lifeless to the ground, only he wasn't really dead. Like a flash, Bond entered the nearest room. There, on the bed, was the most fantastic blonde, really smashing, with no clothes on at all, if you know what I mean, like in books. There, on the table, was his authentic Japanese destroyer.

'Who are you?' she gasped huskily gazing at the handsome stranger.

'I am James Bond and I am 16¾,' he said in as low a voice as possible. 'I have just killed your friend Dr Evil, but he will live.'

He strode to the table and picked up the destroyer. Before he left the room he turned to the girl, well, woman, and said: 'You will get cold lying around with no clothes on, anyway it looks silly, whatever they say in books. I would get a dressing-gown on if I were you.'

Moments later there came the distinctive sound of Bond's super three-speed-gear Raleigh as he pedalled away down the drive.

LORD ARTHUR WENTWORTH'S BLACKBOARD
Oscar Wilde's first play (age 15)

(The scene is a richly decorated room, hung with damask curtains, rich brocade and the finest tapestries, but if you cannot get this your mother's dresses would do. There is a pale scent of incense and also the furniture is sumptuous. It is the Fifth Form at St Topaz's School. A young man is seated at a desk, which is Arthur, who is the pupil. Standing by the gem-encrusted blackboard is a young man, which is Basil, who is the teacher. As the curtain rises, Arthur is lighting a slim, delicate cigarette.)

BASIL: You know it is against the school rules to smoke, Arthur.

ARTHUR: What is the point of rules if we do not break them?

BASIL: You have just made an epigram. Do you know the derivation of the word 'epigram'?

ARTHUR: Like most words in English, it comes from the classics. Without the help of the Romans and Greeks, Englishmen would be hard put to it to express their contempt for foreign languages.

BASIL: I sometimes wonder who is giving this lesson—you or me. Now, where was I?

ARTHUR: You were trying to persuade me that a knowledge of

Canadian wheat production will enrich my career as a poet and artist.

BASIL: My dear boy, one does not have a *career* as a poet. Poetry is too important to work at. One must content one's self with devoting one's self to it.

ARTHUR: Exactly. I shall write a play and with the proceeds withdraw to an exquisite house where I shall dedicate my life to a poem.

BASIL: It is a charming thought. What will your play be about?

ARTHUR: It will be about two wonderful young men sitting in a classroom talking about art, poetry and Canadian wheat production. One must show the public one has taste and also has done one's lessons.

BASIL: And how will the play end?

ARTHUR: Suddenly, without any warning at all.

(CURTAIN)

PAMELA: *'How's your wife, Peter?'*
PETER: *'She died last Tuesday.'*
PAMELA: *'Are you sorry?'*
PETER: *'Sorry? Of course I'm sorry. I liked the woman.'*

FASHION FLASH

Mary Vaughan

What use is a Little Black Dress to me,
With my splendid hippage of fifty-three?
For my stately forty-four of bust,
A Big Black Dress is a vital must;
And, whatever the fashion writers say,
The Big Black Dress is here to stay.
On sunlit sward or in salons shady
It is *de rigueur* for the larger lady.

'It seemed such a shame to move him!'

NATURE IS A TERRIBLY INTERESTING THING

JAMES CAMERON writes Lady Chatterley
in the style of Godfrey Winn

Have you ever wondered, as I do whenever I read of some little act of unsung sacrifice in places like the Midlands, how wonderful it is to love *people*—to the *full*, enjoying the simple things of life even in some honest working man's rude hut?

Ours is really a terribly exciting age, and lots of us refuse to be *blasé* about the wonderful things of nature, which is full of great beauty that quite transcends the difference between rich and poor. I pray with all my heart that nobody would cast the first stone at a woman just because she liked gamekeepers.

This was more or less Constance Chatterley's position, or one of them. She had married Sir Clifford, a well-born marvellous young man with a lovely seat. The seat was called Wragby Hall, and you have no idea how lovely it was, there among the sooty, soulless, gruesome workers' cottages, though they were very sweet inside. How marvellous the honest working wife is at making the best of her simple possessions, under such difficulties.

Constance Chatterley, although a very different type, had her difficulties too. The war came (the first war, and I cannot tell you how rough it was; I am sure you have read about it in those wonderful stirring books by Philip Gibbs and people) and Sir Clifford was called to a Destiny at the Front, as indeed were high and low, including his late Majesty King George VI, whom I met when I was a *matelot* in that self-same Royal Navy, though indeed that was not the same war.

The brutalities of war caused a scar on Sir Clifford's soul, indeed I am bound to say worse. He had always been a clean-living young fellow. But he was to become even cleaner, *in a*

61

certain sense. For Sir Clifford returned from this man's war *very badly wounded.* To be terribly frank, as sometimes we have to be, he had very little of him left below the waterline, nor had that little long.

I wonder if you can imagine how this distressed Constance Chatterley—so young, so wholesome, so ardent, so full of compassion; and of course such a nature-lover. Seeing Sir Clifford there in his wheelchair, so patient and undemanding of her, it was as though she, too, sensed the pangs of loss.

After all, she was still so fresh and gay. In the world of imagination she reminds me of my mother, except of course in a way she doesn't. There was this sad thing about Sir Clifford. The sight of his stiff upper lip brought tears to Constance's eyes. She was such a pure girl, it almost drove her insane. What a terrible thing is mental illness; I pray with all my heart we never stoop to mocking it.

So one day Constance was walking through the woods of the estate, admiring the poignant affection of the daffodils and the tender impertinence of the primroses and the gentle laughter of the cowslips, and various other aspects of the sweet challenge of spring. And into the mind of Lady Chatterley came a deep sense of the essential *rightness* of Nature, and of her husband, especially of what he had once used to have been.

She arrived at the clearing flushed and semi-conscious. There was the shirt-sleeved gamekeeper; his name was Mellors, no more and no less. He was closing up the chickens for the night. But still one trio of tiny things was pattering about on tiny feet, tiny mites, refusing to be called home by the anxious mother.

'I'd love to touch them!' she panted. Before Constance knew it she was touching them. The little tiny chickens ran around 'cheeping' at being ignored.

By and by the gamekeeper gazed at her. Compassion flared in his, well, bowels, and the nettles had evoked a strange stirring in his loins.

'Eeh, but thar't winsome, like,' he said in the vernacular, 'Happen thar'll coom oop to t'oot.' His voice had the simple manly honesty so often corrupted by the veneer of education. Education is of course a marvellous thing, but.

A surge of democracy welled up in Lady Chatterley. As they entered t'oot it grew unaccountably stronger, more urgent, more democratic. I often wonder if everyone understands the real affinity between the landed classes and the simple estate-workers—as our Prime Minister does, though of course rather differently.

This is an age of frankness, and my readers know well that there are times when I am forthright. The ensuing hours in the simple woodland home of Mellors were so tender, so simple, so *real*, so HUMAN, that they have to be described in detail, as a tribute to wonderful Mother Nature. These two young people were in *love* . . . They expressed it in a fashion that I *know* is not customary in the grounds of Buckingham Palace. Nevertheless I am confident that they intended no disrespect to the person of Her Majesty our Queen, whom I had the pleasure of meeting in 1961. This hut was something really quite different. This was direct and *elemental*, and if in retrospect it was a bit sick-making, it was somehow *right*.

Under his shirt was his slim smooth body, rippling with the play of muscle under the silken skin. His rough manly breeches lay like an offering on the homely floor. Constance's costume was quite pretty, too; she was wearing a cinnamon two-piece by my friend Norman Hartnell, at least to start with. In wonder she confronted the gamekeeper Mellors; he looked so confident, so cocksure. Already she was beginning to forget about wheel-chairs . . .

For no one knows how long Constance was aware of nothing but a cleaving consciousness, a rhythmic growing motion like the waves of the sea at Antibes, where I had a marvellous holi-day two years ago; a convulsion of deepening whirlpools of ecstacy in his man-smell and his man-touch and the quivering maleness of his man-handling. She could have swooned at the carnal rapture of those slender buttocks.

She felt slightly ashamed of enjoying it so much. For of course Lady Constance was aware that *this* is only a part of love, which is really made of companionship, and *understanding*, and common interests. I know a sweet old couple whose mar-riage was saved time and again by a shared hobby; in this case fretwork. All this Constance knew well; in her heart of hearts she knew full well that the last moments had been just a phallacy. She thought with gratitude of the tiny defenceless chickens that had brought them together.

But then the wondrous magic took possession again, and all this stuff about wispy lingerie and loins and deep breathing, which I assure you is really *nothing*, though it seems important at the time.

Only when it was all over did she become aware of the oppressive closeness of the hut, the windows closed, country-style, over the airless heat of passion.

'*What* a fug!' she whispered.

'Tha canst say that agen,' he breathed, stretching his great male arms behind his great male head: god-like.

'Tha an' me's a sacred rite,' he said. 'Sex is nowt wi'out shared faith, companionship, bairns. Tha knows t'body's only part, just a private part.'

And for a while Mellors the gamekeeper made with the high philosophical phrases, for we all know, do we not, that the one thing the British working man likes is a bit of cant.

Then they talked about the industrial system for a while, and the need for the workers of the smoking valleys to get a square deal and an eight-hour day.

'Tha mun coom one naight to t'oot,' he said. 'Shall ter? Slaip wi' me? 'Appen Sat'day?'

'As a matter of fact,' said Constance, 'I do have a sale of work Sat'day. But next time I'll really try to come.'

And as she ran home in the twilight, or gloaming, the trees in the park seemed erect and surging as though they were alive, and who is to say that they were not? Nature is a *terribly* interesting thing.

Next week I am going to continue my series on *Passion Without Pain*, with the Love-Life of Doctor Schweitzer. This is a *terribly* ennobling story, and I really *do* hope that . . .

THE SILENCES OF PASSION

Gwyn Thomas

In certain areas of life, I am told, love moves like a great and gifted fish from the current of one desire to the next. I have a strong feeling that I have been hanging about on the banks of the wrong streams, staring at the wrong seas. In the social contexts where my identity was fashioned, love, where it should have left a memorable radiance, created as often as not a mildewed quietness.

In any fairly ravaged industrial area, the face of love can be clobbered beyond recognition. Passionate liking is such an absurd and tenuous relationship it needs strong hints of grace and sophistication to provide it with a reasonable framework.

The early films provided us with many a shock as we saw the sheer floor space in which the better-provided were allowed to develop their pre- and extra-marital antics. It created a fixed bitterness in young lovers who had a narrow choice to make between a back lane and a parlour in which an immovable uncle was tickling 'Abide With Me' up to a Sunday gloss on the harmonium.

In the South Wales of the '20s politics and religion twisted the arm of the libido with a consistent ferocity. We subsisted on speeches, sermons and hymns which declared that the only authentic love was the urge to unite socially with the rest of the species.

Sexual love came into it only to be denounced as an indecency, an irrelevance, a betraying and bathetic bit of farce, a sheltering in stupid shadow, while the vast body of the army was advancing in light towards the uplands of total liberation. The nearest we got to the foot of Juliet's balcony was a demonstration. And we landed on the balcony itself only when we had some letter of scalding protest acknowledged on heat-proof vellum by the Prime Minister's secretary. Many a smooching amorist was dragged from a protective doorway by a father beating him half to death with a knout of knotted pamphlets.

Love needs an oxygen of confidence and when one has known an ambience of grotesque indignity one approaches personal love as warily as one would a gaolbreak. The adulterers I recall from my childhood were few, although I admit that I was not at that time watching out for them. The ones who were brought to my attention by relations anxious to point out to me in a cautionary way the various paths to hell, were jolly, roaring outlaws, not giving the sliver of a damn for their shattered respectability, and defying the pious to apply to them the execution by dog, stone or exile prescribed in the rougher pages of the Old Testament. They were, too, heavily dependent on drink for their excesses and in days of slump tended to crawl back into an autumnal restraint, and the places where extramural love throve, like the warmed wall of the old steam-fan and the back of the dance-hall, fell silent.

We followed these sinners about with praise, encouragement and building foods. They and the revivalists were the only people whose signatures we sought, thinking that in handwriting might be some clue to success.

From the numberless chapels which had splintered off from the Established Church flew many fragments of further dissent. These new persuasions settled themselves in small huts, usually on the moorland fringe of the town. The religious idiom in these places was much more passionately assertive and individual than in the conventional temples. I suppose starting up a new sect is classically a crypto-sexual act, for it is simply a desire to introduce some sensational novelty into one's relations with others. One is looking for a new and astonishing posture, a new chime of echoes for a voice maddeningly muffled.

I did a fair amount of research into these breakaway conventicles, usually on winter nights when sensual fervour ran thin. The sectaries reached a high degree of excitement. They did not favour long, set statements by a chosen preacher or hymns decorously sung. Their fancy ran to accordions, to dancing of a stamping kind, and self-revelations delivered in gibberish and a half-delirium. If the drug coca had been cultivable in those hills I would say that they had stumbled across a fair plantation of it.

My envy of them had edges of unforgettable anguish. Their ecstasy would move swiftly from the mystical to the sexual. The accordion would keep playing, because musicians of this type get their own kinds of satisfaction which are not explicable in terms of other love-techniques. It must have something to do with those straps and a swiftly manipulable keyboard. But many couples would leave the hut, yap up in joy at the frost-bright stars, canter up into the darkness of the hillside, then find bliss disperse abruptly as their bodies touched the freezing surface of the moor.

We wished them well, for they appeared to have reached a superb synthesis of the two passions we most admired, preaching and kissing. And the sight of their slow, sad progression from the heights back down to the blinking censure of the valley bed's streets, led us to the discovery of one of our first principles, that the levels of heat on this earth are disastrously and inextricably uneven.

In the lives of many of the women in that time and place there must have been caves of yearning. Men whose maturing was too often a simple rejection of tenderness, over-large broods of children, tormented by a lack of space and calories into muttering insurrection, hutch-houses where a wish for privacy passed as something sinister, a symptom of contempt or eccentricity, these things did a perfect Jack the Ripper job on more women than even Jack ever dreamed of. Death could often be seen backing in shame from such a lack of fulfilment.

On to the lives of such women the reasoning of demagogues and revivalists fell like an appeasing dew; their candent perorations warmed like brandy. The great revivalists came to revive something more than a limping theology. At their best they relieved more sieges of coldness than the gulf stream. They shattered silences that threatened to become funereal. They set lights swinging in dreams that had slipped betimes into a penultimate shroud.

I am thinking of one such wizard who lived well into my own lifetime. During one summer, when he was in his middle twenties and supremely handsome after the fashion of Henry Ainley, he burst forth from some Calvinistic Death Valley in the far

Welsh west, his eyes mesmeric with conviction, his tongue a thunderclap of sonorous hallelujahs. Every crouching heart in the land rose in a full ecstasy of response. Men paddled into the harbour of salvation after years on a broad lagoon of booze. Four members of the local quoits team, athletes of depravity, confessed their sins publicly and asked for admission into the orbit of grace. The whole audience wept as they saw these scamps sob and forswear quoits, sex, ale and the glee-group. They lapsed that very night, somewhere between the chapel and their homes, lured into a sawdust bar by some voter who had big gambling money involved in a quoits contest which the four converts stood a chance of winning.

But for the women it was a more serious thing. Their need for beauty, which a man can drown in a pint or stifle with a jest, is in them organic and abidingly disquieting. For them our revivalist was a combination of Valentino and Lloyd George; Latin frankness set squarely in the midst of a hymn-singing and radical democracy. The less timid went down to his enchantments like skittles. The pulpit on which he stood was less a platform and lectern than a protective screen. He spoke of the sun of warmth and love that was shortly to rise over the stricken tundra of their days. The brilliance of his invocations exploded with blinding force between them and the image of the muffled necks and belted bellies of their shuffling and beer-logged mates.

There was an occasion when he was found in a fern-bed, in flagrant delight with one of his younger worshippers. It was a great mistake. When one is stoking a communal libido it is tactless to particularise. That evening a whole army of enraged lovers assembled in the chapel and a mood of lynching was in the air. The deacons refused to take any part in the opening hymns. Two sidesmen soaped the rope. Two hundred pairs of female eyes did not leave his blushing face. He dangled from the grudge they bore him. We small ones in the gallery heard dreams topple and hit the ground so hard we wondered if it was just life again or a fresh onset of subsidence.

The revivalist stood up for his sermon. This, we thought, was one torero who would gladly ask the bull to get on with it. He opened his arms and leaned towards us. He said nothing. He was inviting us to brood upon all the places in the lives of men and women where love needed to go and, sometimes, inscrutably went. We brooded. Our spirits went towards him like lemmings, fascinated by the cliffs of his confessed anguish. He began, softly, to conjugate the verb 'to love' in Welsh and English. His voice had a quite unearthly timbre and reach. The precentor, a megalomaniac and a hard man to stop when he felt the mood was with him, began to hum one of our lovelier songs of lamentation. At least three women left the place, weeping, to mark the falling from the sky of yet another love.

At the end of that summer the revivalist, his larynx and most of the rest of him spent, retired into private life. He took with him a curious seraglio, a group of exquisite handmaidens, his favourite gospel-singers. And he left behind him a land that he had come to salve and left even more scarred and apprehensive than it had been before.

I fancied the revivalist line myself. Indeed, I fancied anything that would make me a magisterial and admirable fellow, letting off storms of compassion in the female breast, flanked by women groaning for a fresh sound, sight and touch of me. I practised a few perorations in the kitchen and thought I was doing fairly well until my brothers found a soporific herb and three wrestling grips that kept me out for the count for days on end. Also, my faith withered, and most of my carnal urges with it.

For me, Spurgeon dropped out of sight at about the same time as Casanova. On a blazing day in 1924 I was bitten by a rabid student of Bradlaugh who was crawling about in the Free Thought section of the Library and Institute. I lost my urge to preach and to impress my name and wishes on the melting hearts of women.

Which is a pity, for I, too, can conjugate the verb 'to love' in Welsh and English. And Spanish, too, if the thing ever went on tour.

MY NEXT HUSBAND . . .

Angela Milne

I am married to a civil servant. My next husband can be a civil servant too—most honest Englishmen are these days—as long as he acts a bit more like one. I mean, it's nice having round the house a qualified boots-and-helmet diver who can do sums on a slide-rule, but what a woman needs is a man who'll sit in the same room in the same office all day so that she can telephone him for a cauliflower, a man who'll be home with that cauliflower at six sharp to seize the bicycle lamp and unfurl his civil service umbrella and trudge back into the cold night for the logs and the wet washing. Yes, my next husband is going to have an elusive but unmistakable quality that I can only describe as henpecked. *I* am going to run *him*.

Herbert, for so I think of this wistfully puny figure (twenty-four inches round the shirt, for easy ironing), isn't going to be any trouble to cook for, even though he'll want dinner every single night at seven instead of some nights at midnight and some not at all, because he's going to adore good solid British cooking, the sort you leave steaming in basins or stewing in ovens. Hotpot, steak-and-kidney pud, macaroni cheese, those ought to do him. He'll rub his hands ecstatically over any food I put on the table anyway, even Crunchitex at breakfast. Imagine a husband who eats breakfast cereals!

He won't be practical, though. Other women may dream of a practical second husband, but what *I* dream of is Herbert's amazed admiration as he inspects the fence I've knocked back to the vertical with six nails, a hinge and a batten. 'Gosh, dear, how did you manage it! It's as good as new!' (No giving the fence a sceptical kick that sends it over again; no dispassionate explanation involving strain, stress and rotten wood; just that quiet background encouragement that does so much for a woman's morale.)

Not practical in big things, I should have said. Herbert is

going to be crazy about those gadgety mending jobs with bits of wire and weeny screws. He's going to take the midget screw-driver *from* me, saying laughingly, 'No, dear, this is not a woman's job!' (He seems to be the sort of man who calls his wife dear; I'll have to do something about that.) Another mending job he'll be crazy about is my sewing-machine, which *he* won't shrug off as a bit of feminine flummery. I may even get him on to some simple hemming. Men do sit about so on winter evenings, and I person-ally think one TV Western so like another.

In the summer evenings, of course, Herbert will garden, his *forte* being the individual staking of small kinky-stalked plants. I haven't decided if he shall be midge-proof or just too frightened of me to pour my best eau-de-cologne over his hair in the idiotic belief that it keeps the brutes away; either will do me fine, really, as long as he takes his wellingtons off *out*side the back door and when he gets up on Saturday morning doesn't steam round the house shouting for mythical green ribbed socks to wear with them. But of course Herbert will never shout. Yes, he will though—when he's at the bottom of the garden. 'Coffee, you said, dear? Thank you, dear! Coming!' None of those mean silences broken by 'I HEARD YOU THE FIRST TIME!'

Herbert's firmly developed sense of wonder will often cause him to drop his own breakfast newspaper (*The Times*) to gasp 'Goodness me, fancy that!' when I read him exciting bits from mine. Combined with his acute observation it will ensure that he never gets through the front door of an evening without mar-velling, 'Your cardigan has got different buttons!' *and* 'How well you've polished that little table today!' Something of the fresh-ness of childhood will cling to him too, in the way he revels in the English seaside, and crumpets buttered both sides, and Hamleys at Christmas time. Talking of that, he isn't just not going to mind carrying parcels, he isn't going to raise a squeak at the unwrapped sort, the folded overcoat crowned with pressure cooker and bunch of flowers that modern life so often forces on parked motorists.

I grow misty thinking of Herbert's little likes—British sherry, getting up at ten on Sunday morning, duty telephoning, being clawed by the cat—but I do realise a man isn't born with these endearing foibles and it won't be till I've pinched his coathanger space and made him read a knitting pattern aloud that he realises it's a woman's world and caves in. Dear Herbert . . . just thinking of him makes me positively agog to rush into the cold night for those logs.

THIS IS A STICK-UP

J. B. Boothroyd

I don't know what Miss Whibley will say.

It seemed so simple at the time. The chairman read from the agenda, 'Pistol for Act Three,' and I said, with ballistics written all over me and the confidence of a man who passes a gun-shop daily, 'I'll fix that,' and we went on to discuss dropping the prompter from the programmes. It appeared as 'promoter' last year and caused some bad feeling.

But nothing like the bad feeling I'm going to cause Miss Whibley.

The London gun-shop showed me the very thing. The cost of hire was absurdly low, the blank ammunition ridiculously cheap. Already I felt the glow that rewards a man who has said he'll do something and done it. 'Excellent,' I said, putting the weapon in my briefcase. 'I'll take it.'

The man reached over and took it out again, then went back to blowing down a Spanish musket. 'Not without a certificate,' he said—'Firearms Act, 1937.'

'Oh,' I said.

'Call back any time,' said the man, dropping the pistol in a drawer. 'With the certificate.'

In the light of this I had left things a bit late. The production was four days away, and they asked me about the gun at rehearsal that night. When I made my entrance and said 'Move and you're a dead duck. Bang!' Miss Whibley, instead of crumpling to the floor as usual, said that it was time we rehearsed with a real shot, otherwise I should be saying 'Bang!' on the night. 'I'm getting it,' I said. Miss Whibley said 'There's not much time.' I said 'It'll be here,' and she said she should hope so, and the producer said 'All *right*, "she crumples to the floor." '

Luckily the police station and the railway station are conveniently juxtaposed at Hayheath. I started five minutes early on the

73

next morning and popped in, saying briskly as I entered, 'Firearms Act, 1937,' hoping thus to suggest some slight immediacy.

The constable questioned me closely, as is proper in these violent times. The weapon was for use on the stage? In an amateur dramatic production? *Only* on the stage? To fire blank cartridges? Would I use it personally? Would anyone use it but me? Where was the weapon coming from? How long should I have it? Had I a licence already? Had I any ammunition in my possession? How much should I want? Was there any—?

But in the end I passed with flying colours, and the constable gave me a pink form which, I saw from a quick glance, would need completing in surroundings of contemplative ease.

'I'll bring it in tonight,' I said, and dashed off. I had heard three trains draw out already.

An older constable was on duty in the evening. He knew nothing of my case, but heard me out patiently, tapping the pink form with his notebook. He was surprised when I confirmed that I was not already a holder of a firearm certificate, as the form I had spent most of the day completing was, in fact, an application for a renewal, and in the circumstances entirely meaningless. 'Come to think of it,' the constable said, drawing up a stool to a shelf of reference books and making himself comfortable—'you've raised quite a few queries here.'

Time passed. The constable got down and stretched his legs. He came and leaned on the counter. 'As a matter of fact,' he said, 'you don't want a certificate at all.' He turned away and began taking down particulars of a lost dog from an elderly lady in musquash.

'But', I said, bursting in rudely, 'I can't get the gun without one.'

'Name *and* address on his collar?' he said to the lady. And to me: 'What you want is a Letter of Authorisation from the Chief Constable. You'll have to fill up another form.'

This, when I got it, seemed very much like the other one, but the paper was a different colour. I took it away. I was late for rehearsal.

It was the first constable again next morning. Neither of us mentioned that the form I now brought in wasn't the one he'd given me. It seemed better to let it slide.

'I shall want to collect the gun tomorrow,' I said. 'We shall have to manage tonight's dress rehearsal without it. But tomorrow . . .' I tailed off persuasively.

'Tomorrow, eh?' said the constable, and shook his head. Then he went into the next room and conferred with two other men. He rang up several people, and looked up a few books on the shelf.

'Call tomorrow,' he said, and smiled reassuringly.

It seemed too good to be true.

At the dress rehearsal I shot Miss Whibley with my old briar pipe. 'Bang!' I cried. She gave me a terrible look as she fell.

It was the sergeant on duty next morning. He heard my story in full, which took some time by now. He threw in a shrewd question here and there about the purpose for which the weapon was required, whether I already held a certificate and so forth. At last he said, 'Well, sir, that all seems in order. Suppose you call in, say, Monday of next week.'

Monday of next week.

'Look,' I said. And I told him. About Miss Whibley—everything. I must have been powerfully moving because in the end he came out with a suggestion surely unparalleled in the annals of officialdom. It was irregular, he said, and he wasn't at all sure he ought to do it, he said, but if I cared to tell the gun-shop to give him a ring he would get through to headquarters in the meantime and confirm that my letter of authority, though not producible, did in fact exist. 'Sergeant,' I said, 'I—you—' I broke down, I think.

The man at the gun-shop was screwing a hammer on a blunderbuss when I broke in on him with the glad news. He went on screwing it. His authority to release firearms, he said, came from the Metropolitan Police at Scotland Yard. Where they got *theirs* from was no concern of his. All he knew was that if all the station sergeants in Sussex called him in deputation on their bended knees it wouldn't make a ha'p'orth of difference. He was sorry. Of course, if I'd like to ring up Scotland Yard—but he'd tell me now, I shouldn't get any change out of *them*. It was the

Firearms Act, 1937, that was the trouble. If they—

Scotland Yard is a big place. Rather departmentalised, you might say. In my state, perhaps, it was a good thing. It passed a long afternoon.

It struck me, as I crept into the Memorial Hall this evening at the end of Act Two and began to put on the grease-paint, that I ought perhaps to have tried the Home Secretary. But I was tired, tired. You can only do so much. Now, my muffler knotted and my cap pulled well down, I have barely the energy to scribble this brief account—my vindication, in a way—on the back of a few spare programmes. Act Three is already under way. I have had my 'Five minutes please' from Mrs Tailypew, the call-boy. I can do no more now but make my entrance on cue, through the property window.

'Move and you're a dead duck!' I shall cry. I shall not cry 'Bang!' but I shall bring down, with cruel precision, my silk evening sock full of sago.

I don't know what Miss Whibley will say.

*'Johnson's been looking after father for so long he
couldn't bear to have anyone else.'*

SMOTHERED TEENAGE BRIDE
MARRIAGE-BED TRAGEDY

'I hope this will be a warning to other young girls against letting their heads be turned by boastful talk and the lure of novelty.'

This was the comment of a Cyprus coroner during the inquest on a coloured man, said to be a Moor, who stabbed himself after killing his teenage bride in a fit of what was described as 'insane jealousy'.

The inquest disclosed an amazing story of a girl's fatal infatuation for a middle-aged African, whom a neighbour later remembered as 'lascivious'.

The man had been a frequent visitor at her home. Her father was under the impression that he came simply to have a chat with him about old times. He had a fund of interesting anecdotes and 'tall' stories.

Cross-examined, the father said that when his guest claimed to have seen men with their heads growing under their shoulders he had thought it 'just a manner of speaking'.

Having noticed nothing 'out of place' between his daughter and the visitor, the father was naturally upset when two men visited him late one night and alleged that the couple had just contracted a secret marriage.

'Old Black Ram'

Without referring directly to either of the deceased, but using such terms as 'old black ram' and 'white ewe', they gave him to understand that immediate intervention on his part might still prevent consummation of the marriage.

Later he found that the girl had, in fact, gone to spend the night at her new husband's lodging.

The father first assumed that his daughter had been hypnotised or was under the influence of some 'sex drug'. It became clear, however, that she had been fascinated by the man's 'gift of the gab'.

The husband alleged that it was she who made the first advances.

The marriage had seemed to be going fairly smoothly until a man, at present in custody on various charges, known to the police as Iago or Jago, though probably neither is his correct name, mentioned to the husband that the wife had been unclothed 'in bed an hour or more' with a man friend.

Husband's Obsession

There was, it was stated at the inquest, no truth whatever in this allegation, but the husband became obsessed with the idea that his wife was carrying on an illicit relationship.

His attitude towards her completely changed. He abused her in obscene terms and on one occasion struck her.

Finally, after ordering her to get into

bed, he left the house but returned almost immediately and, after a long tirade of abuse, smothered her.

In a statement later, he said that he had used this method because he did not like the idea of shedding her blood or making scars on her white skin.

MOTHER'S PLEA AGAINST SON REJECTED

Refusing to grant an injunction, a judge said last week that he had come to the conclusion while watching the behaviour of the applicant in the box that she had a tendency to hysteria.

'I believe', he said, 'that in cases where a woman remarries after her husband's death, the child of the original marriage is often under a considerable stress.

'But these things are merely passing, and I am confident that if the applicant and her husband exercise ordinary sympathy and common sense they will find that this young man, Hamlet, will "play the game".

'I dare say you will all three have a good laugh over this later.'

Youth Warned

Turning to the son, the Judge said, 'Your mother seeks legal action to restrain you from uttering threats and menaces against herself and your stepfather. She has said here that you recently accused her of "honeying and making love over the nasty sty".

'I would remind you that your mother and stepfather are legally married, and that charges of this sort are entirely out of place. I am sure I can rely on you to behave yourself in future.'

The son was understood to say, 'That's what you think, wait till Act Five,' as he left the court.

Officers Object to 'Lechery' Charge

Described as a Turkish citizen, a man was recommended by magistrates for deportation after evidence had been given that he had encouraged the use of his orchard for immoral purposes.

A second charge, that he had lived on the immoral earnings of his niece, the daughter of a clergyman, was dropped.

Agreeing that he was the author of the popular song 'Love, love, nothing but love, Still more', the defendant stated that he had believed throughout that he was acting in the best interests of his niece, Miss Calchas.

It was stated that Miss Calchas had recently left the country to join an officer of the Greek Army. 'Everybody called her Cressid,' said her uncle.

Introduced to Officers

The defendant denied that he had received any monetary consideration for introducing his niece to Army officers. She had spoken of them as her 'fiancés' and he had allowed her the use of his orchard on that understanding.

He did not agree that on one occasion he had used the words 'I will show you a chamber with a bed.' He did not know how often intimacy had taken place between his niece and visiting officers.

There were angry interruptions from officers in court during the cross-questioning of a witness who gave his name as Thersites, and was described as a journalist.

Asked about the general moral tone of the camp concerned, he replied 'Nothing but lechery. All incontinent varlets.'

'Newly-weds Could Have Lived'—Vicar

'If the Ministry of Health officials had shown a little more understanding, these two young people would be alive today. Their action was bureaucracy run riot.'

In support of this allegation, the Reverend Laurence told the coroner that his curate, who was carrying a vital message to the young husband, had been forcibly detained on the ground that he had been in contact with an infectious disease.

'Not Nice'

Asked whether he had himself admitted that the letter was 'not nice', witness said he might have said something of the sort. He had, he said, been upset by the thought of 'a living corpse' being 'enclosed in a dead man's tomb'. The coroner said that was very natural.

The message, had it been delivered, would have done much to prevent a misunderstanding with most unfortunate consequences.

He agreed that he had himself officiated when the couple secretly went through a form of marriage at his house.

Asked 'Why the secrecy?' he said there had been family objections to the marriage. He did not think that intimacy had taken place before the marriage.

'Very Much In Love'

'But', he added, 'they were very much in love. So much so that I refused to leave them alone in my study for even a few minutes before performing the ceremony.'

A woman who had been in domestic service with the deceased girl's parents described them as being of a violent disposition.

'SO-CALLED ISLAND OF VICE'

'These disgusting allegations against a distinguished scientist' was counsel's description of newspaper reports which were the subject of a libel action.

'Poison pens and vulgar tittle-tattle', continued counsel, 'have been responsible for all this talk of "black magic", and this so-called "island of vice".'

He was amazed, he said, that any newspaper (not the *News of the Globe*) had dared to give such rumours currency.

Nightmare Stuff

The so-called 'experiments', involving a 'monster' and the young daughter of Professor Prospero, had been perfectly normal scientific procedure. Moreover the daughter was now, he understood, happily married, and had been deeply distressed by the publication of these rumours, which might well be thought to be such stuff as nightmares are made of.

She vaguely remembered a young man whom her father addressed as Ariel, but denied that he had 'meant' anything to her. She had considered him 'effeminate'.

DISORDERLY HOUSE ALLEGED

Policemen who for several nights had kept watch on a house in Eastcheap had brought to light a very serious state of affairs, prosecuting counsel told magistrates at an East London court.

The evidence, he said, left no doubt that the house was in every sense of the word disorderly.

A particularly disquieting feature was that Mrs Quickly, proprietress of the house in question and now in the dock, seemed to make a speciality of providing serving Army officers with what he could only describe as 'wine, women and song'.

Well-known Names

Several officers who had not reported for duty at the proper time were found later to have been frequenting this particular establishment.

'I would take this opportunity', said counsel, 'to warn the court that attempts are likely to be made by the defendant to suggest that the place was under distinguished patronage. It would, I submit, be grossly unfair if these people were allowed to drag in the mud the names of people well known in London Society.'

After some discussion the court gave leave for a young man whose name had been mentioned in connection with the case to be referred to as 'Mr H.'

Called Him 'Cheater'

Mrs Quickly said that one of the officers referred to had, in fact, been her fiancé for many years. She admitted that on one occasion she had tried to have him arrested for breach of promise, as well as for money owing to her, but stated that this had been due to a misunderstanding.

Questioned about her alleged association with a Captain Pistol, Miss D. Tearsheet of the same address agreed that he had on several occasions attempted to interfere with her clothing, but she had witnesses to testify that she had called out to others in the room asking them 'for God's sake' to 'thrust him downstairs'.

She had also told the captain to his face that he was, in her opinion, 'an abominable damned cheater'.

The case was adjourned.

The Rest of the NEWS OF THE GLOBE

☞ Officers returning from Egypt expressed great satisfaction with conditions of service there. Confirming that eight wild boars roasted whole were often served as breakfast for twelve officers, Major Enobarbus said that this was considered a fairly light meal.

*　　*　　*

☞ Mrs Page, of Windsor, wants to present a walking-stick to her local church, but has asked that it should be blessed and hung over the altar. She declined to give any reason for her offer, beyond stating that the stick had 'performed meritorious service'. The vicar, while welcoming all contributions, said this one 'seemed unusual'.

*　　*　　*

☞ Conditions of employment in 'stately homes' recently taken over by the National Trust are to be investigated following allegations by a man working as a porter at a picturesque castle near Inverness that he was asked to do excessive night-work. 'One might', he said, 'be working at the gates of hell.'

☞ The skipper of a ship recently wrecked on the Illyrian coast has described how he helped a girl passenger, whose name he did not know, enter the country disguised as a man. He said he gathered she was collecting material for an intimate picture of the Illyrian court.

*　　*　　*

☞ Because a more than average number of twins were born in the year before the War, cases of mistaken identity are likely to be on the increase, a medical authority said, commenting on a recent case in which confusion had arisen over the identity of twin brothers, both having the same name. Each of the brothers employed a valet, the two valets being also twins, named Dromio.

☞ As a result of the credit squeeze, a judge has warned, money-lenders seem to be growing more exorbitant in their demands. Rebuking one of the latter for demanding what he called his 'pound of flesh', the judge said he had no right to take advantage of the country's economic plight.

*　　*　　*

☞ An ex-officer, campaigning for election to the council, has denied saying that while he was several times wounded on active service, many of the voters had 'roared and run' for no good reason. He said it was absurd to allege that he had told his agent that all he wanted was that the voters should 'wash their faces and keep their teeth clean'.

'What do you mean, you're not in the mood?'

CONFESSIONS
OF A BOOKER JUDGE

Gillian Reynolds

No doubt about it, the prestige of being a Booker Prize judge is enormous. So much so that no one would believe me when I told them that I am one this year (the official announcement having drawn fewer lines in the press than National Earthworm Week), but that's understandable. When Martyn Goff, Director of the National Book League, rang to make me the offer the first thing I asked was who had let him down?

He laughed, but then he is a cheery chap. It wasn't like that at all, he said. The Chairman would be Anthony Thwaite, the others would be Isabel Quigly, Bernice Rubens and Edna Healey.

And so we all went to lunch at Book House, which is on top of a hill in Wandsworth. We asked, after some initial hesitation, basic questions like how many? And when would they arrive? We could, we were told, take the first lot home with us that day.

I walked down the hill to the railway station carrying the large cardboard box. It was a fine day in late May, a bit chilly but a bright blue sky with white clouds, the kind that excites. On days like that people start romances or become blondes.

All the way back, sitting with the box heavy on my knee, hauling it up the stairs and down the escalators, the little shifts inside it were like quickenings. Oh! I am a Booker Prize judge! and what is in here needs me!

I began reading the minute I got home. Random, I said to myself. Be random. No preferential treatment for famous names. Just put your hand into the box, take one out, read it. Treat them all alike.

I went out next day and bought a new little file box. I would do a card on each as I finished it. Anthony Thwaite, masterful person that he is, had told us to have comments on everything we had read, by September. Martyn Goff, the optimist of Book House, had warned there might be as many as 80 novels altogether. In the end there were 120 on the official list, with 36 more that publishers submitted for possible 'calling in'. By this time I had run out of file cards, patience and random intent. However, the very possibility of such events was remote as I sat down, the envy of all my friends ('How wonderful! A whole summer reading the best novels!'), to Book One.

Those were the idyllic days.

But by mid-July I had three unopened boxes in the hall, and heartburn. The books were coming in so fast and in such numbers that at one point the postman, taking pity, offered to take a box away again. Where was the excitement of their little shiftings now? Long gone, vanished in the panic of trying to find a place to put the buggers once they came out of the boxes.

Slit the tape, peel back the cardboard. There they would be, jackets rubbing shoulders, the rivals. Visions of India, South Africa, Canada, Guyana, Ghana, Iran, Australia, Japan, the past, the future. Worlds without pity, terrible souls stripped naked, occasional jokers, women with feelings worn bare, love with holes in, guilt by the cattle-truck load. Random no longer, purposive now, the hand goes into the box and, if it comes out with more of the same as that which lately it held, puts it aside and searches again. It dawns that the reason so many publishers' names are unfamiliar is that what they publish is, on this evidence, crap.

The clock ticks on meanwhile. Arithmetic joins aesthetics in judgement. If it takes a day to do 200 pages, how many pages are left and how many days? Selina Scott's question, much ridiculed at the time, about whether a judge has to read all the books now looks journalistically shrewd.

I haven't been reading fiction reviews, so as not to be prejudiced. But was that wise? I haven't phoned any of the other judges to confer, but when someone has rung me I have clung to the call like a lifeline. I am drowning in the sea of words. I can't remember what 'good' is, or 'bad' for that matter. If I were a novelist I might sue for industrial injury. Is there anything left to say about love, hate, rage, old age and the ways children see things?

At about this time the next book would show there is. Reading on. And on. One day I did three. The next day was like a hangover. I couldn't face the rest of what was in the box until afternoon and even then it took a swift half hour on Paul Muldoon's poems to get me back to the page at all. Reading on. The minute I finish one I put it down with the left hand and pick up the next with the right.

Don't judge by the jacket or the author's biography. Avoid the plot synopsis. Go for the prose. Prose? I've read better on the back of cornflake packets. Left hand drops, right picks up, spectacles fall down nose, delicious waves of snooze. Doorbell rings. More books. Isabel Quigly has 'called in' more. My heart hardens. This is the way publishers get round the rules, get more considered than their official four. Not with me, not this year, not with so many already in and waiting.

Of these, two come as page proofs. Publishers aren't supposed to do that either. But they do, especially with famous authors, knowing you won't resist. Trying to read one in bed, the 'read' heap collapses on the floor and I throw the 'unread' after it. Next day I relent and spend half an hour getting it back into order.

September comes and so do the leaks. Who spoke to *The Times*? Who showed the full list to the *Bookseller*? This last has caused problems. It seems that publishers don't like the whole list to appear as some of them tell their authors fibs about what they have submitted. I have been told by two booksellers what is going to win. I am surprised. They may be disappointed.

There was a time, four months ago, when I used to look in the window of my local bookshop, the Mandarin in Notting Hill Gate, and give myself secret hugs for all the books I wouldn't have to buy. 'I'll get it for the Booker,' I thought, and with Timothy Mo I was right, but with John Le Carré I was wrong. Since then it has been all reading for work, which can sometimes be reading for fun, but not always.

What I miss are biographies, poems and, most of all, Americans. I hadn't realised how thin literary life is without Americans.

84

I hadn't realised, either, how thick the plots around the Booker can be. Lobbies are no longer discreet, pleas for inside information continuous.

Brian Wenham, who was a judge the year William Golding beat Anthony Burgess, says it gets worse on the actual day. On 22 October we turn up, party frocks in hand, at the Guildhall for the final deliberation, the dinner, the TV show and the announcement.

'Would you do it again?' Wenham asks me. We look at each other and say not a word.

'We like the plot, Miss Austen, but all this effing and blinding will have to go.'

REGINA ORME'S GUARDIAN

Stella Gibbons

Guardians in fiction may be divided, when we have a spare
moment, into the Shambling and the Severe, and while in Jean
Webster's story *Daddy Long-Legs* we have an example of the
Shambling Guardian (all arms, legs and wistful charm, making us
long to hit him), in another American novel, *Infelice* by Augusta
Evans Wilson, we have Earle Palma, a regular humdinger of the
Severe sort.

To turn aside unwillingly from him for a moment: in older
novels, the Luvly Gurl who has been made ward of a Severe
Guardian usually wants to ride some tiresomely unmanageable
horse and the Guardian 'gravely' forbids her to. But with a
stamp of her chestnut curls and a catching of her rosy lip
between her teeth she is off and away and the mischief is done.
'Bitterly was saucy little Cissy to regret that defiance later,' and
before things get better she has 'sunk' her vicious little teeth into
some get-at-able part of the guardian, usually his wrist, and he
goes about with it in a sling for simply weeks and weeks, causing
her agonies of secret tears every time she runs into him while
she is culling fragrant blossoms in the great sweet rose garden.

She ends by kissing with her soft red lips the fading scar of
which her imperious temper has been the cause, and then he
catches her soft kittenish little form to his heart—by George—
yes, where were we—well, in the contemporary version of this
the Severe Guardian gravely forbids the Luvly Gurl to visit
some low nightclub to which he, as a Man, may safely go; nay,
may even have already visited; and she rebels. Off he goes in a
huff (at least, in any other man but a Severe Guardian it would
be a huff, but they only get grieved or pained or oddly con-
strained in their manner) leaving her (Unfair to Janis!) kneeling
on the hearthrug and seeing the flames through a strange crystal
blur.

Mrs Wilson was born in 1839 and died in 1909, and she is

described in my reference book as 'an Alabama author', but when she wrote *Infelice* I can't find out, and anyway, while reading it dates are the last thing one thinks about.

'In the gladiatorial arena of the court room, Mr Palma was regarded as a large-brained, nimble-witted, marble-hearted man, of vast ambition and tireless energy in the acquisition of his aims; but his colleagues and clients would as soon have sought chivalric tenderness in a bronze statue or a polished obelisk of porphyry.'

That tells us all we need to know about Palma, I think; but Madame Odille Orphia Orme has seen fit to entrust her daughter Regina, aged fifteen, to his care, and who are we to question the decisions of a mother in a novel by Mrs Wilson?

But for all his icy ways Palma believes in doing himself well. His library fairly intoxicates Regina when she first sees it. Amidst bronze inkstands, ebony and gold *escritoires*, brightly embroidered cushions for his feet to rest on, the final refinement is a velvet penwiper, while in a recess 'hung a man's pearl-grey dressing-gown lined with cherry silk; while under it rested a pair of black velvet slippers encrusted with vine leaves and bunches of grapes in gold bullion.'

Regina is asleep on the hearthrug in this bower when Palma comes in; and after a few playful yet oddly grisly remarks, which give us more than a hint of what his court-room manner must have been when he got hold of a shaky witness ('There is nothing very dreadful in your being caught asleep, like a white kitten on a velvet rug. If you are never guilty of anything worse, you and your guardian will not quarrel'), he chucks her under the chin.

Well, I know it says: 'When he put one hand under her chin and raised it he saw that the missing light in the alabaster vase had been supplied, and her smooth cheeks were flushed to a brilliant carmine,' but if it wasn't a chuck, what exactly was it?

Then, 'throwing his massive head back, he adjusted his steel-rimmed spectacles, joined his hands and built a pyramid with his fingers; while he scrutinised her as coldly, as searchingly as Swammerdam or Leeuwenhoek' (I do like *value* when I lay out ninepence on a book) 'might have inspected some new and as

87

yet unclassified animaliculum, or as Fillippi or Pasteur studied the causes of "Pébrine".'

Putting aside a passing wonder as to who the dickens Swammerdam, Leeuwenhoek, Fillippi and 'Pébrine' might have been, we read feverishly on, and presently Regina is rising eighteen, and Palma is in the bad books of his stepsister, Olga, because for the last eight years he has persisted in trying to prevent her marriage with Belmont Eggleston, the struggling young painter. He has done it, too, and finally his warnings are proved dead right (what else did you expect?) when Eggleston marries another girl for her money.

Poor Olga has brain fever, and, as is customary in Augusta Evans Wilson's novels, the illness proceeds in the greatest discomfort and confusion.

Palma, who has lately been concealing a burning passion for Regina beneath his build-up of marble lips, granite face, steel spectacles and all the rest of it, is away in Washington on a case when Olga becomes ill.

No sooner has the doctor turned Olga's mother out of the sick-room and substituted Regina ('she is watchful, and possesses unusual self-control which you, my dear madam, utterly lack in a sick-room') than back comes Palma.

'I am glad to find Mr Palma has returned,' blethers the good doctor, 'though he knows no more than a judge's gavel of what is needful in a sick-room, *he will be a support and comfort to us all*' (italics mine, and Ye gods! can you wonder?) 'and his nerves never flag, never waver.'

The nerves of a Severe Guardian never do, and Palma's have the additional resource of an inexhaustible supply of cigars which he is always lighting at the gas brackets; but it bears hard on everybody else. What does he contribute in the way of comfort and support, exactly?

He glides between the gas globes (likes to be near them, naturally, because of the cigars) and the bed while uttering a groan from between his granite lips, sits for hours on end gazing at Olga with one elbow on his knee, and at intervals he sighs so loudly that the sick-room party can hear him. Oh, yes—on one occasion he does go and attend to the fire in the furnace room, but only after Regina has become so harassed by his breathing remarks about her faintness and weariness into her ear that she says *anything* in order to get rid of him. Then, 'shod in his velvet slippers, he noiselessly left the room,' but there is something fishy about this, because the house is huge, and full of servants, and surely one of them could have sat up all night to perform this menial task?

Palma and Regina have the usual Row Over the Unconscious Form of the Sufferer which takes place in most of Mrs Wilson's novels, and it ends in a draw. He is reduced to gliding in and out twice a day for a brief consultation with Doctor Suydam, and startling people out of their brief uneasy dozes.

However, after many weary, weary months of misunderstanding and suffering caused by honourable pride—I do wish I had the space to tell you about Madame Odille Orphia Orme's befoolment of General René Laurance in Paris, and how after a scene in which her scheme of vengeance is almost at fruition 'his hat had rolled out of sight and . . . he searched hurriedly for it,' her companion Mrs Waul (One of the Catter Wauls, would she be? Sorry, the sense of period is infectious) 'spoke from her distant recess', and what she said was: 'General Laurance will find his hat between the ottoman and the window'—but to return to Palma and Regina.

On page 497 (good gracious, are we there already?) we are into the home stretch at last.

'She felt giddy, faint, and the world seemed dissolved in rosy mist . . . "My Lily! my proud little flower. You will not come? Then Earle Palma must take his own and hold it, and wear it for ever . . ." After his stern self-control and patient waiting, the proud man who had never loved anyone but the fair young girl in his arms abandoned himself to the ecstasy of possession. He kissed the eyebrows that were so lovely in his sight . . . "my precious violet eyes, so tender and holy . . . my Silver Lily . . . mine for ever".'

Sooner her than us, I am sure you will agree.

THE BRITISH CHARACTER.
Love of Detective Fiction.

'. . . *"This looks to me like 'Dead-Face' Anderson's work," gasped
Detective-Inspector Watkins, eyeing the corpse in the bath . . .'*

THE BRITISH CHARACTER.
Importance of Breeding.

'... "I remind you of who?" I said. And then I knocked the blighter down.'

ANNA

P. M. Hubbard

An analeptic puts you in good heart:
   An anagram makes rat-heel out of leather:
An analytic takes a thing apart:
   An anaconda crushes it together.

An analect is part of a selection:
   An analogue's a thing you reason from:
An anamnesis is a recollection:
   An anapaest's the one that goes tiddi-pom.

Anacolutha lack a proper link:
   The analgesics put you out of pain:
The anabases climb out of the drink:
   The anabaptists pop you in again.

Anacreontics are a kind of song
   (Unlike *Anna's the name of names for me*):
Anna Karenina is immensely long:
   And sixteen annas equal one rupee.

A WREATH OF SAD STORIES

Woven from the Leaves of Life

Claud Cockburn

Teenaged, and a resident of Malvern, Worcestershire, Thomas Blore read some books, and they had stuff in them about Circassian girls, many of them dancers. They were of singular beauty, intelligence and skill, and plus this they were gloriously feminine; passionate and yet submissive; and, if you liked, they would play soft music to you while you reclined on something.

Older, Blore met a lot of girls, but none of them Circassians. Then he went to a party in Paris and he saw a girl across the room, and he said to a man 'Who's that girl across the room?' And the man said 'She's a Turk. Or rather, really, she's a Circassian, actually.' Blore was most awfully bucked, and addressed the girl, and soon married her. He was particularly bucked at the recollection of a comment by S. Freud to the effect that happiness is the fulfilment of childhood desire.

He brought her back to England immediately, and she said that, of course, she did not intend to let marriage interfere with her career. Blore said perhaps she could appear in cabaret, or did she mean ballet?

She said 'Dancing? Faugh!' And it turned out that she was a qualified solicitor, and before marriage had been admiringly referred to as the Benson, Benson, Benson, Benson and Bloom of Ankara South. She said a true daughter of progressive, modern Turkey had no time for dancing, and progressive girls from modern Lebanon, Syria, Iraq and adjacent areas had no time for it either.

Blore, reclining, said 'What about soft music?' She said 'Are you anti-democratic or something? And please don't sprawl when I speak to you. Sprawling is not so progressive.'

She got enrolled as a solicitor in London, and took her meals out with the other solicitors, who called her Cassie. When she got home she was too tired to do any housework, and had to read Toynbee in bed for relaxation. 'In modern Middle East', she said, 'we find Toynbee not very serious. But he is quite amusing, don't you find?'

When she divorced Blore she conducted her own case, and got an alimony award which crippled him for life.

II

The setting sun of yet another day was casting long shadows across the porch of the old homestead in Peoria, Kansas, as Hiram Hendrick, moved by the wonder of it all, vowed—not for the first time—always to be worthy of his heritage. He was clean and keen, and he got to be a captain in the Army. Then they made him assistant Military Attaché in a foreign capital, and the setting sun of yet another day still was casting long shadows across the Chancellery of the Legation in this foreign capital as Hiram, moved by the wonder of it all, vowed never to do anything he would be ashamed to discuss with the people in the War Office of the country to which he was accredited. In particular, he swore never to let his country down, or bring a blush to its cheek, by engaging in espionage and getting expelled as *non grata*.

'Thing about Hiram,' the boys would say in days to come, as they sat 'yarning' round the camp fire in the Union Club, while elk and moose sought their scanty fodder in the surrounding wilds, 'he was always absolutely *grata*.'

The sun set over and over again, and was doing so in Washington, D C, when a man from the Pentagon said to the Minister of the country where Hiram was *en poste*, 'How do you find Hiram Hendrick these days? Is he still as *grata* as ever?'

'More *grata* than ever, if anything,' responded the diplomat. 'I'd say he's one of the grataest men in your service.'

'No suspicion', queried his military interlocutor, 'of his using his diplomatic immunity as a cover for espionage, obtaining unauthorised information through unofficial channels, or by the bribery and corruption of such of your nationals as may be in possession of important military secrets? No hint of anything

94

improper, likely to lead to a peremptory request on your part for his immediate withdrawal?'

'None,' said the Minister.

So a week later Hiram was recalled to Washington and transferred to the command of a military canteen in a little-known area of northern Nebraska.

III

With all the fresh fervour of her eager young heart, little Clorinda dreamed childish dreams, and at her mother's knee prayed and prayed to become awfully, awfully rich, so as to have a series of men at her feet, begging her to marry them.

Then an uncle who had gone out to São Paulo, Brazil, died there, and cut up for a matter of a cool six million, four of the coolest being for Clorinda, and she married a man called Fuzeley, who insulted her publicly at the reception after the wedding, to show his independence and emphasised that, though penniless, he was in no way intimidated or inhibited by her great wealth.

To underline his point he later bought jewellery for other girls and sent Clorinda the bills. When she divorced him he said that had she not lived like some exotic flower, a hothouse plant sheltered by her riches from wholesome contact with life's realities, she would have been more broadminded.

Her second husband, who was Peter Althrop-Thurze, was brutally rude to her at the reception after the wedding, to show that, though penniless, he was not intimidated by her great wealth. He said she had better give him half her money right away so that he could start a business of his own, not wishing to have his friends suppose he was living on her.

The business he started was a nightclub in New York, and he said she had better remain in London. Otherwise, if she came to New York with him, people would say she didn't trust him out of her sight with the money, and he would be humiliated in the eyes of his friends and business associates.

After two years of separation she divorced him in Reno, and he said you could never trust these rich girls, they were spoiled and fickle, not knowing their own minds from one minute to the next.

Mewd, who married her some months later, said at the reception after the wedding that the unequal distribution of the world's goods, the existence of huge unearned incomes, maddened and revolted him, and that he was often disgusted at himself for allowing himself to become involved with a rich woman who had never done a hand's turn of decent work in her life, and probably wouldn't know how to take a bus across London if she had to, and she would have to pretty soon, because the masses weren't going to stand for this sort of thing for ever, and she needn't think they were, and they wouldn't be fobbed off much longer with crumbs, either.

He gave up his job, saying he could not stomach the notion of taking work out of the mouths of fellows who needed it more than he did, and he sat at home all day in a silk dressing-gown, saying the mere, grotesque, utterly unnecessary size of the house, more like some filthy luxury hotel than a sensible home, nauseated him.

He had become, he yelled, nothing but a spiv and a parasite. He commenced drinking heavily, and when Clorinda divorced him, a couple of years later, he said that what she and all her kind were, were ruthless juggernauts, little recking of the havoc of a human life.

IV

The educational inspectors, or whoever they were, asked Toby Neasworthy what he wanted to do when he grew up, and he said he wanted to enjoy a life of almost unparalleled luxury, extravagance and power, comparable only to that of the Roman Emperors. They gave him good marks for clear thinking and vision, and asked how? He said he was going to get to be bossman of a huge circulation newspaper somewhere, which would lash out fearlessly, hit hard, and pillory when necessary.

Also it would expose scandals in high places and low, unafraid to tear aside veils which too long had concealed this or that. Everyone would read it to see who or what had gone off the rails now, and Neasworthy would enjoy a life of almost unparalleled luxury, extravagance and power.

He became boss-man of such a paper, and from then on was

forced to live in an outer suburb with his aunts, because it would be so awful if the boss of this paper got breathed on by any scandal himself. When he travelled by train he had to take two tickets in case he lost one and they hauled him up for trying to travel without paying his fare.

When he finally retired he went off to have an orgy and found he had forgotten how.

V

Paynham-Bridges worked hard for years to get elected to Parliament so as to be in a position to do the country a tremendous lot of good.

'He was one of the best stuntmen in the business.'

HER HUSBAND AND I

Robert Morley

How well did I know the Duke of Windsor? It's a question which I have up to now been inclined to duck, to use a term of which HRH himself was fond. He was in his own pond always ducking and, of course, when he finally ducked the crown I had been half-expecting him to do so. Indeed, I remember wasting a few shillings in a private recording booth to make my own version of his abdication speech long before the event took place, and whenever a ring on the doorbell sounded I would play it while ushering my guests up to the bed-sitting-room I occupied in those days. 'Great things are happening,' I would urge, 'don't talk, just listen.' I always thought my own farewell sounded a good deal more moving than his but, of course, he was never to hear it.

I was not to meet the Duke of Windsor (as he was by then known) until some years later and nowadays when so much is still being written and watched on television and on stage about him, I feel I should no longer keep to myself the story of how we finally became acquainted, thereby throwing what light I can on this eccentric and enigmatic character.

Very well, then. The scene is the Lido, that narrow stretch of sand bordering the Adriatic, one of the numerous islands which share with Venice herself (I imagine the Queen of Cities must be feminine) the lagoon. While some of these islands are given over to lace-making and glass-blowing and one to nothing very much but eating luncheon, the Lido itself (because of its fine sandy beach which compares favourably with our own Weston-super-Mare) provides in the short summer season a refuge for the successful rich. The two states are by no means synonymous. It is quite possible to be successful and poor or unsuccessful and extremely wealthy. But in the years of which I write, and during one of which I encountered the Duke and Duchess, most of us stretched out in front of our cabanas had little to worry about except sunburn.

It may help my readers to understand what exactly occurred at the historic tea party, the circumstances of which I am about to relate, if I were to fill them in with the conditions which in those days prevailed on the sands. The Lido was not the sort of place where anyone could simply stroll on to the beach, drop their trousers and wade into the water. The foreshore was reserved almost exclusively for the patrons of the two principal hotels, Des Bains and the Excelsior. Early on the day of your arrival you paid a large sum to the Concierge Des Plages or indicated you were willing for it to be added to your bill; you were then allotted a cabana which contained two upright chairs and two daybeds, a limited supply of towels and a sunshade. Occupants of the cabana were limited to six in number, and any attempt to spill over into an adjacent beach lot was sternly resisted, not only by the occupants but (if they were absent) by guards who constantly patrolled the dividing catwalks which led to the communal toilets, showers and the restaurant whither everyone resorted between two and three-thirty.

Hidden discreetly from our view was the field hospital and the children's playground. The hospital dealt with burns, stings and heart attacks. The children's playground was little patronised. During the afternoon all games were banned from the seashore, and although during the morning it was permissible to erect fortifications and scoop out paddling pools, the sand was conscientiously levelled at intervals, not by the waves as is normally the case on such locations but by a positive army of attendants who at the same time removed seaweed, transported shells and the occasional ice-cream paper.

Italian children have always struck me as being extremely old for their ages and, although one occasionally came across a small group of them chattering in the shade behind the huts, their behaviour was quite different from the kind of rowdy exhibitionism normally encountered on an English beach. An Italian parent, for instance, never throws a ball at his or her offspring or exhorts him to run races or comb hair. In point of fact, all Italians of whatever sex or age, I find, comb it to excess. My own children (who have never cared for games) were perfectly happy in the water, hiring beach floats, purchasing ice cream or anything in fact which cost money, spotting Henry Fonda in the distance and waiting for the sun to set and life to begin. We invariably went to the Lido during the film festival.

I have never forced culture on my crowd, and they were perfectly content to sit in St Mark's Square on wet mornings and translate the titles of the film posters into basic and indeed box-office English. But towards dusk, they would disappear up the road opposite the Excelsior where the action either was or was likely to start at any moment. They were not in the least upset, therefore, when one afternoon we explained to them that they could get away a bit early and see if there were any returns for the latest Peter Sellers epic while we were bidden to tea with Wallis and David.

They were not themselves giving the party, but their hosts rented the next cabin. There can be no harm, surely, after all these years in revealing the hosts' names—Peter (now I am happy to say Lord) Thorneycroft and his Italian wife who was also, of course, his English wife. This was no *affaire des plages*, which is the place surely to interpolate a story about HRH and my father-in-law who owned a club in London of which the Prince was Patron. As sometimes happens, they had fallen out when HRH had resisted some suggestion of my father-in-law with the phrase 'Buck,' (his name was Buckmaster) 'don't try and hang your hat on me.' My father-in-law was not wearing a hat, naturally (as the exchange took place in his own lavatory) and was at a loss to understand what was meant at the time. Later, when it was explained to him, he was very angry indeed and for some years the two only acknowledged each other's presence with a brief nod.

One evening at the Embassy (what a pleasure it is to recall the old names; the Embassy was a night-club in Bond Street, indeed I believe it is to this day) he was shown to a table next to the Prince. His Royal Highness was all smiles. 'Buck, my dear fellow,' he greeted him, 'I want you to meet Mrs Simpson.' 'And I, Sire,' replied Buck, introducing his own companion by what unfortunately happened to be her name, 'would like you to meet *Miss* Simpson.' The last time they met, on the golf course at

Sunningdale, the Prince drove straight through without even nodding. You can't, as my father-in-law was fond of observing, expect to win them all.

When we asked the Thorneycrofts at what hour we were to present ourselves, my wife and I were told to do so soon after the guests arrived. No exact hour had been fixed, as they were coming by bus. I must say that was quite a surprise. Somehow I couldn't see them in a bus and, of course, I didn't. The bus stops on the upper road and the pair found their own way along the catwalk and joined our hosts. We counted, or rather I did, seven hundred and fifty slowly (I had decided previously on the number) and then walked across and were introduced. I recall that the Prince was not wearing a coat. I recall that, after a time, I returned to our cabana for our chairs and that Mrs Simpson herself handed me a cup of tea. Of the rest of the encounter my mind is completely blank.

I have in my time had occasion to speak with several other members of the Royal Family and can recall exactly what was said. Why then cannot I remember what occurred on that early autumn afternoon while the shadows of two such august personages continued to lengthen on the sands of time? I cannot explain it except to think there was some sort of magic about the couple which confused and at the same time obliterated memory, hence the countless books and utterly divergent plays and films which continue to pour from our presses and screens. All I know is they went home as they came, and we wondered if they found seats. The buses are crowded around that time of day.

LET'S PARLER FRANGLAIS!

Miles Kington

LE PHONE-IN

BRIAN Et maintenant nous allons over à Keith dans Ealing. Vous avez question, Keith? (*Silence*) Êtes-vous là, Keith? Oh, dear. Nous semblons avons perdu Keith dans Ealing.

KEITH Allo?

BRIAN Ah! Nous avons Keith dans Ealing! Et vous avez une question?

KEITH Bon soir, Brian.

BRIAN Bon soir, Keith. (*Silence*) Vous avez une question?

KEITH Well, Brian, il faut dire que je suis un long-time listener à votre programme, mais je suis un first-time caller.

BRIAN Bon, bon. Et vous avez une question?

KEITH Je trouve la programme très enjoyable. Je ne suis pas un bon sleeper, Brian, et votre programme me donne une sorte de company.

BRIAN Je suis glad. Et vous avez une question?

KEITH Well, Brian, il me semble que les newspapers ... at any rate, j'ai lu quelque part dans les newspapers ... non, c'est Wedgwood Benn ... vous pouvez m'écouter?

BRIAN Oui. Carry on, Keith.

KEITH Well, Brian, un ami aux works m'a dit que Brussels a dit au Labour Government que le postman anglais va disparaître. I mean, après 1980 le postman sera illegal. (*Silence*)

BRIAN Et votre question?

KEITH Non, well, I mean, cela me semble not right. C'est un terrible liberty. N'est-ce pas?

BRIAN It happens que je n'ai pas lu cet item particulier dans les newspapers. Vous êtes sûr? Que le postman va devenir illegal?

KEITH Oh, oui.

BRIAN Well, Keith, si c'est vrai, je suis d'agreement avec vous.

Le postman est une institution. Sans le postman, il y aura beucoup de chiens avec rien à look forward to!

KEITH Ce n'est pas le point, Brian. I mean, je suis, moi, personellement, un postman. Je ne veux pas disparaître en 1980.

BRIAN Bon. Merci, Keith dans Ealing.

KEITH J'ai seulement une chose de plus à dire, Brian. Qui blâmez-vous pour le football hooliganism?

BRIAN Je crois que tout le monde est un peu guilty. C'est un social question.

KEITH Because je crois qu'un bon whipping leur ferait un world de good. Quand j'étais un kid, mon père m'a battu chaque jour. Cela a fait un homme de moi.

BRIAN Merci, Keith, thanks for calling. Et maintenant Elsie dans Lambeth. Vous avez une question, Elsie? (*Silence*)

'. . . and two long range weather forecasters. That's the lot.'

THE PEN IS MIGHTIER THAN THE ORCHESTRA

VINCENT MULCHRONE
on his two years as a music critic

It takes a lot to stop a newspaper office in its tracks, like a Bateman cartoon, but the Chief Sub did it one night with an almighty yell across the editorial floor, 'What the bloody hell's a flattened fifth?'

He wouldn't have dared shout at the music critic like that had that worthy been some venerable old codger. But the music critic, by now paling a little, happened to be me. And my career as a critic was exactly one concert old.

What added to the piquancy of the moment was that I knew something the Chief Sub didn't know. I was a phoney music critic. And he knew something I didn't know. He had his own string quartet.

It had all begun a few hours earlier when the Editor asked me, 'Do you know anything about music?' It was a fair question, for I wore my hair unfashionably long in those days. Like an idiot, I said yes, and followed him into his office humming a snatch of 'Danny Boy', one of the few tunes I knew all the way through.

'London,' he said (it was in the days when you genuflected at the word), 'London says we've got to get a bit of culture in. You're the music critic. We'll give you a guinea a time for doing the Hallé.'

But not immediately, it seemed. His Northern caution told him to try me out first. It so happened that a string quartet was playing that night in the Holdsworth Hall. A Fourth Division engagement if ever there was one. But they'd try me out on that before launching me on what the County Palatine is pleased to call Hallé's Band.

I was to write a 'stick', newspaper jargon for twenty lines. I made a quick calculation, and a happy discovery. It is that if you write 'The Zoltan Slumbacher String Quartet played Ludwig Frankenstein's Variations on a Theme and Fugue by Ladislaw Hochenheimer at the Henry Longbottom Memorial Concert Hall, Manchester, last night' you are half way home and dry.

But I was in a panic over the other half, a panic I stilled with a visit to Manchester's magnificent music library. One of the jewels I dredged up was that the composer of the evening's major work was a bit of a lad for flattened fifths. Whatever, to this day, *they* may be.

So I worked it in. And the Chief Sub screamed. I did not deign to explain, but proffered the suggestion that these things could always be checked. He sent to the library for Groves and other text books. And—oh, the relief—one of them said that Charley boy was a positive fanatic for flattened fifths.

The crit appeared, and the biggest phoney ever to close his eyes and beat time with his programme in the Free Trade Hall was launched.

It's easy. Honest. It was at the Hallé that I discovered programme notes, a précis of the form and intention of the work, but to me a heaven sent crib. To one who cut his teeth on *Roget's Thesaurus*, it was child's play to substitute one's own adjectives and adverbs. Add a small knowledge of painting—'across this broad canvas, Sir John took the woodwinds, pricking like *pointillistes . . .*' and the job was done.

Even so, I always prayed for incidents. Sir John Barbirolli reproving latecomers was always good for ten lines on the decline in concert-going manners. A breakdown in the air conditioning was another, especially if the humidity made the strings hoarse. And if a famous soloist left his sickbed for the performance, criticism might be reduced to a single word like 'splendid', or 'mellifluous' or, occasionally, 'magnificent', though I was always sparing with the latter. Well, I mean.

Occasionally I would indulge a flight of fancy and, for example, remark that it was a fortunate day for all of us when Bartók abandoned the existing diatonic system and the chromatic system based upon it, and took up the style in which the twelve notes of the chromatic scale are considered as independent entities.

I have my friend Percy to thank for that. Percy A. Scholes, who wrote the *Oxford Companion to Music*, the phoney critic's bible. Percy put it all down from Absolute Pitch to Zymbalum, which you will know to be the Hungarian name for a dulcimer.

But of all the tools of the critic's trade, the most effective in my case was a pint. Bitter, to be exact. The best bitter in Manchester was to be found in the pub behind the Free Trade Hall. There the orchestra's brass section repaired during the intervals to slake their livid embouchures.

Three of them recognised in me a fellow devotee—of bitter, that is—and we became good friends. It was they who taught me, in their down to earth way, anything I know about music. At first, though, they were just another source of information about that night's concert because, between pulls at their pints, they would discuss the major work to come in the second half.

Of course I had to translate a bit. There was nothing hoity-toity about these musicians, none of your Green Room talk in the boozer. One might say, talking of the conductor, 'He's making a balls of the scherzo. You'd think he had a bus to catch.'

That, after another pint and a quick check with Percy, would appear as, 'We know Beethoven was the father of the scherzo as we know it today, bustling, humorous and sometimes droll. But in the Fifth his intention was to introduce a touch of deeply reflective and even mystical poetry—a poetry which Sir John read last night a trifle too quickly for my taste.'

After a couple of years of this some small smidgeon of musical know-how, if not actual knowledge, began to rub off on me, and I was getting to the stage of venturing some of my own opinions when the blow fell. With no consideration for me, Vaughan Williams produced a new symphony, the *Antarctica*, and gave it to his old friend Sir John, and the Hallé, for its first performance.

You see the difficulty. No programme notes. And worse than that, Sir John insisted on conducting his rehearsals in strict secrecy. Not a note was to leak out of the Free Trade Hall before the big night. All that was known was that the symphony was based on the composer's music for the film, *Scott of the Antarctic*, and that there was a wind machine in it somewhere. And, a final nail in my coffin, all the big music critics were coming up from London.

I needn't have worried. The camaraderie of pint drinkers won the day. I think it was a trombone who blurted out in the pub, 'It isn't a bloody symphony at all. It doesn't have a proper symphonic structure.' It was a frequent subject of discussion, and the boys were all for a first movement deepest in musical thought, the second slower and more lyrical, the third in a dance lilt, and the fourth, if there was to be one, a quick dessert for the others, yet all with a certain homogeneity.

I was at the first performance, thought I agreed with the pint men, swallowed hard, and took the plunge. The next day, I was the only critic to suggest that this was something less than a symphony. And the same day, at a chance meeting with Sir John, heard him say, 'Quite right, Mr Mulchrone, quite right.'

It was the high point of my critical career, and the last. I had foolishly bruited the remark about, and the Editor announced that he was going to extend my beat to cover the Liverpool Philharmonic. I tried to envisage the years ahead, and the hours I would have to spend building up contacts in the Liverpool brass.

So I got a transfer to the London office, where they had a real music critic. It's not that I had anything against the Liverpool Phil. Great Orchestra. It's just that I couldn't stand their bitter.

THE LAST AUSTRALIAN HERO

Barry Humphries

The filming of The Adventures of Barry McKenzie

Mucky Pup (*'It's Hilarious!! Watch your friends' faces!!!'*) is a curious substance sold in novelty emporia and Tottenham Court Road joke shops. Manufactured in Tokyo, it is a convincingly glistening dollopy scroll of bright brown plastic which people with an irrepressible sense of humour place mischievously on their friends' drawing-room Axminsters. If there is a dog or a kiddie around you can imagine what a load of fun is in store for the Mucky Pup purchaser.

On a sunny January morning in Earl's Court a group of Australian film makers could be found scattering about twenty pounds' worth of factory fresh Mucky Pup on the immaculate pavements of kangaroo valley. A street scene in *The Adventures of Barry McKenzie* was about to be shot and our chosen location just didn't look authentically English. To make matters worse it wasn't even raining, and an adjacent phone booth was conspicuously operable. In fact, it must have been the last unvandalised public telephone in London. Clearly the person whose job it had been to discover film locations which typified English squalor and desuetude had blundered badly, and the Australian designer and his assistants were frantically sprinkling fish bones on the footpath and piling overflowing garbage cans in people's doorways.

In the back of a van our graphics designer was hastily writing a sign which said 'Remember, Leprosy Inoculations are Compulsory' while highly paid extras attired themselves as bowler-hatted beggars and starving stockbrokers. Disguised as a Cypriot crone, an actress waited patiently, at the upper window of a derelict dwelling we had requisitioned and suitably defaced, for the cameras to roll. When Barry McKenzie stumbled out of his taxi (which had taken him from Heathrow to Earl's Court via

Stonehenge) it was this lady's task to deject the brimming con-tents of a chamber-pot into the street below whilst another extra, picturesquely disguised as a beefeater, rummaged hungrily in a faked-up dustbin. But still it hadn't rained. The weather was positively bloody Australian, in fact.

The enormous cost of making the real England look really English was borne by the Australian taxpayer. Long before, when it was first proposed that a major motion picture be made of Barry McKenzie's scabrous comic strip adventures, the prob-lem had been who was going to foot the bill. One of us knew the ageing whizz-kid who wrote the then Prime Minister's speeches, and a daring ruse was hit upon. Affairs of State in Canberra being what they are, it was rightly assumed that the PM rarely had time to check his copy before holding forth to the House, and so it was that one fine morning he overheard himself pledging a quarter of a million dollars of the taxpayers' money to finance a courageous new film venture which would spearhead the fledgling local cinema industry and put Australia in the centre of the cultural map where it belonged. The money duly changed hands with a murmur of incredulity in the Press and a rancorous howl of protest from Australian film critics, who all had the grubby and time-worn screenplays of their own cinema epics stuffed in the bottom drawers of their copy desks and naturally resented two hundred and fifty thousand of the green folding stuff finding its way into rival pockets.

The Art of the Film is a serious business, even in Australia, and public monies should properly be spent on cinema drama-tisations of aboriginal folklore, or 'relevant' and 'viable' social documents about the agony and the ecstasy of 'real' Australians in settings of kangaroo-infested bushland or gleaming Sydney skyscrapers. Fantasy, humour and downright ribaldry were the enemies of antipodean culture. Barry McKenzie might achieve a cheap and contemptible success at the box office, but in do-ing so it would demolish our international reputation as a race of suave sophisticates. People might even think we were *all* common.

Hardly believing our luck, we leapt aboard the first plane out of Sydney to spend the money so generously entrusted to us, but not before a little man from the Ministry of the Environment, Aborigines and the Arts (a Cinderella portfolio customarily assigned to the Party dunce) had rushed across the tarmac and uttered the amazing line: 'I hope you won't be using any Australian *colloquialisms* in this movie of yours!' We assured him that our artistic intentions were impeccable, not to say ponderous, and that no one viewing the finished product would thereafter suspect Australians of vernacular usage. We said something like that anyway, and privately wondered if any of those chastely spoken experts on the environment or the abos had ever glanced at our script.

The yarn we were about to spin on celluloid concerned the vicissitudes of a foul-mouthed Australian virgin (or latent heterosexual) marooned in London and prey to a horde of perverted rapacious Poms. The hero, of course, bore the name of Barry, antecedent of Monty Python's Bruce and the popular forename of most likeable and intelligent Australians. According to an encyclopaedia of Christian names, Barry is Old Welsh for 'a spear'. Time and long usage have rusted and blunted its meaning, however.

In photographing Barry McKenzie's misadventures it was necessary for our expatriate film company to acquire a London office and a vehicle. Thus, within a week of arriving in London, we bought a second-hand van which irretrievably packed up outside Harrods and might still be there, and we rented a flat in Soho which enjoyed the propinquity of Wardour Street without the advantages of hot water or electric light. Although the landlord was a Greek and the car salesman a fellow Australian, we were already experiencing at first hand the commonplace discomforts of English life. In a grisly fashion, life was beginning to imitate art, and Barry McKenzie's fictitious persecutors beleaguered his biographers. The pinguid landlord's name was, astoundingly enough, Mr Damocles (which is old Greek for Barry) and the coin-operated telephone in our jerry-built high rise apartment jangled constantly with plaintive calls from previous Pakistani tenants demanding refundment of their £200 deposit.

One of the film's most important props was an elaborate

meter which was to adorn Barry McKenzie's hotel room. Since it was supposed only to accept pound notes and emit flashing lights the machine had to be specially constructed and a quiet and ingenious little Englishman was given a very large sum of the Australian taxpayers' money to build it. We never saw him again, though in all probability he went into the accommodation business in Earl's Court, profitably equipped.

It still hadn't rained. London had rarely looked lovelier in January. Short of shooting the film in our own flat we were at our wits' end to convey the ghastliness of English life, when Miss Undine Voide turned up at the Savoy. Miss Voide worked for the Dept of the Environment in Sydney and had been assigned the onerous task of flying over and checking up on how we were spending the cash. The heart-breaking pleas from the Pakistanis were now interspersed with telephone calls from this suspicious hireling of the Australian Government who was demanding to see our accounts and, worst of all, our rushes. Luckily we had a fair bit 'in the can', as they say in Hollywood, but try as we might, a few proscribed colloquialisms had some-how crept into Barry McKenzie's dialogue. The next fortnight was spent hiding the film from Miss Voide and simultaneously granting her access to *some* of our impeccable bookkeeping. Luckily she was more interested in staying at the Savoy and shopping at Fortnums on her expense account than sabotaging our work of art, so that she was somehow sent back to Sydney with glowing accounts of our progress and integrity without once meeting a single member of the production company.

Meanwhile there were ominous rumblings from a famous air-line which has certain Australian associations. We proposed to film part of Barry's trip in one of their planes and they were deeply distressed by a line of dialogue in which the hero, in response to the hostess's 'Is there anything I can do for you sir?', bluntly proposes a spot of dalliance in the airborne toilet. A cele-brated Melbourne brewery was likewise apprehensive lest their distinguished product become linked in the public's mind with such a coarse and undesirable consumer as Barry McKenzie.

However, in the face of injunctions, boycotts, threats and outraged protests a film was made. It opened in Australia a year ago to a scream of abuse from the critics. In eight weeks, thanks to our colonial customers, the government got all its money back and they have now made so much profit that the Department has been able generously to subsidise other film makers, our talented critics amongst them. *The Adventures of Barry McKenzie* is now unleased upon an unsuspecting Pom public. Columbia Warner thought it might be a good idea to add subtitles: e.g.

BARRY (to irritating Englishman): 'I hope all your chooks turn to emus and kick your dunnee down.'
SUBTITLE: 'I hope your poultry transmute into ostriches and demolish your outdoor earth closet.'

We tried it but there wasn't enough room left on the screen for the picture. Alas, as for the Mucky Pup, it ended up on the cutting-room floor.

'And do you think this will last any longer than the winemaking?'

ON SADDLERS

Jacky Gillott

'I'm looking for a pelham.' The woman leaning on the counter to make her request seems to be wearing very ancient army camouflage clothes.

'Cob size? Full size? With a port . . . without? Vulcanite mouthpiece or steel? And what sort of chain—double linked?'

'Well, I was thinking of a Kimblewick—with two slots in the rings.'

'Very severe, a Kimblewick. Can break a horse's jaw badly used. Have you considered a Scamperdale or a Banbury?'

And this is just the tip of a conversation on bitting overheard at the saddler's. It goes on to lament the number of small girls who, made insensible by the sight of Eddie Macken riding in a hackamore, are now clamouring for bitless bridles to put on their own truculent ponies.

'You've got to have beautiful hands for a hackamore . . .' the saddler's customer sighs mistily. 'Eddie's got a lovely pair of hands.'

We all silently think of Eddie's divine hands and wonderful seat.

'Perfect balance!' muses one of us. It could have been me. I am easily carried away by the language and lore of the horse world. A shop window in some high street crammed with curry combs, poultice boots, saddle soap, sweat scrapers and spurs and I'm in there, turning over all the small items within easy reach—rein stops, rectal thermometers, stock pins, plaiting thread, hoofpicks. The smell of leather and neat's foot oil is intoxicating. The conversation, its special vocabulary is stimulating beyond anything at a gowned High Table.

'You need a springtree model with cut-back pommel to avoid pinching that animal's withers,' advises my favourite saddler, 'and a saddle flap that will set off his shoulder to advantage.' He must be six foot four, an ex-Life Guard from London who makes his own saddles in a wooden loft above a barn. He has Radio Four on the entire time he stitches. The sound of Robin Day's voice hectoring some luckless civil servant is oddly freakish in this room whose shelves spill over with equine remedies for which all horse owners have an hypochondriac passion.

Liniments for this and that, powdered seaweed, wormers of all kinds (guaranteed to rid the horse of bots, ascarids, strongyles), Vitamin E to promote fertility and an amazing conditioner called Spectrum-14, one of whose mystery ingredients is dried *Irish* grass. As used by Eddie Macken, is the claim, so many a dazed lady rider spends £15 on a tub of the stuff although how *much* Irish grass (albeit dried) it is possible to fit into so modest a container is almost a theological question in this strange and hallowed world.

Do people who consider buying a horse fully realise that the creature's wardrobe must needs be far more extensive and expensive than their own?

Your horse must have a day rug, a night rug, a travelling rug, a sweat rug, and a New Zealand rug. It requires stable bandages, tail guards, over-reach boots, hock boots, running martingales, standing martingales, Balding girths, numnahs, Grakle nosebands, drop nosebands . . . I could go on. And on. The litany enchants me.

Although Mac, my other favourite saddler—a Scot who once patrolled a London beat—stocks jodhpurs and crash hats and is a moderately clothes-conscious man himself, insisting on the kilt at Hogmanay and secretly donning a Masonic apron on other undisclosed nights of the year, he knows very well that horse owners clothe themselves only either at second hand or in desperation.

For this reason he does rather less well in the human dress department than the stallholders who, balaclavaed to the nose, where a single droplet swings, position themselves at various horse events round the country. These events are always held in punishingly exposed places like Salisbury Plain at fiendishly unseasonable times of the year. The anorak tents bulge with blue-lipped people lagging themselves like water tanks with one layer upon another. Over the second Guernsey sweater goes a quilted waistcoat followed by a sort of duvet with armholes topped by a thornproof, a wholly weather-resistant garment with a waxed surface which—as you drive home in your warm car—begins to melt unpleasantly and gums you to your seat.

Shoes are the horse owner's other major expense. Not his own, you understand. For his own feet green gumboots make a perfectly adequate home.

Once upon a time Mac did horses' shoes too until a succession of brutish animals did for his back. Freddy, who now does my shoeing, was at one time (like Mac) a London policeman. He was on mounted patrol in Richmond Park but all he ever came across was people up to things in the back of their cars and he didn't feel like dismounting himself just to discourage them. So now he taps on a set of shoes once every three weeks for £8 plus VAT, plus travel, with hoof cushions to prevent bruised soles as an extra. While he hammers and trims away he has me listen to his latest tapes—every weekend he goes up to London for singing lessons so that he can be the vocalist with his brother-in-law's band. So, above the blast of his portable furnace, I bend an ear to his latest Mario Lanza rendering and shout that he's coming on just fine.

His assistant is a champion disco dancer and bangs the anvil with a nice rhythm.

The hoof burns, the hammers ring, 'Santa Lucia' swells intermittently above the din and we talk of contracted heels or possibly feathering the shoe to reduce the risk of brushing. Darkly, we condemn other blacksmiths who dump the toe.

There is the sharpest possible pleasure in this exchange of special language. And at the end, when the last clench is secured and Freddy stretches his aching back, he'll say: If you haven't got the cash today, next time will do. They say it at the saddler's too. Oh, put it down, they say. Any time. After the enjoyment we've had from mulling over such matters as healthy frogs, slipped stifles and coronets, money can only be a mere incidental.

'Henry—you've forgotten your glasses again.'

'Well, I'll marry you if you insist—but who do you suppose you're speaking to?'

TRY UNDER 'DIABOLICAL'

E. S. Turner

It is time the Worshipful Company of Index-Makers (assuming it exists) looked to its art and mystery.

Indexing today lacks human interest. It may be accurate, systematic and compendious, but who wants that?

Samuel Palmer, who indexed *The Times* for our hairy forbears, believed in making his work *readable*. He scorned elaborate classification and was happiest when indexing items under straightforward headings like 'Dreadful', 'Disgraceful', 'Distressing', 'Disgusting' or 'Diabolical'.

Thus, rubbing shoulders with 'Disraeli' and 'Diplomacy', would appear 'Dreadful Scene in a Police Court at Rochester', 'Disgraceful Wedding at Bradford', 'Disgusting Barbarity of a Wrestling Match at Accrington', 'Disgusting Cruelty to an Ox by Two Ploughmen', 'Diabolical Attempt to Blow Up a Powder Mill at St Chamas' and 'Diabolical Amusement—Throwing Vitriol over Ladies' Best Dresses in New York'.

When the nature of the Dreadful or Disgusting occurrence was not specified a clue could sometimes be found elsewhere in the index. Take that disgusting wrestling match, for instance. Under 'Sport and Sporting' is another entry which reveals that the match was fought between Two Naked Men. But there is no other clue as to what happened at that disgraceful wedding at Bradford.

The letter 'E' sometimes produced notable entries, like 'Extraordinary Occurrence—a Box with the Body of a Child in it Found in a Goods Van on the Exeter to Bristol Line'. There might also be entries under 'Curious' or 'Interesting', but for real pulsing human interest the 'Ds' had it every time.

It was not only under adjectival headings that Mr Palmer let himself go. Under 'Executions', for instance, appears the item: 'Execution of Boyse and Alsen, Two Robbers, at Assens in

Denmark, Shocking Scene at, Two Young Girls Drinking Their Blood'.

Depravity held a strong fascination for Mr Palmer, but he was even more impressed by the ingenuity with which the human race shed its limbs, put out its eyes and fragmented or pulped itself. Consider these entries, all of about a century ago, under 'Accidents':

> to Patrick Haggerty, from a Needle Entering and Breaking in his Chest as he was Embracing a Young Woman;
>
> at the London Docks, to Two Young Women who, Looking down on the Hydraulic Lift, had their Heads Cut off Coming down on them Suddenly;
>
> to Count Radetzky, who in Rising to Bow a Lady out of his Room, Fell and Broke his Leg;
>
> to a Child of Colonel Broughton, Poisoned by the Chemist's Apprentice Sending Black Drop for Black Draught;
>
> to Mr Lawrence at Berne, from the Lightning Splitting the Apple Tree from Top to Bottom, against which he was Leaning, so that he Fell in and on its Springing too (*sic*) Held him as in a Vice;
>
> to Mr Drummond, of Alloa, who Stepping Back from a Runaway Horse, came Suddenly on a Sharp Axe held by a Boy and had his Nose Cut off;
>
> to Master Gillian who, on Applying his Tongue to a Frosted Lamp Post, was Held Fast and only Released by Cutting the Tongue;
>
> to Mr Gobert, Shot by a Pistol he was Showing to a Customer, on which the Customer Blew out his own Brains from Terror.

So it went on, a gripping chronicle of folly and ill-fortune— somnambulists impaling themselves on railings, gamekeepers tripping over their own spring guns, brewers falling into their vats, miners plummeting into the earth. Whenever possible, Mr Palmer mentioned that the victims were Cut in Two, Blown to Pieces, Dashed to Pieces, Literally Cut to Pieces, Smashed to Atoms, or Reduced to a Skeleton.

Mr Palmer did not go into such detail when dealing with less fascinating subjects than accidents. Under 'Bankruptcies', for example, he listed merely names of individuals, with never an indication of the frailties or villanies which had led the victims to ruin. Even under the heading 'Police' he could be laconic.

To the reader who is not merely browsing, but is seeking to track down some specific news item, Mr Palmer's system is not, at first, easy to follow. If one is writing about suicides at Niagara it is no use looking under 'Suicides' or 'Niagara'; instead, one turns to 'F' and finds 'Fearful Leap of Mrs Flynn over the Bank of the Niagara River'. Again, if one is writing a treatise on the press, it is vain to seek under 'Press'; the looked-for item may possibly appear under 'Cheap Press' or even 'Hireling Press' ('Hireling Press and *The Times*' runs one entry). With practice, one learns; though Mr Palmer, surely, is being unnecessarily elusive with the entry, under that hard-worked 'D', of 'Dirty Box Picked up at Lucknow Full of Diamonds'. Incidentally, if an item does not appear under 'Distressing' it is worth turning to 'M' to try 'Most Distressing'.

With all its imperfections Mr Palmer's index is more vividly alive than the current Official Index of *The Times*. His only rival in his sphere today is the indexer of the *New York Times* who, while he does not file entries under 'Diabolical', also imparts information in such detail as to render consultation of the files superfluous. Thus, the progress of a presidential illness may be followed in column after column of small print: 'White holds President would have had coronary attack years ago but for his golf . . . President says handicapped persons inspire him to do job without feeling sorry for himself . . . Professor Link reveals Eisenhower has used anticoagulant Warfarin since 1955 heart attack; says that in larger doses it is effective rodenticide, causing rats to bleed to death . . .'

If Mr Palmer could see this index he might even consider that it was a shade garrulous.

GLOSS FINISH

*Fashionable and fashion-conscious photographer LORD
LICHFIELD talks to DAVID TAYLOR*

One's upbringing was practically Victorian. Maturity has been
more baroque. Always one has been accustomed to a life of
exquisite style and usually to a life of great wealth. One's not at
all dim—knows perfectly well one's an easy target: the trendy,
picture-snapping, racy-living earl and all that. One shrugs off
any tart asides, like water off the proverbial whatsit's back, and
gets on with one's professional and private lives—both of them
immensely full—simply because one has always been suffused
with this conviction that there really isn't a moment to lose.

Take today: one's sat here in a frightfully smart bit of Camp-
den Hill and oh, Lord knows how one might describe it: a bijou,
creeper-clad house in a street so tiny it could be mews, interior
largely muted greys set off with splashes of bold plum, furnished
in a smokey glass and chromium style, I suppose, packed with
gadgetry which one adores, desk and chair in functional black,
corduroy highlights, map of the world with gaily-coloured pins
showing where one's photographed on location (simply everywhere except, inexplicably, Wales and some of the Gabon) and a
much-thumbed *Reader's Digest Great World Atlas*, much-buttoned
telephones galore, a digital clock which—blast it—has stopped,
snazzy little Jap TV, pin-sharp Olympus camera gear (one's
on contract to them as well as Burberry's), beautifully-turned
collections of one's work and—can hardly miss this—photographs gummed to every available square inch.

Where were we? Taking today. Right—back from Scotland
overnight by jet to this, one's metropolitan working pad, whilst
Leonora took herself and the children in the Range-Rover down
to Shugborough, one's seat. Must look in on *Vogue* and talk to
Nescafé, be in Eastbourne at first light to photograph macs
against the Seven Sisters, got a job in Singapore coming up
and have just done a talk in Monte Carlo—no, sorry, that's

tomorrow—and must try and wangle a seat on Concorde to save time on the way back from the Far East—terrific amount of work has just come in—plus there's this exhibition just opened: the collected works of Bailey, Beaton, Brandt and Lichfield (crikey, sounds like a firm of commissioners for oaths, does it not, with oneself the junior partner) and that's right, it's the show they publicised by chartering a light aircraft and chucking out leaflets to flutter down all over the West End, a charity do, in aid of spina bifida kids.

Look, I'm sorry, I should have done a formal introduction. This is Thomas Patrick John Anson, 5th Earl of Lichfield, 6th Viscount Anson, 6th Baron Soberton, cousin of the Queen, married the old Duke of Westminster's daughter, photographer chap, everyone calls him Patrick. Fact is, he's not at all formal: used to cause the most frightful rows by pratting about in embroidered Mr Fish shirts and kingfisher tweeds, had a fetching hair-do, all at a time when that sort of thing wasn't really on for a chap of pedigree just out of the Grenadiers: people took him for a Sixties dilettante.

Doesn't mind the Sixties bit, but dilettante smarts. Patrick Lichfield has always been conscious of an obligation to work twice as hard at his chosen career in order to persuade colleagues one's not just amusing oneself. His great mate is David Bailey—opposite end of the social scale—and when first they met at *Vogue* they did nothing for months on end except exchange furtive glances: Patrick shy of being in the presence of grass-roots genius, David half-suspecting he was up against a toffee-nosed toff. Finally they were introduced underneath a Paris bedstead, each having dived for cover during an episode we'd better not dwell on now that his Lordship is a respectable family man.

Respectability at Shugborough, when he was a lad, was of the Victorian sort, I began by suggesting, for Patrick was reared in an atmosphere of quintessentially upper-crust barminess, largely influenced by his septuagenarian grandfather, the 4th Earl, who ruled the household, staff and family, with preposterously despotic vigour—a feudally-minded, eccentric martinet who meant kindly but often disguised it well.

Lest Patrick should take on cissy airs, for instance, he was from his earliest days despatched by the 4th Earl to a room in one of Shugborough's outside towers, so perishing cold that for six months of the year the ink froze over in the inkwells. Patrick took his food in the nursery until seven, then graduated to the servants' hall until he was fourteen and finally considered fit to join the family at table. He started off there in disgrace. Grandfather instructed him to pass the port off the sideboard and Patrick, to date experienced only in decanting pop, held on to the stopper and shook vigorously to bring up the sparkle. The butler was told, by a written note, to fetch a fresh supply. The butler always got told what to do in writing—the 4th Earl never uttered to staff, even when in the same room. His style was succinct. Patrick still has an example which reads: 'Beans cold. Butler farted.'

Escape into a less cloistered world came by way of prep. school, Harrow and Sandhurst. The discipline was, and remains, useful. The travel was enjoyable. For the rest, says Patrick Lichfield, the thing he remembers most clearly about the army is leaving it at 2.30 p.m., 24 October 1962. He was twenty-three.

He was also lumbered with Shugborough. Not that he doesn't adore the place—one finds it totally relaxing—but the 4th Earl had in the 1950s made over all 9,000 acres of it to Lord Lichfield's father. Father died first, followed two years later by the 4th Earl, a tragedy further clouded by the fact that Father had remarried only three months before his departure. The results of this tortuous piece of probate were that Patrick, though an Earl, was strapped for cash to maintain the family seat which had lost two lots of crippling death duties in two years, and he could not hope to pursue his passion for photography with any real zest until he had seen to re-roofing Shugborough as a necessary condition before it could be handed over to the National Trust. Fortunately, he was greatly helped with the hand-over by his stepmother who, he admits, probably loved the place more than did any of the family. She moved to Cornwall. Patrick moved into a private wing.

He also moved into London society and into an informal apprenticeship with Dmitri Kasterine, the beautifully-spoken ace photographer much featured in *Radio Times*, who taught him all the rudiments of the photographic craft. Contacts brought him to *Vogue*, for which he still has great sentimental affection, and the glittery world of fashion photography. People, he now says, remain his favourite subject: he has never entertained being a sharp-end photographer assigned to the horror that is war, nor until recently has he favoured meaningful snaps of harsh or cryptically-cropped landscapes. Society pictures by Lichfield appeared in *Queen* (now *Harper's* and same) and he graduated to the weekend supplements.

He has never sniffed at advertising. Probably the best-known snaps by Lord Lichfield are self-timed snaps *of* Lord Lichfield, belted up in a Burberry, with a couple of stout labradors in one hand and an expensive-looking blonde in the other. He also went through a frightfully commercial patch of being seen in a succession of flash cars, not to mention flash motor-bikes, the latter resulting in his being admitted to casualty no fewer than thirteen times. He has always suffered, he avers, from a rather childish tendency to suppose that everyone's a jolly good sort and was, for a time, in danger of 'making rather a Horlicks of one's life' in over-earnest pursuit of fun. Marriage changes a chap, though. Today he's totally house-trained, he says, besotted with his children (one of each) and at pains successfully to combine his private and professional lives. Leonora, though musical and a gifted illustrator, does not share his passion for pictures, he says. This is a positive advantage. One has the benefit of perspective.

One also has—though it does seem churlish to drag it in—total freedom from financial worry. Not that it stops one worrying—one's 'an optimistic worrier'—because we're back to the old chestnut of is he, or is he not, taking his photography seriously? One unequivocally is. One has a staff of five and work up to *here*. One is emphatically not in the business of gumming happy snaps into a vellum-bound album. One is clicking, against stiff and unforgiving competition, and determined to uphold one's (justified) reputation as a photo pro.

One is, after all, a Taurus. And superstitious as hell. Wet as it may sound, one does experience, from time to time, inexplicable insights—OK—rather paranormal things. But there honestly isn't the time to get bogged down with *that*. One's only sudden feeling right now is that the chauffeur-driven Merc is outside and the traffic may be hell between here and lunch. As seems always to be the case, one must tidy one's self up and dash.

'It's very nice but I thought there would be more people in it.'

I'M NOT A VEGETARIAN

Patrick Barrington

Although I never pandered
    To cruelty or greed,
I set too high a standard
    Entirely to succeed;
I'm not a vegetarian—
    I never felt inclined
To so unhumanitarian
    An attitude of mind.

I can't help feeling sorry for a radish;
    I can't help feeling pity for a pea.
How a man can be so narrow with a vegetable-marrow
    Has always been a mystery to me.
I look on it as cowardly and caddish
    To massacre a peanut in its shell;
My views may be mistaken, but I keep to eggs and bacon;
    And, after all, I manage very well.

I hate to see the life of a tomato
    Inhumanly and mercilessly wrecked;
I look upon a beetroot as a sensitive and sweet root
    Deserving admiration and respect.
I hate to see an apple in a tart, oh!
    Imprisoned like a felon in a cell.
Humanity, awaken! Oh, return to eggs and bacon!
    And, after all, you'll manage very well.

I weep for all the metres
    Of asparagus they grow
For the vegetable-eaters
    Of sinister Soho.

In some later generation,
    Dare I hope will be revealed
Rather more consideration
    For the lilies of the field.

My creed, which many look upon as crazy,
    Was formulated many years ago.
I believe that souls of ours go to dwell in fruits and flowers
    When their human life is finished here below.
A stockbroker may turn into a daisy,
    A barrister become a heather-bell.
This faith of mine's unshaken; that is why I keep to bacon,
    And, after all, I manage very well.

I like to think a plum may be a PLATO
    For anything that anyone can know;
I like to think an onion may contain the soul of BUNYAN
    Or a lettuce be the dwelling of DEFOE.
KING PTOLEMY may lurk in this potato;
    This celery be SHAKESPEARE—who can tell?
Oh! leave its spears unshaken. Not on SHAKESPEARE but
                                                on bacon
    I'll live. And I shall manage very well.

'Here! I've been deposed!'

FLAMENCO

Susan Jeffreys

When I got to the *Instituto* I was sweating like *un puerco*. It was hot that summer and I had run with the buses. That thing with the buses when you run for one and do not catch it so you run to the next stop and do not catch another bus until in the end you have saved yourself the fare.

'The courses started last week,' said the official one behind the desk. 'If you wish to do Cake Maintenance, Smocking for Weight Control or English as a Second Helping, you are too late. These classes are all full.'

'I do not want such classes, *camarada*. I wish to learn the flamenco.'

'Do you reap the bitter harvest of *los giros* or are you on *el regular earner*?'

'A bit of this, a bit of that,' I answered.

'Then you must pay the full fee.'

'Take it,' I said and threw the money at him, 'but I will do only the summer course.'

'That is what they all say,' he replied as he swept the money into a drawer and locked it. 'But you will become like the others. Obsessed.'

I went to the hall where they did the flamenco, it was empty. From the room above came the urgent, rhythmic hammerings of the upholstery class. Terrible gaspings came from the courtyard below where unfit men played five-a-side football. The evening sun streamed in through the windows, blood red across the sand in the *balde de fuego*, the fire bucket.

An *inglés* came into the hall, he was pale and wore glasses. He unbuttoned his shirt so that his string vest showed. He took out a handkerchief and tied a knot in each corner. He put the handkerchief on his head.

'*¡Madre de Dios!*' I said. 'Is this how you dress for the flamenco?'

'Well, I get sweaty,' he said and rolled down his socks.

Two more *ingleses* came into the hall. They carried plastic bags from Waitrose.

'*Salud*,' said the one in the string vest.

'*Salud*,' they replied and took out shoes from the bags. The woman's shoes had steel on the heels and toes. The soles of the man's were studded with small silver nails.

'Do you practise much?' I asked.

'¡*Nah*! ¡Leave off!' they said. 'We live in a maisonette.'

More people came into the room; they greeted each other and were friendly and pleasant.

My heart sank. I was hoping for blood feuds, card reading and perhaps a knife fight. I had hoped for hooped earrings, tight trousers and yards of black lace but these people shopped at Marks and Spencer. They were *gente bastante regular*, ordinary people.

I got up to leave; as I did so, three *hombres* came into the hall. They carried guitars and reeked of garlic. Their cheekbones were sharp as blades and their sideburns met under their chins. My heart rose and I sat down again.

They began to tune the strings of their guitars. One of them took a thin *cigarito* from the corner of his mouth and parked it on the neck of his guitar. He leaned towards the others and hissed, 'I see that Arsenal have signed Charlie Nicholas.'

'¡*Mierda*!' I thought. 'I will learn *nada* here, I have thrown away my money for nothing. I obscenity on your Adult Education.' In disgust I turned to look down into the courtyard where the unfit men were playing five-a-side football. One of them seemed to be dying, with little dignity and no priest.

When I turned my head again the *profesor de flamenco* had arrived. He wore flared trousers and plimsolls. He looked Welsh. Again I got up to leave. If I had left the room then, I would still be *una mujer libre*, a free woman. But the way was blocked, I was trapped in the room and now am trapped in an obsession.

What happened next was like that thing with Clark Kent and the telephone booth. The class barred the doorway, very straight and still. The *profesor* clapped his hands, the guitarists struck a chord and the *gente bastante regular* were transformed. Smouldering fire burnt in the eyes of women who had entered the hall respectable matrons. *Macho* arrogance oozed from every pore of men who had seemed mild-mannered. The man and the woman with the steel-bottomed shoes looked as if they slept in the cold, open field and had never been in a maisonette in their lives.

As for the *hombre* in the string vest, he was like a tiger. Every movement he made seemed fierce yet graceful, he looked lithe and dangerous. Even his string vest looked virile.

With a rhythmic *zapaedo* the class swept across the floor past the fire buckets, drowning out the noise of the upholstery class and the five-a-side football. Their fingers snapped and their eyes flashed. They clapped their hands and slapped their thighs. They were not the *gente bastante regular* who had first come into the hall.

I stood on my chair and shouted '*¡Ole! ¡*Triff and brill! ¡Keep it up, chaps!' as the dance reached its climax.

When it was finished I went up to the *profesor de flamenco*. I approached with great respect, he was no *hombre regular*.

'Can you teach me to do that?' I asked.

'Well, it's a bit tricky, see,' he said, 'but we'll have a bash. You need to practise, mind.'

And he was right. You must practise often if you wish to clap with the dry, sharp sound of the *palmada* and at the same time stamp out the rhythm with the feet. I practise much, usually in bus queues. I keep warm and soon get the stop to myself.

I am not good at the *pito*, the finger-snapping. All the fingers on both hands must make a loud sound if it is to be done well. With the right hand it is not too bad but the left has the resonance of a bunch of bananas. I practise all the time even in bed and now live a life of great solitude.

For me the *caida* is nothing. It is that moment in the dance when the rhythm is at its most furious and the dancer falls flat on the face. For me this is easy, but I have much work to do on the *getting up again in the same breathtaking moment*.

I like to do the hammerstep. For this you must jump forward on to your left toe and slam the right heel down behind it. It is a powerful step and banned above ground level in all Adult Education *Institutos*. It pulls the floor away from the walls. A team of flamenco anarchists could destroy every bridge in London. I practise it wherever I find a parquet floor.

But there is one thing I can never master however much I practise: *el haughty look*. For this you must stand very straight and look over the cheekbones to the proud swell of the bosom. I practise all the time but all I can ever see is my feet.

Why do I do this thing? Why spend all my spare time stamping and twitching and my spare cash at the shoe menders? Why do the rest of the class do it?

There is a printer who started so that he could keep his back from stooping and some nurses who find it gets rid of the tension that comes from being nice all day. There is a man joined because he could not get into the photography class and some more who joined either because they saw *Carmen* or take their holidays in Spain. But these excuses are not the real reason.

I pretend I learn the flamenco for that time when I am an old one and take the Senior Citizens' Winter Break to Spain. In those times I will wear tweeds, thick stockings and sensible shoes. The flamenco dancer who will be brought in to entertain the old *inglesa* will see me and choose me to be his partner to make a fool of me. But I will be magnificent. I will whip out my false teeth and as they chatter out the rhythm, my stout brogues will stamp out the *taconeo*.

But this is also an excuse. It is not the truth. For the truth is that the flamenco is a drug and once you have spent an evening sweating, stamping and oléing you wish to spend all your evenings doing it. Every time you master a step you have an appetite for a harder step. Each dance you learn makes you all the hungrier to learn a new one. It serves no purpose. It is an obsession.

But at least it got me off jigsaw puzzles.

CHANGE AT CREWE

George Melly

Just before we moved into Ronnie Scott's for our annual four-week stint, I flew down to the South of France to visit a friend who was cooking for two months for Quentin Crewe in a hill-side village called Le Grand Bank. It's not really a French village any more. It had become a ruin but was bought and rebuilt *in toto* by the engineer Jeremy Fry, who fills it in the summer with his friends. Quentin, however, occupies a house full-time and in winter is the only resident. Confined to a very advanced wheel-chair, which was designed by Jeremy and Snowdon, he needs considerable assistance: a secretary to type his current book on a word-processor; someone to help him in and out of bed, bath and car; a chauffeur and, of course, a cook.

One evening at dinner I asked if we were anywhere near the Ideal Palace of the Postman Cheval, a long-time shrine of the Surrealists. In the late nineteenth century the Postman built, on a piece of ground next to his house, this extraordinary concrete folly inlaid with stones and pottery shards, writhing with naïve statues, and pierced by corridors and grottos. Quentin said a friend had told him it was about two hours away and proposed a visit.

We set out at 10.00 a.m. There were five of us: my friend Alex at the wheel, Quentin by her side with his portable chair in the boot, and, in the back, his secretary Mags, myself, and Francis Fry, Jeremy's son, who was doing some building in the village. Luckily Mags is small and Francis thin, but even so it was quite a squash.

We set off in white mist, up into the mountains, down into valleys and across plains. Eventually we stopped for lunch in a small town where I foolishly ordered tripe sausages which have of late disagreed with me. Over coffee Quentin consulted the map. His face fell. By avoiding the autoroute we were not even half-way there.

We reached the outskirts of Hauterives as the light was fading and it was almost dark before we found the Ideal Palace, although the caretaker still let us in. It was impossible to see the details but the dreamlike towers and pinnacles were visible against the afterglow. Having come so far it would have been absurd to turn round and drive straight back. We would find a hotel and return next day to pay our proper respects to the visionary Postman. The caretaker told us that his sister-in-law kept an excellent hotel in a town some fifteen kilometres away. When we finally reached it, Francis, who apart from Quentin spoke the best French, got out to consult the landlady. I, too, got out. The tripe sausages had decided to assert themselves and, leaning against a wall, I was violently sick.

In between spasms, I could see across the street the landlady becoming more and more animated. Francis has this effect on people. He is both very polite and good-looking, but something in his manner, in the way he forms his sentences, always leads to a kind of *Alice in Wonderland* chaos. At all events the hotel was not suitable for Quentin as there was neither a ground-floor bedroom nor a lift. The landlady had told Francis there was another hotel at the end of the street but it turned out to be an abattoir.

We drove round and round that unwelcoming little *ville* to find ourselves at last in a district of small factories with high wire fences. To our surprise, as we'd been told, there was a hotel, a low shabby building with a pebbled forecourt. Sticking up from the pebbles at the entrance was an iron wedge to prevent the gates from swinging both ways. This tore the exhaust of Alex's car from its moorings and almost severed it. Francis and I rushed into the hotel for different reasons: he to test out the accommodation, I because the tripe sausages had changed their strategy. Standing on one of those awful French loos, I could hear Francis beginning to wind up the enormous proprietor and his only customer, a near-dwarf. There turned out to be no bedrooms but we were assured that a further thirty kilometres ahead was a modern hotel on the side of the autoroute. Indeed, after a long, slow journey, with many wrong turnings and the exhaust beating an irregular tattoo beneath us, we found it. It was called '*Halte OK*' and was exactly the sort of place where the Feetwarmers and myself stay on the outskirts of, say, Derby. We had rooms, there was a lift, and even dinner, in my case a bowl of clear soup and some grapes. The waiter managed to spill an elaborate fish dish incorporating both pastry and a thick sauce all over Quentin. 'I don't mind you laughing,' he said with remarkable restraint, 'but I do think the staff at least might try to control themselves.'

At dawn Alex and I got up and limped through the mist a further thirty kilometres down the autoroute to Valence, the nearest place, according to the helpful hotel manager, which had a garage specialising in exhausts. They did indeed have a close approximation to the one we needed and, while they were fitting it, we sat in a café where the plump proprietress fed her poodles on segments of oranges part-masticated by herself.

We arrived back at '*Halte OK*' as the others were eating lunch and afterwards we returned to Le Palais. For me, at any rate, all our disasters were worthwhile, in a way almost appropriate. Here I was at last confronting a structure I had seen only in photographs, a work of poetic necessity with no other function. 'Yes, Monsieur,' said the caretaker in response to my question, 'Monsieur André Breton came here several times.'

We drove back along the autoroute. It took us two hours exactly.

A SHORT HISTORY OF MARRIAGE

Alan Coren

PREHISTORY

According to Professor Leakey, the earth is 4,600,000,000 years old. The year 400,000,1981 AD will therefore be a really big anniversary, possibly Plutonium, and it would be unwise to forget it. Civilisation could end up not talking to you for weeks. Start thinking about a suitable anniversary present now, even if you end up rushing out to buy it at the last minute. Something personal, certainly nothing for the kitchen.

2,000,000,000 BC Unicellular life appears. It reproduces by parthenogenesis, involving no one else. It is therefore pretty happy, especially as nobody asks it where it has been all night.

30,000,000 BC Earliest apes appear. This is the Oligocene Period (from Greek = 'few'), and the handful of apes thus has a very good time, since you can lope for weeks without running into an ape of the opposite sex, which means that when you eventually do, you are extremely grateful. Ugly apes have as much fun as attractive apes, and do not have to stay in all the time washing their hair. As a result, however, apes naturally begin to proliferate, so that within hardly more than about six million years some apes are starting to get choosy. Thus, the more repulsive apes take to trying to hang on to their mates permanently, in case the chance doesn't come again. It is the dawn of matrimony.

1,700,000 BC Earliest known hominids appear. Hunting and food-gathering begins. Slight shift in bonding-patterns emerges as female hominids able to make lizards taste good gain edge over female hominids with nice legs.

400,000 BC *Homo Erectus* stage. Body hair starts thinning. As big busts therefore become more evident, there is a commensurate swing away from lizard cuisine again.

350,000 BC Date of Heidelberg jaw. From its size and

elaborate hingework, palaeontologists have now been able to sex it with confidence, and also attribute to it the beginnings of domestic conversation. Phonetic experts believe it to have been capable of delivering complex structures at rapid speed, viz. 'What time do you call this, I have been slaving over this bloody lizard crumble all day, I was given to understand you were out gathering moss for afters, it does not take eight hours, whatever they are, to pluck a few handfuls of lichen, doubtless you have been lurching around after that top-heavy slag up the cliff, what is that curly red hair on your club, well I have not given you the best years of my life in order to . . .'

350,000 BC (*later the same evening*) Date of Heidelberg headache.

200,000 BC Discovery of fire. It is now possible to get a decent steak. An entirely new area of marital discord is ushered in, since it is even more possible to get a lousy steak.

80,000 BC Neanderthal Period. Tools become much more sophisticated: the needle is refined, making it possible to invent the nightdress. Cohabitation enters its darkest phase to date.

50,000 BC The First Ice Age. Neanderthal man, maintaining that it was Neanderthal woman's job to get the firewood in, bloody hell have I got to do every little job myself, and while we're on the subject it wouldn't kill your mother to get up off her backside now and again, becomes extinct.

30,000 BC Emergence of Cro-Magnon man, and the Aurignacian culture, bringing with it cave-painting and violent arguments about what colour to do the dining-room. Chisels become more sophisticated, and Cro-Magnon woman suggests that a shelf be put up in the kitchen.

25,000 BC Cro-Magnon woman asks how the shelf is coming along.

18,000 BC Last Ice Age. Cro-Magnon man reckons that it is hardly worth putting up the shelf now, and becomes extinct.

12,000 BC Rise of Proto-Neolithic civilisation. The wheel is invented. The woman is not allowed to roll it.

THE MODERN ERA

3,500 BC Sumerian civilisation flourishes. Cuneiform writing is invented, radically changing the whole nature of marriage, since it is now possible to write notes saying:

I miss you my darling, when is that ratfaced husband of yours going on nights again, s.w.a.l.k.

As it is also possible to find them lying around in pockets, a new vitality enters married life, together with surgery.

3,000 BC Cretan civilisation. First recorded example of bridegroom saying: 'It is a small thing, but Minoan.' The period is also remarkable for the rise of gold, silver and copper ornamentation: the sweet-dish is born, and becomes the first example of an item made not for using but for giving. Such is the glut of production that weddings alone will not mop up the fearful flood, and the engagement party is invented. This is an extremely successful marketing operation, and even allows the silversmiths to diversify into cruets.

2,000 BC Abraham leads the great emigration from Mesopotamia into Canaan, but it does not help: his mother-in-law finds out where he is from the butcher.

1,988 BC God commands Abraham to slay his son Isaac. His mother-in-law commands him to make the boy a solicitor. It is no contest; by 1,982 BC, Isaac has eight junior partners, plus a branch in Hebron specialising in corporate financing.

1,184 BC Menelaus goes to Sparta on business, and while he is away, Paris comes in to service the dishwasher. He then persuades Helen to elope with him to Troy, whereupon the Greeks lay siege to the city. The siege lasts ten years, which means that, while Helen was undoubtedly the most beautiful woman in the world at the start, by the end she is lying third, behind Miss Guatemala and Julia Morley. Menelaus takes Helen back to Sparta, but sees a lot of Miss Guatemala on the side.

753 BC Rhea Silvia, left short of housekeeping by her husband Mars, takes a part-time job in a Latium boutique, but has nowhere to leave the twins. She contacts a domestic agency for a child-minder, but because of a misunderstanding they send a wolf. It does not matter, the wolf is very good with kids and knows some terrific games, plus being a stickler for neatness. Anyone leaving toys lying around is liable to lose a leg. In consequence, Romulus and Remus grow up right, and found Rome. Dr Spock may have known a thing or two, but he wasn't in the wolf's league.

432 BC Outbreak of appalling marital disorder in Greece: not only are the divorce courts run off their feet with cases in which the evidence leaves even hardened barristers vomiting, but the genetic consequences afflict society for years to come, as sisters find themselves to be uncles and men turn out to be their own grandparents. Sociologists blame it on watching too much Sophocles.

46 BC Carpet containing Cleopatra delivered to Caesar. CLEOPATRA: 'Have you told her yet?' CAESAR: 'She hasn't been feeling very well lately.' This is the first recorded example of this popular exchange.

0 BC Breakthrough in attitude to one-parent families.

60 AD Revolt of Boudicca, who fits sword-blades to her chariot wheels and leaves a pitiful trail of Roman sopranos in her wake. Later, she edits *Guardian Women*.

618 Foundation of the T'ang Dynasty in China, ushering in the 128-piece dinner service. This is to revolutionise marriage, since the only way anybody can afford one is to have a formal ceremony, a large number of guests, and a list at Harrods.

663 Synod of Whitby installs Roman Christianity in Britain, which causes many problems, not the least of which is that very few people can spell 'rhythm'.

868 Earliest printed book appears in China. However, since several hundred couples suffer serious damage attempting page 32, it is quickly withdrawn.

879 Following the second Danish invasion, King Alfred seeks refuge in a peasant woman's hut. Her husband, who has been asleep in the garden, is awakened by the smell of a neglected oven, but proves an inferior swordsman to the king. This comes as no surprise to his wife.

1000 Leif Ericsson discovers North America. He is met by a tall woman with wonderful teeth who is prepared to enter into a one-to-one meaningful relationship in which both partners respect one another as persons. Leif Ericsson gets back in his boat.

1066 Normans introduce contraceptive to Britain. It is called garlic.

1099–1204 The Crusades, or I Have To Go Abroad On Business. It is hardly surprising that the English contingent fares so badly: of the 18,400 crusaders who set out, 9,200 are secretaries, and only a handful get further than Brighton.

1327 A bad year for marriage. Edward II, King of England, comes out of the closet. Since he is subsequently killed with a red-hot poker, it is also a bad year for coming out of the closet.

1536 Execution of Anne Boleyn radically changes English sexual mores. Husbands are encouraged to believe that it is no longer necessary to bring home bunches of daffs or engage in enervating foreplay: all you do is stick an axe on the bedside table. Women, however, respond by waiting for

1558, when Elizabeth I introduces the fashion for virgin spinsterhood. Nobody gets married, and there is very little sex, which is particularly hard on Sir Walter Raleigh, who has just invented the cigarette for afterwards.

1590+ The rise of English drama. Hardly have people begun marrying again when they have to start going to the theatre all the time. In arguments about who had the tickets, where to park the horse, who fell asleep during the first act, whether to eat before or after, and whose turn it is to take the baby-sitter home, thousands die.

1669 Nell Gw

1981 Hack's wife bursts in, enquiring whether hack realises it is now 3.30 a.m., not of course that it is a question of hack choosing between her and typewriter, hack exclaims bloody hell, politely, I have only got to 1669 and not yet dealt with rubber-wear or mortgages either, hack's wife says what is hack writing about, hack says marriage, hack's wife goes ha bloody ha.

RAILWAY NETWORKS

Anthony Carson

Once I worked as a clerk in an office and I grew thinner and my suits fell to bits and I watched the seagulls out of the window. The months passed and I knew I had taken the wrong road. 'You're not paid to watch seagulls,' said the manager. In my spare time I went to Victoria Station and bought cups of tea and watched the trains. The ceiling of the station shook with the thunder of wheels, and men with fur collars and attaché cases disappeared in clouds of steam. There was a faint imported smell of sea, a catch in the throat, a volley of shouts, and an explosion of children like fireworks. The Golden Arrow drew in. Out came the eternal over-wrapped exiles from operas and roulette, pampered ghosts from Anglo-French hotels, lovers, swindlers, actresses, impostors, believers, bores and magicians. But all that mattered to me was the gold and blue of the places they had been to, the singing names, like Leman, Maggiore, Garda, Ischia, Ibiza.

Eventually I joined a travel agency. I almost lived in trains, pushing hordes of people round monuments, cramming them into cathedrals, and winkling them out of gondolas. Once, on the Paris–Vallorbe run, my train split in two. Half my clients disappeared down a gradient. The runaway carriages reappeared half an hour later at Vallorbe station and were greeted by hysterical shouts, as though they had come back from Siberia. But the train didn't pull up. It puffed off busily in the general direction of Italy, and I found it quite impossible to control the pandemonium on the station platform. Even I, the courier, wasn't aware that this divided train was returning to another platform.

I lived in a world of smoke, station buffets, Customs offices and rattling corridors; the antiseptic rush through the Simplon tunnel; the gleaming run beside the lake of Geneva; carriages of priests, soldiers, Chianti and garlic between Pisa and Rome; and the eternal stolid caravanserai of British clients getting constipated from pasta and ruins. I was still a prisoner entangled in a web of questions, complaints and prejudices. But through the window, past the vacuum flask and the knitting needles, I could see the running rainbow feet of beauty.

After a time I began to weary of trains and to long for London. But I could not escape. The demon which had haunted me in the office and dragged me to Victoria Station to gape at the expresses would not release me. It was my living. Sleeping past Lyons, breakfast at the frontier, loving past Stresa, eating past the Apennines. Eventually I broke up a highly organised tour of Italy by running off with one of the clients, was sacked by the agency and took up writing.

A summer and a winter passed and London lay on my stomach like a lobster supper. I was making no money. The current was turned off, and I dreamed of the Continental railroads like swallows whose wings flutter in their sleep. Somewhere, someone was waving to me. 'You should be here!' Again I haunted Victoria Station. Then I paid a visit to another travel agency. 'I am a railway expert,' I said. 'Can you speak Spanish?' asked the manager. 'Certainly,' I replied. 'We are experimenting with a place called Sitges in the north of Spain. We would like you to take about fifty clients there from London. Would you be prepared to do that?' 'Yes,' I said. 'Be careful with them,' said the manager. 'Some of them are old ladies and not used to travel. You start in a fortnight, and if you call in tomorrow I will give you the list.'

We went on the Newhaven–Dieppe–Paris route, and left for Port Bou from the Gare d'Austerlitz. So far it was an uneventful journey, except that four of the old ladies recognised me from my last Italian tour, and I could see them rustling up and down the corridors with scandal. The next morning we steamed into Cerbère, and I was smoked out of my carriage with questions. Do we change here? Is this Spain? Is Franco here? Shall we change our money? Can we use the lavatories in this station or would they arrest us? Can we get coffee? Tea? Aspirins?

Before I need answer all the questions the train slid through a tunnel and we arrived in Port Bou, Spain. Directly we got down on to the platform it was obvious that all the officials hated us on sight. Many of them were armed to the teeth. We were driven into a gloomy barrack-like Customs shed, our suitcases were wrenched open and the contents scattered right and left. One of my old ladies burst into tears. Have you any drugs, firearms or pornographic literature? an official was asking her.

There were six ticket-windows operated by six dour, sadistic railway employees. When you presented a form to be stamped each one said 'Wrong window.' Finally, at the risk of being shot, I got out on to the Port Bou–Barcelona platform and made enquiries about my agency reservations. A very old man in a peaked cap with RAILWAY SERVICES written on it pointed at a carriage. 'They are there,' he said. The carriage was bursting with people. 'But I have fifty clients,' I shouted. The old man looked at me with terrible patient sadness. 'That which has to be . . .' he said and crept away.

Finally we arranged ourselves on the train. I stood next to a plump Spaniard in the corridor who was looking out of the window at the embittered tourists flapping about the platform like intolerably harassed poultry. 'In an odd way it pays,' he said, offering me a cigarette. 'All of you foreigners, after this ghastly experience at the frontier, are expecting the worst from us. But when you find how friendly we are, and how much we hate our railways, it will seem all the better. Where are you going to?' 'I am taking fifty English people to Sitges.' 'Be prepared for the worst,' said the Spaniard, 'and beware of the tunnels.' He gave me details of the journey.

We reached Barcelona in the afternoon. Three of my old ladies had fainted, and there were ten cases of diarrhoea. ('You should have told us about the water.') There were two trains to Sitges. One said 'Very Fast' and the other 'Highly Rapid'. I chose the Highly Rapid and chased my party into two or three amazingly empty carriages. There was another train which I had not noticed. It was called 'Supremely Quick'. This left almost immediately. We waited in our train, starving, for about an hour, while it gradually filled up. When it was obviously crammed it left for the next Barcelona station, Paseo de Gracia.

Here was a waiting cargo of fresh passengers. Women lay on the floor like threshed wheat, suckling babies. Aerated-water sellers climbed through a trellis of arms and legs and half the station got on to the train to say goodbye. At the next station the beggars were waiting, followed by the lottery sellers carrying dolls and bags of sweets.

An hour later, remembering what the Spaniard at Port Bou had advised me, I squeezed my way through the train and warned all my party to take down their luggage and put it on to the outside platform. 'The train only stops for a minute at Sitges,' I told them. In the middle of this operation we entered the first tunnel. The carriages filled with smoke and the lottery sellers, coughing with rage, stumbled over their dolls, aerated water rolled over the floor and pickpockets got to work. In all, there were nine tunnels and they were very long and the train was slow. Finally we came into the light, and the town of Sitges, white as ice-cream, glimmered into view.

We poured out of the carriages, the fists of the lottery sellers pistoning through the windows, grappling with a cascade of luggage. Suddenly, with horror, I remembered I had placed some old ladies on the front carriage. I could see no sign of them. I ran forward to the platform behind the engine.

They were there. Five of them. Their faces were quite black. From one desperate feathered hat I could distinctly see a little spiral of smoke ascend, like the aftermath of a Red Indian massacre. 'This is Sitges,' I said in a small voice. But they just looked at me. And the train, with no warning, as much as to show that it *was* a train, made off towards Valencia.

I am back at Victoria Station again. Meet me at Platform Eight.

DRAWN FROM MEMORY

A VISIT TO ANDRÉ GIDE

Constantine Fitzgibbon

It was early in 1944, and I, a very young and junior officer, was passing through Algiers on the orders of my military superiors. An acquaintance there introduced me to Antoine de Saint-Exupéry, the poet and airman. Saint-Exupéry was grounded at the time, a sort of punishment, I heard say, for reckless flying. He seemed, nevertheless, to be in excellent spirits, and drove us out in his jeep to a black-market restaurant where he arranged that a most delicious meal be cooked for us. There were five or six of us at table, the bottles came quickly, Saint-Exupéry talked brilliantly in his bluff and witty fashion, and by the end of the evening I decided that I had seldom met a man I liked as much. A tough, intelligent and sensitive Frenchman takes a lot of beating.

In the course of the evening it came up that I had once, before the war, translated an essay by André Gide which had appeared in one of the high-class American college reviews. Saint-Exupéry asked me if I had ever met Gide. I had not, though we had corresponded—about copyright and so on. Would I care to meet him now, since he was living just outside Algiers? I most certainly would. Very well, Saint-Exupéry was going to see him late the following afternoon and he would take me along.

At that time I regarded André Gide as the greatest living writer. I had, I think, read every published work of his. His personality, particularly as revealed in his journals, fascinated me then—and indeed still does. I was young enough to believe that an author's conversation has a close relationship to his writing, that it resembles perhaps the unquarried marble from which he may carve his books. And in view of the charm, the force and the skill of Saint-Exupéry's talk, I foresaw a true intellectual feast, made all the more delectable by contrast with the dull rations of ideas available in the officers' messes that I frequented in those days. Also, of course, there was the appeal to snobbery, improved by the fact that I should not be visiting Gide as a completely unknown person. Algiers sparkled under its winter moon as I made my way back to my billet.

Next afternoon I went around to Saint-Exupéry's apartment, waited while he finished a game of chess with a sardonic individual whose name I did not catch, and then we drove out to Gide's house. Saint-Exupéry was in a somewhat less communicative mood today, and the drive was largely silent. Which was just as well, since he treated his jeep much as I imagine he had handled those planes, screeching around corners on two wheels, dodging in and out of carts and phlegmatic Arab families, his horn blowing almost continuously. At one point he burst briefly into song, while I clutched my seat and banged my knees against the metal protuberances with which jeeps were so well endowed. We arrived with a slither of brakes at six o'clock.

Gide's house was one of those Arab ones that face inwards, presumably towards a courtyard, though this I did not see. Its outside was therefore bleak and in the chilly half-light, for dusk was falling, somewhat forbidding. Saint-Exupéry, who like me was in uniform, stamped his feet while waiting for the bell to be answered, and hummed to himself. At last the door was opened by a small and solemn African boy, whose blue-black face glowed in the shadows. We followed him along a short, dark hallway and waited in a sort of ante-chamber, where we left our overcoats.

This room, too, was poorly lit, by a single hanging lamp so far as I recall. I remember blueish tiled walls, and large brass objects—jars, presumably—glinting faintly, and cacti, and heavy pieces of mahogany furniture lurking in shadowy corners. We waited for some time. Another boy, an Arab one, looked in, stared at us silently, and vanished again. Then, after some five minutes, a third boy appeared and we followed him along another dim corridor where scimitars hung upon the walls. We were shown into the great man's study.

He was seated behind a desk or table, on which there stood a heavily shaded lamp. His bald head caught what little light there was and seemed, as a result, even larger than its actual size, his great domed forehead even more impressive. So I was surprised and somewhat taken aback when he rose to his feet to see that he was a short man. He was wearing, I think, a smoking jacket or perhaps a dressing-gown—at any rate some quite informal garment. He gave me a long appraising look as we were introduced, and under the scrutiny of those penetrating old eyes I felt clumsy and embarrassed.

'*Asseyez-vous*,' he said gently, pointing towards a Victorian sofa. I did as I was told, and found that the piece of furniture on which I was seated was remarkably uncomfortable, its hardness and narrowness being emphasised by a superabundance of cushions. These, and the sofa itself, were covered in a sort of carpeting. I sat there, upright in the half-darkness, while Saint-Exupéry pulled a chair towards the writer's desk and into the circle of light.

'*Vous êtes à Alger depuis longtemps?*' Gide asked me politely.

'*Depuis trois jours*,' I said.

'*Ah!*' said Gide. He turned to Saint-Exupéry.

'Tell me,' he said, 'are you getting your American royalties through yet?'

It appeared that Saint-Exupéry was not. Gide was, since last week or the week before. There was a certain colonel at Allied Force Headquarters who had been helpful, most helpful. It was all a question of a word in the right ear. Furthermore, Gide's agent in New York . . .

I sat there, listening attentively, and was delighted when one of the distinguished writers lit a cigarette, for this enabled me to do the same. But now there was the problem of an ashtray. I saw one in the shadows, a sort of bowl, but when I went to pick it up it was immensely heavy.

'Not that one, if you don't mind,' said Gide, and I suddenly felt that this solid bronze bowl was either extremely precious or else had an incalculable sentimental value for the old gentleman. After a certain amount of trouble another ashtray was found. I carried it away to my sofa in the shadows.

At this moment a small boy came in bearing three cups of black coffee.

'*Vous aimez le café?*' Monsieur Gide asked me politely.

I replied that I did, though if the truth be told I do not usually drink strong Turkish coffee at a quarter past six. Furthermore, I had now to perform a sort of juggling act with coffee cup, cigarette and ashtray until I had managed to arrange the cushions so that they provided a firm ledge. Gide and Saint-Exupéry continued to discuss the relative virtues, loyalty and skill of their respective New York agents.

When this subject had been at last exhausted, Saint-Exupéry told our host that I had once translated an essay of his into English.

'*Ah?*' said Gide, and looked across at me.

I mumbled something about the honour that it had been.

'And it was sold?' he asked.

He clearly had no recollection of our brief correspondence, of the words of praise he had so generously bestowed on my translation, or even of the fact that there had been a translation at all. I assured him that it had been sold.

'Where?' he asked.

I told him.

'*Ah!*' he said, and, after a pause: 'When?'

I gave him the date of publication.

'*Ah!*' he said, and finished his coffee. Then, turning to Saint-Exupéry: 'Tell me, has Robert Aron asked you to write for his new review?'

'Yes,' said Saint-Exupéry, 'though I'm not sure whether I shall or not.'

'How much has he offered you?'

'Three francs a word,' said Saint-Exupéry, leaning back in his chair.

'Hm, seems reasonable. He's only offering me five. Now tell me, what sort of backing has he got?'

For some time they discussed the finances behind this review, passing on to the finances of other French language magazines in various parts of the world, rates of pay, speed of payment and convertibility of currencies. A little boy came in to take away the coffee cups.

'You're sure you wouldn't care for another cup?' Gide asked me politely.

I declined, and the conversation about the magazines was

resumed. There were, I gathered, many personalities involved, all unknown to me and mostly, it seemed, at loggerheads with one another. If one wrote for so-and-so in London it was quite inconceivable that one could also be published by so-and-so in Casablanca. The reasons, political or literary, behind these strong mutual antipathies were not explained, for presumably Saint-Exupéry knew all about them already. I smoked another cigarette.

This conversation, too, came at last to an end. Saint-Exupéry glanced at his watch.

'Good heavens,' he said, 'it's gone seven. We'll be late!' We were meeting friends for dinner again.

He got to his feet, and I did likewise. So did André Gide, and again I noticed how small he seemed with his great domed head in the shadows. Behind me the tin ashtray slid, with a faint clatter, to the carpeted floor.

When I had finished picking up the cigarette butts, Gide turned and asked me politely: '*Vous restez quelques jours à Alger?*'

'Two or three more days, I think,' I replied.

'*Ah!*' he said, and held out his hand. 'It has been a great pleasure meeting you.'

'For me, a pleasure and an honour,' I replied.

'*Ah!*' he said.

We left him, standing behind his desk. In the ante-chamber, now almost in total darkness, one of the small, solemn, unsmiling boys helped us into our overcoats.

When we had climbed into the jeep Saint-Exupéry said to me: 'Well, what did you think of the greatest French writer of the age?'

EPITHALAMIUM
by the Poet Laureate
[E. S. Turner]

Loud above the sooty Minster clash the bells in brilliant air!
Every shop has gorgeous photos, hearts entwined are everywhere.
Come on, Elsie! Come on, Shirley! Gosh, the flags at C and A!
Taj Mahal Sends Loyal Greetings, Indian Meals To Take Away.

Anne and Mark . . . United Dairies weep to see your happiness.
In your honour Clockwork Orange puts itself in fancy dress.
Virgin Harvest, SINderella, Nymphet, Film Without A Name . . .
All are wreathed in smiles and bunting, all cry out with loyal shame.

O the pushing! O the straining! Glint of sun on laddered thighs!
Cockney voices from the trannies yapping to the happy skies.
God be thanked for Rediffusion, in whose windows fifteen screens
Show us fifteen brides and bridegrooms, smiled upon by fifteen
    Queens.

Ankle-deep in loyal litter, see the pigeon-haunted Square.
Joy is rising up like incense, dung is dropping from the air.
Loyal dames from Cincinnati join the ever-swelling shout.
How the Hare Krishnas caper, how their top-knots jig about!

Round the Palace in their thousands, writhing like a bag of eels,
Surge the mums from Penge and Merton, fugitives from Meals on
    Wheels,
Tugging at the sacred railings, trampling over helpless Japs . . .
Come on Snowdon, Beaton, Lichfield, hurry up and take your
    snaps!

Here they come . . . the shining sports girl, firm of seat and tart of
    tongue.
She will do her captain's bidding. Would that I were rich and young!
Now beside its Slumbereezees kneels a nation linked in prayer,
And a star shines over Sandhurst, God knows what it's doing there.

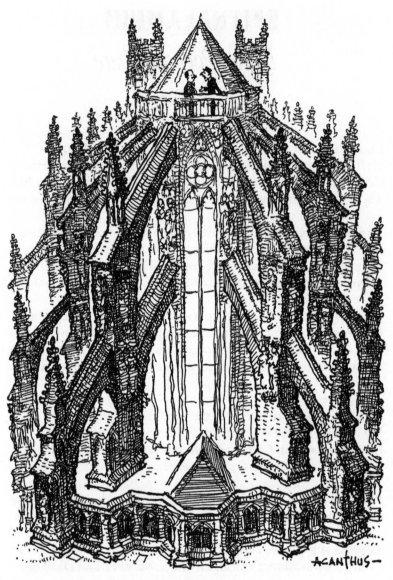

'You'd never think this cathedral is supported almost
entirely by voluntary contributions'

HEAR IT NOT, DUNCAN!

Duncan Campbell

Finally, I think, the time has come to tell the whole story of the Zircon spy satellite. Spill the beans. The entire fruits of my research. All the documents, the plans, the diagrams, the lot.

The Special Branch are hardly going to be keeping an eye on *Punch*, are they? They'll be watching the *New Statesman*, getting the binos focused on the second floor there. They're not going to get a restraining writ slapped on the editor of *Punch*, are they? What would the judge say?

Well, here goes. The Zircon spy satellite programme contains . . . hang on, a minute, couple of blokes moving around in the garden, wearing belted mackintoshes . . . they must have lost their way.

Anyway, as I was saying, what I discovered about the Zircon satellite was precisely that . . . now where have those blokes in the garden gone? Is that someone downstairs . . . What's that you say, officer? You've found a stack of documents relating to the Zircon programme . . . must have been a friend that left them there . . . Aaargh!

No. I cannot tell a lie. And those of you who started reading the above because you reckoned you were going to get the whole inside story of the Zircon business will just have to pop along to *Punch* and ask for your money back.

For there are two of us. There's the Duncan Campbell who works for the *New Statesman* and who researched the Zircon spy satellite programme and is called a traitor by Lord Chalfont, and there's the person writing this piece. If you're confused it's nothing to what it's like for us.

When the Zircon business first happened I was lying fast asleep on a winter Sunday morning. The phone rang. It was ITN. They wanted to know if I could come in and be interviewed by them. Always happy to oblige, I asked them what for.

'It's concerning the story about you in the Sunday papers,' said the man from ITN.

Now there is no speedier way to wake up on a chill winter's morning than to have someone from ITN phoning you up and asking if he can chat about the story featuring you in the Sunday papers. It was like a syringe full of adrenalin in what rugby commentators refer to as the 'upper thigh'. It was only when the heart slowed down a bit that I realised that they wanted to talk to the Other One.

The Other Duncan Campbell arrived on the scene and on his bike in the mid-Seventies. He was a freelance journalist from Brighton and I was working at *Time Out*. Even then he had a nose for a story and he was soon shaking the twigs of the Branch.

He first hit international fame when he was arrested with another *Time Out* journalist in 1977. He had been researching a story about signals intelligence when the SB pounced. He was hoisted off briefly to Brixton prison.

I went along, naturally enough, to his appearance at Tottenham magistrates' court and, as the *Time Out* news editor, spoke to the press outside about the case. Someone took my photo and it duly appeared in the *Scotsman* the following morning.

Beneath it was the caption: 'Duncan Campbell before his court appearance on Official Secrets charges. His widowed mother lives in Dundee.' (The local angle is always important and to caption-writers of the day at the *Scotsman* the fact that a bloke came from Dundee was almost an admission of guilt anyway.)

The photo puzzled my mother, since my father was sitting opposite her at breakfast when the paper arrived. Neighbours dropped in notes of condolence. My sister phoned from Hong Kong with an offer to stand bail. The confusion which has pursued us for ten years had begun. It has not been made any the less by the fact that both of us are journalists working sometimes in the same field, him at the *New Statesman*, me at the *London Daily News*.

Sometimes it has worked to our advantage. When the Other One was working on a story about some unpleasant mercenaries, he needed a witness to one confrontation. We both went along. 'I am Duncan Campbell,' he said to our quarry. 'And this is Duncan Campbell.' They never recovered.

I've had cheques of his—and income tax demands—and he's had telephone calls from people whom I met on a beach in Puerto Rico in 1968 and who, seeing the name Duncan Campbell in the London telephone directory, reckoned there might just be a vague chance it was the same one.

We did discuss altering names. But if we were to use initials, I would have to be I. Duncan Campbell, which sounds like a last will and testament. The National Union of Journalists, unlike Equity, doesn't stipulate that hacks must have different names when they enter the profession. Eventually we decided that the confusion had its own advantages.

'That unpleasant article about you? Oh, that must have been the *other* Duncan Campbell. Shocking business, yes, terribly confusing,' we can say when we bump into someone who has been given a nasty time by either of us. I tend to remember the difference between us when I am invited to a no-expenses-paid meeting somewhere very far away; but having been along to some public meetings about Official Secrets legislation and seen the sad, wee faces when the punters realise they've got the wrong Duncan Campbell, well, I'm not going to cause any more unhappiness.

The Zircon business has, of course, started it all over again. 'You look very different on television,' people say. 'It's a disguise,' I assure them. 'You can't be too careful these days.'

Campaigners against obsessive official secrecy pump my arm when they meet me at parties. Keep up the good work. I nod modestly. When they try and ask about details of What It All Means I give them one of those Can't-talk-here looks.

Up in Scotland where there are many Duncan Campbells, there's no such problem. I mean, I knew a Duncan Campbell who won the tilt-the-bucket competition in the Oban Games when I was only eight and I've bumped into others ever since. But down in London people can't believe that there are two of us bouncing around in the same area. I've even had quite amicable conversations on the phone with people who think we're bosom buddies and who feel quite indignant when I say after a minute or two that I don't think we've ever met.

Last summer I played cricket for the *New Statesman* cricket team. This was taking it all too far. I used to get wickets just because opposing batsmen would be so sure that any satellite-spotter would have some damn cunning way of spinning the ball that they were transfixed to the crease. Sometimes between innings an opposing player would murmur some secret tale under his breath, clearly expecting that I would be following it up the next week.

I *know* other people have the same problem, although I don't think The Who's Peter Townshend ever really got mistaken for Princess Margaret's ex-fiancé. But it's quite comforting to have another self. When I go to football games and hear fans chanting 'One Charlie Nicholas, there's only one Charlie Nicholas,' I can even feel sorry for him. Take a tip, Charlie, the pressure's a lot less intense when there are two of you.

'Norman, maybe it wasn't such a smart idea for
you to have left everything to science.'

CORONET AMONG THE CORKS

Libby Purves

The middle-aged party stumped into the earl's dining-hall, and stared at his crested chairs. A wild-haired Irish woman lilted 'Welcome to Henham House,' and took a quid apiece off them. 'Is there a guidebook?' boomed the senior male tourist. 'Well, no, we've not had the time. We're only open a week.'

'Quick decision, wasn't it? This opening the house?' said the man sceptically. Anna from Wexford waved her hands lyrically. 'Ah, that's the sixth earl for you. A man of quick decisions.' The senior female tourist broke her silence. '*I've* just made a decision. I'm never having a dark green carpet.' Around her feet, notice-able as scurf, lay fragments of white petals from the rose-tree at the door.

'We hoovered this morning,' said Anna, descending sharply from poesy. And to me: 'We've been up to our eyes, organis-ing cream teas and unpacking the didgeridoo collection. It was held up in Customs.' She led her party off to inspect a model of the proposed Humphrey Repton Park, a gallery of cross-looking countesses in painted ballgowns, and some glossy snaps featuring Winston Walberswick Rous, aged ten weeks, twelfth child of the sixth and current Earl of Stradbroke. Left alone in the hall with the sun streaming in from the park, I was just reading the family crest on the door, *Je vive en espoir*, when a tall man in a bush hat loped through it. 'Stradbroke,' he said. 'Call me Keith.'

You will forgive me if I digress. I have to explain that if you happen to live along the Suffolk coastal strip, within gossiping distance of the Henham Estate, such an encounter is tanta-mount to meeting J. R. Ewing in the supermarket car-park. The life and times of Keith Stradbroke, even as reported in that sober organ the *East Anglian*, have built a legend. When the fourth and fifth earls died within a few days of one another in 1983, and the title fell on an Australian sheep-farmer with a vast fortune made by debt collecting and missing persons bureaux; when the said Australian turned out to have eleven children and a sensational divorce astern of him (23 co-respondents), and appeared with the lot of them (children, not co-respondents) in sleepy Wangford to spend a year camping in a broken-down rectory, heating the bath-water in a gigantic galvanised tank mounted over a wood-fire, and fighting a bizarre lawsuit for possession of his land, it was unnecessary for local newspapers to do anything but report it all with a straight face. Any neighbouring *bourgeois* not yet *épaté* was neatly swept into the legend by the announcement, in quick succession, of projects for the recovered estate: a Sunday market, a nudist camp, an Australian zoo, a life-size model of Captain Cook's ship *Endeavour* and a giant ski-slope. Round here, if you see a headline like NO ONE IN VILLAGE WOULD NOTICE 300 NUDES, SAYS EARL you know, straight away, which earl.

But it was the advertisements, for me, which brought him to life. There was the one for a nanny who would receive a bonus of a thousand Australian dollars if the countess became pregnant; there was the invitation-to-tender for the construction of a memorial stone to his wolfhound Reigel (deported after savaging too many pheasants) with the legend *The 6th Earl of Stradbroke, Countess Roseanna, and 11 Stradbroke Rous children wish Reigel many good Roo hunts and successful mating with female wolfhounds.* Then, dull months later, suddenly down among the agricultural small-ads, one would glimpse a mad exotic bloom; and families would gather round to read another Henham bulletin opening:

> All the tenders listed below are of course subject to Council permission and your English laws, etc. I require some good bushmen with local knowledge of conditions . . .

Finally, three weeks ago, came the irresistible invitation:

So I came, and by luck his Lordship himself was over from Sydney. He normally costs a thousand quid an hour for interviews, but waived all charges for *Punch*. We passed through the Grott Shop, which sells souvenirs, ships in bottles and antique clocks largely because Anna the guide deals in them. She first struck up a friendship with Keith over her stall at his doomed Sunday Market. The sensible middle-aged local couples swivelled their eyes in polite English fashion at Stradbroke's leather bush hat. There was a definite sense of relief in the air; at last the maverick absentee squire was doing something as comprehensibly earlish as opening his house and flogging cream teas. Give the man a chance, they seemed to be saying. He'll understand what's what, how to behave, join the county.

Oh no he won't. I had feared that the author of the surreal newspaper ads for bushmen had been working on his image as an Antipodean Uncle Matthew for years, practising for the big moment when he would shake Suffolk rigid. But no. He was surprised. 'I thought the old fourth Earl would breed kids. After all, my Dad was sperming kids till he was 77, he left me five illegitimate ones. We sperm a lot of kids, Stradbrokes. So I didn't think I'd inherit.' As for the county, he has not even noticed it. And not one of the wild tales or outré projects reported of him has been meant as a joke. The local rumour that his son Wesley, aged 11, attempted to start a pig farm is perfectly true. 'Wesley's a very smart bloke. He wanted something to do, to make some money. I was rabbiting for money when I was six.' The nudist deal fell through because they wanted a 20-year lease. The ski-slope was serious, at the time, as was the replica ship; the 50-bedroom glass mansion on the estate has got to the model stage, and the sheep-farming is under way, with local bushmen. A conservation project is taking shape, because that is his new idea; the Australian museum is growing as fast as Anna can unpack the didgeridoos.

Wild, light blue eyes glittered at me over his mug of tea. 'I had a peculiar childhood. I couldn't read or write until I was about fifteen. Granny wrote to me on my fifth birthday saying, "Dear Keith, you are now the head of the family, here is one guinea, put it in your war bonds." Same every birthday, but never enclosed the guinea. I don't have to keep Henham. I could sell it tomorrow.' But he keeps it. It's a challenge. He has a fax machine in the corner near the scones. 'I'm a commission man. I'm about profit. The thing tells me my Sydney office is making a profit and my English office—this lot—isn't. It's going to.' He stared moodily out at his pretty, derelict acres.

It is odd, it *must* be odd, to emerge from a family of alienating inbred weirdness, get kicked out of Harrow, build yourself an uncomplicated fortune in a hot new land—only to be clobbered from across the seas by a chilly, failing estate, a press of merciless taxes and an unsought title, bestowed by a subtle and decadent old country which has the nerve to think that *you* are the oddity. He thinks we are.

'England has lost the pioneering spirit. Rich kids get spoiled and poor kids cheat on the dole. Now *I* give my kids two cents at age two—right—my son Henham gets two cents. For that he does the washing-up. At three, he gets three cents. At five they all get an allowance and buy their own clothes, and if the shoes don't fit they go barefoot. They all know damn well I will not pay for college and university and Sloane Ranger courses. They can pay their own way. Take my daughter, Ingrid, okay, she's a model, but she can still slaughter four sheep and cut them up before breakfast, any morning. Now the coal strike—'

Since you ask, he did attempt to take his seat in the House of Lords. 'Went up there, one kid under each arm, said to the police bloke at the gate, I've come to make my maiden speech, I've got 25 minutes. They asked me what my interest was, so I said 17½%. Turned out they meant what would I speak about, so I said, the coal strike and dole cheats. So the bloke says, sorry, milord, we need your father's death certificate and your birth certificate and your mother's marriage certificate—*thirty certificates* in all.' He gives the short, bitter laugh of a man who has been looking for certificates for so long that the coal strike has ended. 'Even then they want me to talk about marshes or some non-controversial bird or something. Well, I won't. I'm an earl, all right, but I'm different.'

Outside in the sunshine, beneath the white roses, wild-haired Anna is weaving a soft inaccurate Irish spell, trying to make him not so different. 'Wouldn't it be nice', she dreams, 'if there was a family legend, now. For the American visitors. We could have a white hart that appears in the park there whenever one of them is going to die, now that would be grand . . .'

I am strangely uplifted. On the way to my car, Keith and I plan a lucrative horse show, a nature trail, and the reopening of the sad secret byways of Henham. I am two miles up the road before I remember that I never asked him whether he got the memorial built to the dog Reigel. The one who turned out, in the end, to be too wild to live in England.

FIRST FOOTER

T. E. B. Clarke

More than a century having passed since the first Cup Final, it is surely quite something to have been given a first-hand account of the game by one of the players—and that without benefit of a medium.

Shortly before the 1938 Final between Preston North End and Huddersfield Town—which also seems pretty astonishing today—this (then) young reporter was assigned to find out whether any of the original 22 players was still with us. Even at that time I was doubtful, for the FA Cup was first won by the Wanderers back in 1872, when they beat the Royal Engineers 1–0 at Kennington Oval; however, my investigation turned up one sole survivor. He was Thomas Charles Hooman, a retired schoolmaster living at Hythe in Kent.

Mr Hooman opened the door to me himself: a fine-looking old gentleman of 87, powerfully built and still straight-backed, with a fierce expression that grew fiercer as I stated my business.

'No use for the Press,' he barked. 'Good day to you.' The door was firmly closed on me. As a one-time itinerant seller of teaspoons I should have used my experience to keep a foot in it; but instinct told me that this fearsome one-time footballer might still remember the effectiveness of a tackle over the top. And in our brief encounter I had observed that he had on the blue, red and pink striped tie that I too was entitled to wear.

I rang again. He reappeared. 'You heard what I said. Be off.'

I said in hurt tones, 'This is not the kind of reception I expected, sir, from a fellow Old Carthusian.'

He gave me a long uncertain look. 'Name? House? Year?' I supplied the wanted particulars. 'Wait there.'

Through the window of a front room in which he had been having his tea I saw him cross to a bookcase and lift down an O.C. List. A minute or so while he put on his glasses and thumbed through its pages, then the book was snapped shut and he returned with sprightly step.

'Come in, my dear fellow. Good to see you. Welcome, welcome. The tea's cold but have a piece of he.' I had long forgotten that 'he' was Charterhouse slang for cake. Not he—meaning Mr Hooman.

I sat nibbling my he while the years were rolled back. 'Great game. Mind, we were a shade lucky to be there. Had a walkover in an earlier round, then played a goalless draw with Queen's Park in the semi-final. Surprise you to know a Scottish club once played in the FA Cup? Jolly fine side, hadn't had a goal scored against them in four years. But they had to scratch. Couldn't afford to stay in London for a replay, and we hadn't the oof to travel up to Glasgow.

'So there we were at the Oval. Disappointing crowd, one shilling admission was too much to ask. Not more than two thousand, most of them cheering for the Sappers. The military had the advantage over us, they could drum up support under threat of the lash.

'They had some bad luck, though. Game hadn't been on ten minutes when one of their best men broke his collar-bone in a throw-in.'

'He threw so hard?'

'No, no, in the scrum. When the ball went out of play the first man to reach it took the throw. Not a bad idea, gave the crowd a bit of participation. I've lain there hugging the ball with four of the other side and half a dozen spectators in a heap on top of me.'

'You didn't have substitutes?'

'Good gracious, no. In that case it wasn't necessary. Plucky chap played on. Made one feel a bit of a cad barging him. Still, *versa rota fortunae*, what?'

I agreed with an effort to look knowledgeable. This I had soon to regret.

'And here's something you'll find hard to believe: we didn't have one single foul in the whole of the match.'

'Clean play or a lenient referee?' I ventured.

'Neither.' Mr Hooman chuckled at the memory. 'Plenty of

strife and we didn't have a referee, only a timekeeper. The captains had to agree on whether a free kick was justified and of course they never did.'

I said I would like to hear about the goal that won the game.

'Wonderful moment! I still see that ball streaking under the tape. No crossbar then, just the two uprights. Teddy Lubbock set it up from midfield, passed out to Vidal on the left wing and we attacked *omnes quinque inordine.*'

Something about five . . . Five forwards up? I was struggling afresh in the Lower Fourth.

'I received the final pass from a chap I'm not naming and then it was just a case of *celerine cucurri.* Don't want to boast but I did sprint for England. Goalie came out but I managed to dribble round him and there it was. Can't say in the back of the net because we didn't have one.'

Now we reach a mystery that will never be solved. According to official records the all-important goal was scored by the forward Mr Hooman declined to name, who was playing under the pseudonym 'A. Chequer'. Yet nobody could have been less likely to steal another's thunder than this fine old English gentleman. Age may have dimmed his memory of the incident, but I have a preferable theory. Mindful of the scorer's anxiety to avoid publicity, he was perhaps making a gallant last-ditch effort to preserve his secret. Why a leading footballer should not wish it known he was playing in the Cup Final is of course beyond contemporary guesswork.

Before I could question him further Mr Hooman said abruptly, 'That'll do. Talked enough.'

I rose, brushing the he crumbs off my lap, and thanked him for a splendid interview.

His handshake was still formidable. 'Been a pleasure. Don't come again, I shan't be here. It won't be long now before the Great Headmaster calls me for my last *adsum.*'

He was dead right: the G. H. added him to the roll six months later. I am glad he didn't live to see a Cup Final on television: the embraces accorded a modern goal-scorer would have brought a well-aimed boot crashing through the screen. *Illud pro certo habeo.*

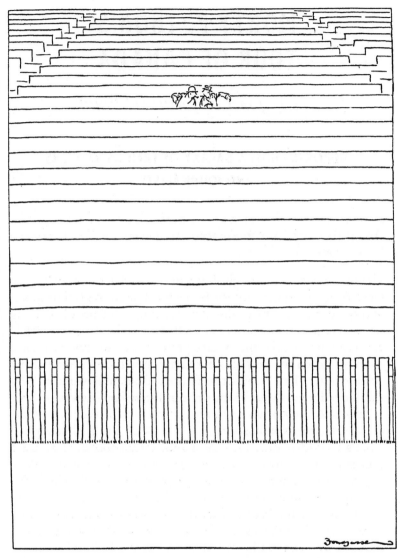

'Of course, there's one thing that no foreigner will ever understand,
and that's our enthusiasm for cricket.'

MONTY PYTHON'S TOUR OF CANADA

Terry Jones and Michael Palin

REPORTS FROM A GALAXY OF FAMOUS WRITERS
AND JOURNALISTS

June 2nd THE TRIUMPHANT ARRIVAL IN TORONTO.
An on-the-spot eye-witness account of events as they happened
by BERTRAND RUSSELL

Hello! I expect you thought I was dead. Well, let's get one thing
clear from the start: I'm not Bertrand Russell the philosopher,
and quite frankly I'm getting pretty fed up with people coming
up to me at parties and saying: 'Oh I thought you were dead.'
It's the sort of joke that wears pretty thin, you know. I can't
even go down to the Labour Exchange without some halfwit
yelling out, 'Here comes the famous dead philosopher!' Not
that I need to go down to the Labour Exchange anyway . . . well
. . . not a lot, but times are a bit . . . how shall I say . . . a bit . . .
er . . . thin for us philosophers . . . Not that I'm a philosopher!
That's the other one. *He's* the famous philosopher. I'm just a
journalist trying to scrape a meagre pittance out of the filthy,
degrading commerce of the gutter press and its ilk. Urgh! Oh
yes! *My* thoughts on the meaning of life and the Development
of Thought in the Western World didn't even make the About
Town section of the *Toronto Herald.* 72,000 close-typed foolscap
pages—with practically no margin—on the Cultural Achieve-
ments of the Modern World, and all I get is a rejection slip!
All right—perhaps it *wasn't* good . . . perhaps I *had* got one or
two little things—piddling little unimportant, pointless little
things—wrong, but does that give someone else the right to
pour scorn on two whole weekends of toil and labour? They

could have just pointed out that there were a few inaccuracies in the text . . . like Bertrand Russell (yes—the *other* one) not being a dwarf . . . and asked me to change them. Heavens above, I can take a hint! Anyway, now we've cleared that up, and I do assure you that I haven't taken it quite philosophically, I can get on to . . .

June 4th THE GLAMOROUS FIRST NIGHT AT THE ST LAWRENCE CENTRE, TORONTO.
A report from WINSTON SPENCER CHURCHILL

Hello! Let's get one thing clear from the start: I'm not *that* Winston Spencer Churchill. Nor am I his son. I'm not going to go on about it like Bertrand Russell (not the famous philosopher) does about *his* name, because, thank goodness, I've come to terms with it. It doesn't worry me. Mind you, it does become a bit of a bloody bore when people come up to you at parties and say: 'What was Stalin really like at Yalta?' And I'm not saying I don't sometimes wish I had a perfectly ordinary name like Len Nol or Merlin Brando or Ben Rosewall. At least then I wouldn't have to waste my entire column explai

June 7th MONTY PYTHON ARRIVES IN MONTREAL.
A report from our showbiz correspondent from the packed Place des Arts: HENRY KISSINGER

Hello! It's me, Henry! Yes! It's difficult to believe that in between negotiating new policy agreements with Red China, co-ordinating business interests in the new Soviet–US Trade Agreements, consulting daily with President Nixon on a wide-ranging series of topics, constant liaison with the press and White House officials, keeping myself informed on the latest internal and external developments in the Far East, as well as doing all the shopping and helping with the housework, I still have time, as showbiz correspondent, to see these wacky Python boys at the Place des Arts. I'd seen the show already in Cardiff, Glasgow (where I managed to see both performances), Manchester, Birmingham, Brighton, Southampton, Edinburgh,

Norwich and Toronto, but then my mind was far too preoccupied with the truly awesome problems of East–West reconciliation for me to be able to spare more than a cursory glance at the stage. So this time, with the Chinese Commodity Controls Agreement virtually signed and sealed, and the Central Clearing Banks agreement ratified, I was determined to give the show my undivided attention. As the curtain went up on this zany sextet, I couldn't help thinking how pleasant international diplomacy can be in such a convivial and relaxed atmosphere. One of the funniest items in the Python repertoire set me to thinking how I had slipped a vital clause into the 1967 Cambodian Trade agreement, whilst watching Doris Day and Rock Hudson in *Pillow Talk*. My Cambodian friend was laughing so much that he readily agreed to an advantageous purchase of 127 Phantom fighters in addition to the ground-control system I had clinched during the opening scenes. Yes! I thought to myself, as Marty Robbins Circus drew to an end, World Diplomacy *is* a wonderful thing.

MONTY PYTHON IN BOTSWANA.
Our correspondent writes:

Hello! Still no sign of Monty Python here in Botswana.

June 13th WINNIPEG. FRESH FROM HEADY TRIUMPHS IN
    EASTERN CANADA, THE MONTY PYTHON TEAM
    ARRIVE IN THE PRAIRIES.
A report from the Centennial Theatre, Winnipeg by YEHUDI
MENUHIN

Hi! Wow! Zapee! Am I having the good time out here in Winnipeg! Zow! Bam! It's grrreat! These Python boys certainly can grab an audience! I haven't seen an audience so zonked since I played the Bartók unaccompanied violin sonata last month. I played as I've never played before. My fingers seemed possessed, dancing across the strings, as if each one had a life of its own! How the audience roared their approval! It was fantastic! They wouldn't let me leave! I took bow after bow and still they asked for more! Of course, these Python boys didn't get anything like that sort of reception, but the audience were pretty enthusiastic. If you can call a bit of applause enthusiastic. Personally, when you're used to the sort of response I usually get from an audience, it seems pretty thin. In fact, I felt if only I could have leapt on the stage and given them a few bars of the unaccompanied violin sonata I could have raised them to a pitch of excitement little short of frenzy, then I could have led them across Canada towards the West Coast, and taken over Vancouver and so on to World Domination. But what was the reaction of a Canadian audience to this essentially British show? Well they certainly laughed. But what is laughter compared to the rapture of an audience maddened with the wild rhythms of the unaccompanied violin sonata, lifting them higher and higher, driving them to the very rim of self-control, when the pent-up passions of the human soul crave for expression, crave for a leader, a leader who will stand at their head and point the way to the future—the way to a better world, where the destinies of ordinary men and women are controlled by a musical genius with a distinctive name! I will triumph! I will succeed! All human life will be at my command!

June 11th CALGARY, WITHIN SIGHT OF THE CANADIAN ROCKIES AND THE MID-POINT OF PYTHON'S TRIUMPHAL TOUR.
A report from the logging correspondent: LIZA MINNELLI (No relation)

It was 197 below, when the coach left Frozen Creek on the 4,000-mile journey to the Southern Alberta Centre for the Arts. Even the milk was frozen in our milk chocolates, and a pack of wolves attacked us as our tickets were being given out by the Drama Group Organiser, Red Larsen. Red, the strongest, most fearless juvenile lead north of Goose Bay, was lucky to escape with a torn ear and two broken legs—no one knew who they belonged to. Blizzards whipped the icy snow into 74-foot high drifts, as we drove south along the frozen Mackenzie River. Old-timers at the back of the coach said it was worse than the terrible journey of 1957, when only four members of the party survived to see *Blithe Spirit* at the Little Theatre, Saskatoon. On the 4th day out of Frozen Creek, I was finishing a Douglas Fir sandwich, when suddenly the glacier fell away, and our coach plunged a thousand feet into the raging waters of McMurdo's Gorge. I felt myself grabbed by Big Frank Kelly, who made such a fabulous Natasha at the Yellowknife Festival of Arts and Lumber in 1971, and together we opened the emergency exit of the bus, grabbed the nearest stalls tickets, and struggled out into the icy tide. I felt Frank's grip weaken, as the raging torrent hurled us past rocks and through vicious whirlpools. With our last breath we agreed to meet in the Foyer at 7.15. There was a sickening thud and all was black. Three days later I regained consciousness to find myself stranded in the weird subterranean darkness of the Athabaska Caverns, only 400 miles from the stalls entrance, I–K. Nineteen days after leaving Frozen Creek, I reached the theatre. I couldn't believe it. There, in the bar, were Frank and Red Larsen, Moosejaw Morgan, and the one-eyed trapper Fenson. Red was hurt so bad he could hardly hold his programme, and Moosejaw died of his wounds halfway through the first act, but I was just glad to be alive, even though I was sitting behind a pillar.

June 20th VANCOUVER. THE END OF THE TOUR.
A summary by our medical correspondent: CHRISTIAAN BARNARD (A relation, but not of *that* Christiaan Barnard)

Hello! Medically the tour was a great success. Heartbeats remained fairly constant, and blood pressures were generally average. Minor skin irritations were an ever-present threat, but none developed into full-scale fungal infections. In fact it was bloody boring, medically. I just read most of the time. Once I was on a tour when the leading lady caught scurvy. Othello came off one night and said he thought Desdemona had badly swollen gums. I gave her an examination after the bedchamber scene, and she claimed that Othello had a severe neck rash. And, believe it or not, it turned out that *she* had scurvy, and *he* had pellagra! Iago refused to go on, until they were both on a vitamin diet, but one night an anonymous note was slipped under my door to the effect that Iago had worms. I later diagnosed bilharzia not only in Iago, but also in Roderigo, his friend from Venice. Two nights later, anthrax decimated the chorus, Cassio's fight-scene had to be adapted because of his colostomy bag, and Brabantio couldn't go on without an enema. Shakespearean productions are by far the most interesting medically, but I have seen cases of Yellow Fever in the *Seagull*, some very unpleasant boils in an otherwise perfectly hygienic revival of *Private Lives*, and a severe foot and mouth outbreak in *Babes In The Wood* at Leicester, during which the chorus had to go on through a dip.

THESE PIG CHARACTERS
COP ALL THE SCRATCH

ALAN HACKNEY rewrites Animal Farm
under the inspiration of Damon Runyon

I am standing cropping this grass, which I am enjoying more than somewhat when this other citizen, who is by way of being a goat, comes up and speaks as follows: 'Benjamin,' he says. 'There is a political meeting tonight and we are looking forward to seeing you.'

I say nothing, because politics makes me nervous.

'Well, are you showing up?' says this goat. 'It seems this pig, Major, being a senior citizen of this farm, wants us all to hear about this dream he has and maybe later to join in this song.'

'I'll be there,' I say. 'But my trap stays shut,' because for a donkey it is not good to commence opening his big trap.

Well, there is this meeting, and all the citizens are there, like the hens, ducks, Boxer the horse, and up front all the other pigs because they are intelligent citizens and likewise the dogs. Then this old pig begins this spiel.

It seems he has this vision in a dream where he sees all the animal citizens enjoying themselves like crazy because Man has vanished from the scene so they are all standing round singing about these joyful tidings of the golden future time because this guy Man who has been exploiting them has blown as a result of this revolution by the animal citizens. All the citizens agree with this proposition only there is this guy Jones who is a Man who owns the farm and who is therefore more than somewhat of a snag.

Well, this respected citizen, Major, next day snuffs, so we do not hear any more until one day when this guy Jones is drunk and forgets to feed us, so we take a look around the corn store where this guy Jones finds us and commences making with the whip. All the citizens are very indignant and take exception to this, so they begin to take a pop at Jones, biting him or maybe kicking, depending on which character is operating. Naturally Jones figures this is unhealthy and commences to retreat, which he does right out of the farm and later we hear he snuffs in some home for incurable drunks somewhere.

Well, all the citizens are more cheerful than somewhat and it seems the revolution is here already, likewise the golden future time. Two of the pig characters, called Snowball and Napoleon, tell everyone we must make certain the spirit of the revolution does not get lost, and they write up on the barn wall these Seven Commandments which start with the proposition that going on two legs is bad and going on four legs good, and ending up with 'All Animals Are Equal'. Also, we can now operate the farm ourselves and cop all the scratch, with each citizen having a piece.

Well, next day all the characters set to work doing what they can, only it is noticed that Snowball and Napoleon do all their work figuring the best way all the other citizens should work, which is maybe all right but anyway I keep my trap sewn up and do not make any observation.

Anyway, we get in the harvest and it seems all the apples get set aside for the pig characters, which is where the milk goes too every day. However, there is an explanation and a fat guy, this pig called Squealer, comes and gives it.

'I do not doubt you guys are worried about this,' he says. 'But you have maybe not heard of Science. Pigs do not like apples and milk but it is necessary they eat them for their health which they need to organise this whole layout. Otherwise they would maybe wither away and this guy Jones would step back in and make with the whip like before.'

So we all see this is very logical, especially the sheep who seem to be becoming regular nod-guys for the pigs, so that when the horse Boxer is going to ask another question, these sheep all yell out 'Four legs good, two legs bad!' and there is no more discussion, and old Boxer says he will in future get up a bit earlier so he can work longer hours which is what we need.

Well, time goes on and there are these plans for the future. This pig Snowball tells everyone we have to spread the news and get other citizens on other farms to have themselves revolutions like ours, also we must build this windmill for electricity so we do not have to work so hard and we can stand around singing about the golden future time. Napoleon, the other big guy among the pigs, says all this is baloney.

Anyway, we have this meeting and Snowball tells everyone about how he figures the future when all of a sudden Napoleon gives this loud squeak and the farm dogs whom we do not see for some time all come in making a racket and chase Snowball out of the barn and right out of the district.

All the citizens are very upset but Napoleon says everything will go on as before except we do not have meetings any more because it is a waste of valuable time. When the dogs come back and gather round Napoleon the citizens admit he is maybe right.

Later the pig Squealer comes round and explains. 'I hope all you characters appreciate the extra work Comrade Napoleon is taking on,' he says. 'We have all got to work harder likewise or we get this guy Jones moseying back in here, which is not to be recommended, so we must get busy with making this windmill and then life will be easier.'

'I do not hear Comrade Napoleon say he is for this windmill,' says old Boxer. 'I hear him say he is against it.'

'On the contrary,' says Squealer. 'Napoleon actually invents this windmill himself and this shnook Snowball steals the plans, so he is an undesirable character and is thrown out. This is tactics.'

The old horse Boxer does not understand tactics, but he respects what goes on in Comrade Napoleon's noggin so he says as follows: 'If Comrade Napoleon says so, it must be right. In future I get up earlier still to work on building this windmill, which is a great idea.'

Personally, I do not say anything.

Well, we get the stone and other material for this windmill and we go short of food and drink while we work at it, except for the pig characters and the dogs, who have to keep their strength up for thinking, and one of the things they think up is abolishing Sundays so there is more free time for work. This is a proposition old Boxer agrees with because the windmill is very important for his old age when he cannot work so hard any more.

Well, a couple of years and the windmill is nearly finished when there is this big storm and it falls down. Meanwhile the pigs and the dogs move into the farmhouse, which surprises a lot of the citizens, except that Squealer explains they need the better working conditions in order to write out all their memoranda. We do not see much of Napoleon these days, except that he comes out and looks at the broken windmill and tells all the citizens he is very outraged because it was Snowball who came back and wrecked it in the night. This guy Snowball had evidently been a crooked operator from the start, which is in contrast to Napoleon who has never spared himself, so he deserves this new title 'Animal Hero, First Class' which he has just invented. Also, one of the younger pig characters has just written this new song which is all about how Napoleon is the friend of the fatherless that watchest over us all. So all the sheep, who are still nod-guys, bleat out 'Four legs good, two legs bad! Long live Comrade Napoleon!' which sounds to me a lot of foolishness and most unbecoming of grown guys and dolls, but I do not say anything at the time.

Anyway, one day old Boxer, who is by way of being a friend of mine, is working after hours dragging stones for the windmill when he suddenly drops and is not able to get up again on his horseshoes. All the citizens are very much worried about this event because Boxer is an old and very lovable guy. Squealer turns up and is very sympathetic. He commences to say that Comrade Napoleon is very concerned. 'Do not worry your noggins, comrades,' he says. 'Comrade Boxer will be looked after in this local hospital. There is this van coming.'

But when this van comes, I read on the side it says 'Alfred Simmonds, Horse Slaughterer and Glue Boiler', which disturbs me more than somewhat. I begin to holler out for the first time. 'Boxer!' I say. 'These guys are taking you for a ride. Get out of it you great stoop!' And Boxer attempts to kick his way out of the truck, but no dice, and later we hear he dies in hospital. It is this guy Squealer who tells us this. 'Boxer was a loyal comrade,' he says. 'Napoleon would consider it a favour if you remember Boxer's motto, which was: "I will work harder and get up earlier." Meanwhile, there is tonight a feast in honour of his memory up at the farmhouse, though you cannot all be invited on account of there is not enough room, except for the pig comrades and the dogs.'

So they have a lot of crates of whisky shipped in for the nose-bag session and I suspect they get the scratch to buy it from the glue boiler.

Anyway, time goes by and all the young animals do not remember anything about how it was before, except me, and I do not remember it much different. There is always this work for the citizens to do and maybe the corn is cut down a bit more, except that Squealer says this is Readjustment of Rations. We do not see a lot of the sheep characters because they are taken off somewhere on the layout for re-education.

Then one day I cannot believe my peepers. What is this? Everyone is staring and likewise do not believe what they see. Here is all the pigs, coming out of the farmhouse into the yard, trotting around every which way *on two legs*. Then all the sheep line up and bleat out 'Four legs good, two legs better!' Also I notice Napoleon has got on one of Jones's very sharp jackets, likewise the other pigs. Furthermore I notice all these pigs are now carrying whips, just like the former Jones guy.

Then this nice old broad who is the mare of the late deceased Boxer says to me: 'Benjy, maybe you better show me on that old barn wall where they write up these Seven Commandments back at the start.' So we go over there and I read them out for her. Only I find there is only one Commandment that has not been rubbed out, and it reads a bit different to how I remember it.

'Honey,' I say. 'I do not personally remember it like this, but I will read out to you the words which are written up on this wall. It says: "All Animals Are Equal But Some Animals Are More Equal Than Others." '

'I do not believe this before,' says the old broad. 'But maybe this is why the pigs take out newspaper subscriptions today and negotiate how they get this radio fixed in up at the farmhouse. Also, although I seem to remember there was these Commandments, "Two Legs Are Enemies" and "All Animals Are Dry", I hear these pig characters propose they have a party, with liquor and with various Man characters they invite.'

'This I do not quite believe,' I say. 'But let us go and take a look.'

Well, we go and look in at the window of the farmhouse, and the old broad is right. Inside is all the neighbours from the farms in the district and these characters are definitely Men. Likewise, we see Napoleon and the other pig characters are also there and they are all drinking liquor together and making with decks of cards. Napoleon gets to his feet and proposes this toast. 'Friends,' he says. 'Personally, I am glad to see an end to any previous misunderstandings. Today I take you round and you very kindly congratulate me on my achievement in this lay-out. You have problems with your lower classes of citizens just like we do with our lower animals. I want you to know I decide to change back the name of this joint from Animal Farm to what it is originally. From here on out, this is once again, The Manor Farm. Gentlemen, I give you this toast. To the prosperity of Manor Farm!'

There is much applause inside but they soon get down to their poker games again. However, there is suddenly this knock-down drag-out fight starts. It seems Comrade Napoleon and one of the big local farmers both produce the ace of spades simultaneously. When they start this scrap the old mare and me are in some confusion, because although we try very hard to make out which is pig and which is Man it is already impossible to say which is which.

Personally, I would not give you two cents for the whole roomful, but that is neither here nor there nor elsewhere.

MY LIFE IN AN ADVERTISING AGENCY

Andrew Barrow

PERSONNEL DIRECTOR. Half your work will be TV.

COPYWRITER [*on telephone*]. Red hot ideas lying among the junk. Yes, quite.

PERSONNEL DIRECTOR. Unless anything happens either way you'll be in Group D until September.

ACCOUNT EXECUTIVE [*after meeting with client*]. Briefly, they've turned down everything.

GROUP HEAD [*answering telephone*]. You've got the wrong number. This is a creative group.

[*Extract from TV commercial script*]. Mysterioso. Slow pan down. Camera halts on fat Alfred Hitchcock type gourmet.

[*Copywriter's description of lengthy market research report.*] Don't worry about that. It's horse-shit.

SECRETARY [*trying to understand entry in diary*]. What's 'Meeting, Monday'?

[*Memo, about job applicant*]. Miss Smith is a tall, good-looking, unsophisticated girl with an attractively diffident manner.

GROUP HEAD. We need to have a brainstorm on this with Wendy and Lorna this afternoon.

ACCOUNT EXECUTIVE [*describing advantage of new type of flour*]. Better dispersal of the self-raising element.

COPYWRITER. If only I could get a job where I could work at home and not have to go to bloody meetings.

[*Headline of half-written advertisement*]. Five ways to serve turkey at Whitsun.

ART DIRECTOR [*on being given a difficult task*]. Charming!

WOMAN COPYWRITER [*whispering about her salary*]. I'm getting three thou'.

[*Extract from TV commercial script*]. Zoom in to tight shot of housewife wearing outsize sunglasses.

GROUP HEAD [*to Creative Director*]. Come and meet Andrew Barrow.

COPYWRITER. What we urgently require is . . . an advertising idea.

CREATIVE DIRECTOR [*getting my name wrong*]. I've got much better things to do at the moment than meet Andrew Barry.

TYPOGRAPHER [*discussing a certain typeface*]. The cap M is the ugly sod in the family.

COPYWRITER [*explaining office politics*]. Robert sees Donald as a potential ally.

SWITCHBOARD MANAGERESS [*to new telephonist*]. I hope we get a call to America today. Then I can show you how we do it.

MANAGING DIRECTOR [*during lecture*]. Can you hear what this chap's saying? Look! We chaps at the back can't hear what you're saying.

PERSONNEL DIRECTOR [*writing to unsuccessful job applicant*]. Try us again in a year or two's time.

WOMAN COPYWRITER. The BBC, that's *the* place to work. I used to work for CBS in America. I *loved* it.

GROUP HEAD. I haven't heard much yet but apparently the client wasn't exactly jumping about with joy.

COPYWRITER. Hey, wait a moment, perhaps that idea of Trevor's isn't too bad.

ACCOUNT EXECUTIVE. Strawberry Delight is a great success story.

[*Extract from TV commercial script*]. Pan down to tight shot of sugar in bowl and package alongside it.

COPYWRITER. The thing is, I've sat in offices like this, talking to people like this, for ten years.

[*Memo from Account Executive*]. You are invited to drink ale with me on the historic occasion of my leave-taking—at the Rose and Crown.

GROUP HEAD. Job two is the launch—probably on television—of the Chocolate Superman.

COPYWRITER [*on telephone*]. Did he ever get his novel published? Oh, what a shame!

[*Memo, about launching of new product*]. This has been grossly complicated by an appalling pack design which none of us are happy with.

CHAIRMAN [*addressing large meeting*]. Above all, you have brought humanity and common sense to advertising.

COPYWRITER [*who has been transferred to Paris office*]. Apparently they want some copy expertise over there.

[*Beginning of brief autobiography by job applicant*]. Me—in a nutshell. I was born into a world of ration books and rebuilding. Winston Churchill had saved the country.

COPYWRITER [*showing his child around the office*]. Silly words? Yes, they are silly.

[*Phrase from recipe on side of a pack*]. Add the flavour and freeze again.

SECRETARY. The client is a devil really.

[*Telegram, sent by copywriter in answer to job advertisement*]. Creative Directorship—Hold everything till you get my letter.

ACCOUNT EXECUTIVE. It sounds on the face of it as if they've decided not to use it.

[*Memo, about job applicant*]. My earlier prejudice has vanished. I like the chap. He appears to have an original mind.

[*Extract from TV commercial script*]. Amazed housewives run from homes and attempt to catch packages as they are tossed towards them.

COPYWRITER. I've never had a scrap of bloody luck at any time in my life—except getting a job in advertising.

GROUP HEAD [*reading from his diary*]. I've got 'Friday the 3rd, boardroom, 9.30 to 5.30, client presentation'.

PERSONNEL DIRECTOR [*answering enquiries about long-term office arrangements*]. Well, that's all in the melting-pot, isn't it?

COPYWRITER [*on telephone*]. We're trying to make the world conscious that this product is on the map.

[*Extract from TV commercial script*]. Cut to close-up of Mr Adams kissing goodbye to his wife.

PERSONNEL DIRECTOR [*after I give in my notice*]. You're buzzing off. Why's that?

A COLONIAL CHRISTMAS

Anthony Burgess

I will call the place Tahi Panas. The literal translation of the
name is indecent, but it is commonly used to designate prickly
heat. There was no prickly heat this tropic yuletide, for the mon-
soon had struck, and all the roads were under water. Cars stood
marooned, their differentials drowned. It felt cool enough for
turkey and pudding and brandy sauce.

I had written new words for traditional carols, thus:

> *Here we come a-pocketing*
> *Our lawful Christmas bribes.*
> *Prices are a-rocketing,*
> *So now the towkay tribes*
> *Must put more in our banks,*
> *Be more generous in their thanks,*
> *So we'll give them the contracts they so heartily desire,*
> *And we'll all be well off when we retire.*

A towkay is a Chinese boss; the imagined singers of the carol
must be thought of as corrupt, and hence mythical, officers of
the Public Works Department. There was another carol for the
sons of Islam:

> *Muslims, awake!*
> *Salute another day*
> *Of whisky and Dog's Head stout and BGA.*
> *Great is the law,*
> *The law the Prophet taught.*
> *Don't give the bloody thing another thought.*
> *You're six hours late for lunch:*
> *Food is cold, of course.*
> *Don't fret.*
> *Go out and get*
> *A new divorce.*

BGA being, of course, brandy and ginger ale, a popular beverage with the teetotal Mohammedans. These carols, and the others I wrote, seem to indicate a certain cynicism on my Christmas part. But, when the muezzin announced that there was no God but Allah, and Christmas Day had begun, the old magic began to work. Peace on earth, and all that jazz. The Queen's speech, garnished with crackling, to look forward to. Tears for lost innocence.

To Muslims, the Christian feast is not some other unintelligible importation of the white man. Jesus Christ was one of the prophets who preceded Mohammed, and his name—Nabi Isa—is honoured as much as Nabi Adam, Nabi Ibrahim and other patriarchs the two faiths have in common—perhaps more than Nabi Lot, the patron saint of homosexuals. So the Muslims are happy to celebrate along with the Christians—no pork, this being *haram*, but plenty of alcohol, this being also *haram* but not quite so much, 'alcohol' being a holy word, being Arabic. Christians were supposed to be happy to receive Muslim visitors, even strangers, and the visits could begin at dawn. The fact of the raging hangover from the club Christmas Eve party was to be discreetly ignored. Hindus and animists could come along too.

My first Christmas visitor (7 a.m.) was a Tamil engineer and a sophisticated black magician of *magister templi* rank. He had been anxious to get a drink of something in my house for a long time, this being a means of obtaining magical power over me. He took a glass of water. But on Christmas Day I would be safe. Then came one of the local prostitutes to drink cherry brandy. Then came a hadji and his Arab wife to drink all that was going. Then came a small electrician whose blood combined Dutch, Indonesian, Chinese and Portuguese corpuscles. He got through a whole bottle of Benedictine at a sitting. The hadji, high-flown, told the prostitute she was a prostitute, and the prostitute alleged that his wife was an adulteress, and the electrician was sick into an ashtray. The magician said nothing but turned off his shadow—a common and ominous trick of black magicians. At eleven a.m. I had to turn everybody out, since I was due at my boss's house for Christmas drinks. The hadji accused me of race prejudice (a white man had bidden him leave his house) and the prostitute offered me a whispered free short time and then was offended because I would not accept. The electrician said that all religion was bloody nonsense and accused the magician of supernatural practices—forbidden, as it was well known, by Karl Marx.

Approaching my boss's mansion I found small children being carried off in stupor. It has always been customary in the tropics to keep drinking water in the refrigerator in used gin bottles. The children had been given orange cordial mixed with water, had complained that it tasted nasty mummy, and been told not to make a fuss in somebody else's house, especially on Christmas morning. A live bottle of gin had, of course, found its way into the refrigerator. Those children had to have their Christmas dinner the day after the day after Boxing Day.

I was invited to have my own Christmas dinner in another town. A road did not, in those days, connect Tahi Panas with this town, and it was necessary to drive a Land-Rover along the seashore. One had to consult a tide-table first, but something went wrong, or the monsoons had messed it up or something, for, just beyond the point of no return, the Land-Rover had its differential drowned and was lapped around by urgent billows of the China Sea (which Milton's 'Nativity Ode' had said would be quiet, along with other oceans, but Milton, Nabi Milton, was never much of a prophet). I stood waist-high in tepid waters and cried for help. I did not like to swim for the distant palm-trees, for crocodiles—which lived normally on the young monkeys that abounded there—had already started off in the direction of their Christmas fare, me. The thing to do was to mount the half-submerged Land-Rover and kick at their encroaching snouts. Thank Nabi Isa I was drunk. I was also lucky, for a fishing *prahu* picked me up and dropped me, doubly soaked, at a quay not far from the rest house of the town where my Christmas dinner was now long over.

I entered the rest house dripping and found a fancy-dress dance going on. I could not get to the bar, as the costumes were being judged, the competitors going round in a ring I was made to join. I won third prize as A Castaway, and was congratulated on the painful realism of my get-up. Then I started to drink.

That night in Tahi Panas, so I heard, the multi-racial electrician had run amok with a *parang*. The dilapidation of the dome of the new mosque continued—something to do with the drop in temperature—and bits of its gold skin peeled off, falling to earth to convince the fisher folk and paddy-planters that Nabi Isa was no ordinary prophet. A pack of pye-dogs stole a turkey and there was a hell of a fight with a rival pack. Broken bottles were brandished in the bars. Belatedly, I produced a final carol:

> *Silent night, tropical night:*
> *Dogs howl, sandflies bite.*
> *Some are busy with bottles and knives,*
> *Others sleeping with other men's wives.*
> *The mosque is losing its dome.*
> *There's nothing to do but go home.*

I never heard the Queen's speech, but I had heard it the year before.

What exactly, incidentally, *is* a differential?

'He's dictating postcards.'

*In response to the Vatican's support for Latin as
the European language, here is MILES KINGTON's*

LATIN TOURIST PHRASE BOOK

Quid pro quo	the sterling exchange rate
Post hoc propter hoc	a little more white wine wouldn't hurt us
Ad hoc	wine not included
Adsum	small extras on the bill
Exempli gratia	token tip
Infra dig	terrible accommodation
Primus inter pares	the stove has fallen in the fire
Compos mentis	mint sauce
Carpe diem	fish frying tonight
Non anglii, sed angeli	fishing absolutely prohibited
Curriculum	Indian restaurant
Casus belli	gastro-enteritis
Sic transit gloria mundi	the nausea will pass away, and you'll be fine by Monday
O tempora! o mores!	*The Times* is no more, alas!
Quis custodiet custodes ipsos?	do you keep the *Guardian*?
Post meridiem	the mail does not arrive until midday
Fiat lux	car wash
Rara avis	no car hire available
Volenti non fit injuria	the accident was caused by a badly fitted steering-wheel
Reductio ad absurdum	road narrows
Nil obstat	River Nile impassable
Nil desperandum	River Nile overflowing
De minimis non curat lex	Lex garages cannot undertake to service small cars
Terminus ad quem	bus station for Quem (small Romanian town)
Caeteris paribus	restaurant facilities are available on the Paris coach

183

Post mortem	mail strike
Expostfacto	not known at this address
Sub rosa	a rather unattractive Italian girl
Sal volatile	a rather attractive Italian girl
Gloria in excelsis	a very attractive Italian girl
Noli me tangere	I do not wish to dance with you
Ars longa, vita brevis	unsuitable bathing costume (literally: big bottom, small briefs)
Hic jacet	old-fashioned coat
Ecce homo	gay bar
Timeo Danaos et Dona Ferentes	that nice couple we met in Portugal
Mens sana	male massage parlour
Ex libris	dirty books
Ex cathedra	ruined church
Inter alia	an Italian airline
Summa cum laude	peak holiday period
In loco parentis	railway family compartment
Quondam	part of Holland reclaimed from the sea
Dum spiro	stupid Greek person
Festina lente	shops shut on Continent (literally: Lenten holiday)
Aut Caesar aut nihil	an Italian football result
Tertium quid	33p

'That reminds me, dear—did you remember the sandwiches?'

DEATH TO THE FLANNELLED FOOLS

*ROBERT MORLEY prods the pitch, appeals against
the light, takes guard and declares the game of cricket is out*

I have a friend, W. Rushton, an actor like myself, a creature of
the dusk who earns his living lampooning prime ministers on
the Box. I came upon him the other afternoon in a meadow,
dressed all in white, a forlorn uneasy moth of a fellow unaccus-
tomed to the daylight and in boots which seemed to be causing
him discomfort. He was, he affirmed, playing cricket for money:
the fact that he wasn't going to get the money himself didn't
seem to disturb him as it surely would have done on a more normal occasion.

Living as I do in Berkshire, I am used to oak trees displaying
posters advertising charity cricket matches—indeed am grateful
for the warning not to approach too closely on such occasions—but Rushton, not for the first time, had caught me
unawares. I withdrew hastily. I would rather watch a man at his
toilet than on a cricket field, but such is the madness of the players that in time they come to believe that the spectacle they
make of themselves dressed in white wielding a willow (to use
their own revolting phraseology—and why not?) is something
their betters should pay to see.

'Car Park: two shillings' the posters proclaim. 'All proceeds to
HRH Duke of Edinburgh', and blow me if the public don't
drive their cars through the gate over the cart tracks, park in the
cow dung, wind down the windows, turn up the radio and tell
each other that they are getting a bit of fresh air.

It is not of course everybody who rolls up on these occasions, mostly people who still have drawing-rooms and take the
Telegraph and *Punch* and who like myself were brought up in the
shadow of The Awful Game.

I have never got over the shock of seeing my first cricket ball. I simply couldn't believe that there was anything so dangerous loose in what up to then had seemed a safe sort of world. A terrible master at a terrible prep. school introduced us. 'This is the bat, Morley,' he said, 'and this is the ball,' and flung it at me. A small red leather bomb, which for some reason failed to explode. I have lived in terror of the thing ever since. In vain I pleaded to be allowed to continue playing with a soft ball. 'I might even learn to like the game,' I told them, 'if I played with a soft ball.' Of course I lied. I had already played with a soft ball and hated it. My governesses were always urging me to join up with other children standing in front of groynes or spread out over the pebbles while Father bowled. (Never my Father, thank God.)

Blind in one eye, I discovered early on that I was never to stay long by the breakwater. While others made a meal of their innings, my own were brief to the point of incomprehension. A moment of top dogmanship holding the bat, a quick swing and back to Long Stop for the rest of time. Later at my public school I used even to hasten the process by taking guard and then before the ball could reach me knocking down my wicket. A protest which enraged the jolly cricketing house captain, who beat me nightly in the bathroom.

Right-minded boys were supposed to like cricket. The masters used to read out the scores of the county cricket matches after prayers. They believed in a God who liked cricket and prep. schools named after his saints.

Not being of the faithful I particularly dread the Test Match season, always fearful that switching on the radio or television I shall be exposed to a cricket commentary by Mr Arlott.

I cannot explain why I dread being told that Sun Yet San has now bowled more overs in his sweater from the gasworks end than any other fool in first-class cricket, but I do. Readers may think me mad if they wish. I am, but I am also brave. The other day, taking some of my old phobias out and examining them, I decided to go back to cricket for the day and to see what really goes on at Lord's during a Test Match. When I arrived nothing whatever was going on. It had been raining and although the sun now shone, the wicket was covered over with what appeared to be collapsed sight screens, and a number of mackintosh sheets of various sizes and colours were laid out to dry on the turf. Someone had obviously been shopping at the army surplus supply stores and was now keen to display his trophies. No one seemed keen to play cricket. While I watched, two men in blue took the field with the measured tread of police officers approaching an incident which they trust will have sorted itself out before they get there. 'Umpires inspecting the pitch,' one of the custodians informed me. They go in for custodians at Lord's. Sports which were once the privilege of the few and are still run by the gentlemen of England—Polo, Cricket, Racing—concentrate as far as conditions still permit on the 'enclosure within the enclosure'. At Lord's there are stands marked Members Only and others bearing the legend Friends of Members. Always one to dramatise my situation, I asked how I could make a friend. 'It's no use today,' the custodian informed me, 'friend or no friend, it's another fifty pence.'

By now the umpires had reached the centre of the ground, cautiously lifted one end of the tarpaulin and sniffed. I wondered what they were looking for, could it be wet grass? Inscrutably they returned to the pavilion. I bet Mr Betjeman likes the pavilion, I bet he likes cricket. 'The players', announced the public address system, 'will take lunch . . . another inspection will be made at two thirty.'

'But I've paid,' I told the custodian.

'You should read the small print.' No one having asked me to lunch, I lingered by his side while he reminisced about the time when as a boy they paid him sixpence for eight overs. 'Who paid sixpence?' I asked. 'Why the players, of course . . . we were glad of the money in those days. Cricket is dying,' he went on, 'it's been dying ever since I can remember.' I went over and read the menu outside the restaurant. Everything was cold. I was cold. I took a taxi and went to an Indian restaurant up the road. If I wasn't going to watch them playing cricket at least I could watch them cooking my lunch.

When I got back they were ringing bells, just like they used to at St Christopher's. An Indian stood outside the Tavern shouting at one of the players coming out to field. 'Encouraging him?' I asked. 'He is my kid brother, he insulted my mother, now he can never go back to India. I shall cut him in small pieces.' He insisted on buying me a gin and tonic. 'Keep the bottle to throw later,' he advised. He was a very cheerful fellow.

I sat down beside a man who knew all about it. He had spent a lifetime playing and watching the game, a helpless hopeless addict. Perhaps he was happy, perhaps they were all happy even the little man in a turban who bowled and kept rearranging the fieldsmen and seemed more grown up than all the others. The Father figure on the sands, he bowled all through the long afternoon, slowly, cunningly, patiently, and the children got out one after another trying to prolong their time at the wicket, not really scoring, just staying there so they shouldn't have to field in their turn. Nothing had changed. Halfway through the afternoon I found myself almost enjoying myself. It was the bars I suppose. Lord's is full of bars and barmaids. I always like barmaids. 'We come down from Lincoln every morning,' one of them told me. 'We enjoy the change.' If they could why couldn't I? The very last ball of the very last over bowled Edrich. He had stopped trying to score half an hour earlier. He wanted to bat another day. I was glad he went.

I watched them all go home, the old men and the boys, the mothers and the custodians, the waitresses from Lincoln, the decent quiet people of England—and, Oh my God, you should have seen the filth they left behind.

THE ENGLISH CONVERSATIONALIST

Colin Howard

'Tell you what, old boy, give me a ring some time.'

'All right, then, I'll give you a ring . . . When shall we say?'

'Any time, really, so long as I'm there. Tuesday?'

'Tuesday? Yes, I can manage Tuesday.'

'Fine! You'll be ringing me, then?'

'Yes, I'll give you a ring Tuesday. If by any chance I don't, I'll try to get it organised for Wednesday.'

'Fair enough, old boy. You've got my number?'

'Don't think I have, not exactly.'

'I'd better give it you, then.'

'Yes, all right; you give me your number and I'll write it down.'

'That'd be the best thing. Ready? Birkenwell 4832.'

'Birkenwell? That's the Exchange, is it?'

'Yes, and 4832 is our number. When they answer, ask to speak to me.'

'All right, then, old boy, that's settled. Tuesday. Failing that, Wednesday.'

'O.K., then, you'll be calling me.'

'Yeah, I'll be calling you. Think that's the best thing, don't you?'

'That seems the drill to me. Or tell you what, old boy. *I* could call *you* . . .'

WHAT HAPPENS AT SATURDAY MORNING CINEMA

PETER BUCKMAN is one of the few adults ever to have been and come back again. This is his incredible story

When you'd rather climb Everest than take them to the Zoo again, when another minute of 'children's television' will make you join the Angry Brigade, when there are absolutely no films in which you can honestly and decently answer the inevitable 'What are they doing, mum?'—then perhaps you ought to consider the blessings of Saturday Cinema. At about 9.30, every week, some 350,000 kids riot in the stalls of our local cinemas. No adults are allowed, except supervisory staff. I was granted special dispensation to bring you this report, and I can honestly say that, for me, the cinema will never be the same again.

I remember once being allowed to go as a kid, and thinking what a noisy clubby place it was, with everyone shouting for the characters they knew and I'd never seen in the flesh, such as Batman—still going—much more baggy and saggy than the seamlessly tunicked figure of the comic strip. Well, the noisy clubby bit hasn't changed at all nor, at least where I live, the fact that the audience is predominantly working class, in fine contrast to the well-modulated tones of the characters on screen.

In our local ABC, where I crept first, the manager was opening the proceedings with a *bonhomie* that did him credit so early in the day, and which the kids totally ignored.

'What're you all here for?' he bellowed jovially through a microphone.

'**** off!' the kids replied, without malice.

'Are you happy?'

'NO!'

'Glad to be back at school?'

'BOO-OOO-OOO!'

'Now if anyone's got all the badges you can buy at the kiosk, I want him to come up here and he'll get a prize.' Two kids fell over themselves to mount the stage, as bemedalled as generals. The manager spelled out the first one's display—it read 'ABC Minors'—and gave him a box of chocolates. The other boy received a clip round the ear. Then the screen lit up with the words of the ABC Minors' song: the kids sang lustily, though not, as far as I could tell, the words on the sheet. The manager retired to loud cheering, which continued as the first film began.

All eager, I leaned forward to catch the credits and the opening dialogue. I was apparently alone in my interest. No one went shush, or looked around indignantly, or muttered things under their breath. The kids nearest me—and they weren't very near, as if I had a contagious disease—had their feet on the seats in front and were unwrapping sweets with no attempt at decent mufflement. I considered composing my features into a stare that would both chill and silence, but there was no point in starting a fight in the first five minutes.

The cartoon, which I alone received with respectful attention, was an all-American one concerning a firefly whose light dimmed, who had it mended, and who then saved an aeroplane single-handed. It was followed by *A Deb in Sicily*, featuring little Deborah taking a Sicilian holiday all by herself. There were only two moments when the kids gave this any sort of notice: the first when a bikini-clad model appeared on the beach, bringing whistles and cries of 'Cor—Lovely!' from boys who at full height would scarcely have grazed her navel, and the second when a jolly fisherman prepared a sea-anemone for eating, at which the entire cinema echoed to the sounds of retching.

The third film brought resounding cheers: the week's instalment of *Panther Girl of the Kongo*, a black-and-white American number made, I should judge, when Bundles for Britain were still a necessity. Though I thought she had nice legs, Panther Girl herself was so completely asexual neither the boys in the audience nor those on screen were at all aroused by her. When, in fact, she was attacked by a crocodile, the cheers were stupendous.

This film ended in mid-fight, and immediately the lights

came full on—none of the subtlety reserved for us weary grown-ups—and instantly the tart usherettes and the rheumy-eyed caretaker were wagging fingers at the kids in an attempt to control them. What went on in the interval, apart from the consumption of an incredible amount of confectionery, appeared to be a series of mobile fights for territory. The older kids looked after the young in their care, making sure they got to the loo and sweet-tray, and that they weren't attacked too often. Gangs of small girls incited similar gangs of boys to attack them. Black fought with white in a sexual war. As far as I could tell there was no necking in the back.

The lights went down and a film from the Children's Film Foundation was announced, to prolonged booing. Now I had been told that the CFF is immensely popular, that, financed as it is by the British Film Industry itself ('no Government sponsorship whatsoever'), it was the principal and most trusted provider of material for these shows. Certainly its morality would cheer any parent: no violence, plenty of action, 'a constructive production policy aimed at increasing international understanding'. But whether four hundred kids, on their own in the dark, appreciated such uplifting sentiments was not clear to me.

The film was *Tim Driscoll's Donkey*, and the kids' noise did not cease throughout its length—at one point becoming so noticeable that the usherettes came shining their wrathful torches amongst the aisles. It made no difference. The hero of the film was an Irish lad much attached to his donkey, which he allowed to be taken away through the knavery of a jealous contemporary. For this, the audience jeered him, in terms such as 'Bloody stupid idiot'. While any extended piece of dialogue only increased the noise in the auditorium, they proved they were following the action by screaming at the screen when they didn't want something to happen, and working themselves up into an orgy of participation over a chase sequence. When all ended happily, to prolonged cheering, many kids dashed on to the stage and dived under the curtain. They were chased off by the caretaker with a broom. Were they, I asked, looking for the incarnation of their fantasies? 'Not bloody likely,' I was told. 'Just making trouble.'

My visit to the Odeon the following Saturday was more eventful. Things seemed quieter during the first half—sometimes they began with sing-songs ('when there was the staff available' the manager somewhat mystifyingly explained), but they had abolished the Odeon equivalent of the 'ABC Minors' song, because some critics told Lord Rank it was indoctrination. The opening film was the last episode of *Jungle Girl* (indistinguishable from *Panther Girl* in age and tone), and this was rapidly followed by the first episode of a CFF serial, *Treasure in Malta*. Though the heroes of this seemed to me to be insufferably public-school, and the characters so stereotyped as to be laughable to any kid who watched television, it was received in relative calm. It was during the interval that the kids showed what they truly thought.

As soon as the lights came on full, they were running up and down winning easy victories over the chasing staff. Anyone who was caught was threatened with the bogey of the manager—'If you don't watch it, he'll have you out. WALK, don't run.' And as soon as the kid was released, he was off again. It was a permanent game of Relievo in adult territory.

Absorbed, I was approached by a diminutive and dirty kid who jumped on the back of the seat in front of me. 'Hello,' he said, and I thought how kind it was of him to befriend me, considering I stood out as a pipe-cleaner amongst matches. 'Can you', he continued, 'give me sixpence?' I fished in my pockets, embarrassed by my wealth, trying to decimalise, and found two new pence, which I gave him with a warm adult smile, and asked if that was enough. 'No,' he said. But he vanished towards the sweet-tray, returning some minutes later. 'There's nothing I can get with it,' he said. 'Oh,' I returned. 'But I haven't got any more'—a black lie to this innocent, but what was I to do, give him the money I was saving to buy comics with? He vanished without further comment.

During the second half, as I was getting absorbed (again I was the only one) in an American comedy, *The Incredible Mr Limpet*, about a brow-beaten man who turns into a fish and then leads the US Navy to destroy the entire U-Boat fleet, I felt a tug at my sleeve. 'Here, mister,' said a voice, 'I've lost my tooth.'

Automatically I became the concerned adult and began looking for the missing object. I was not yet on my knees when it struck me that teeth are not easy to find in the dark. I straightened, and addressed my friend soberly. 'You should get sixpence for it,' I said. 'Yes,' he said and held out his hand.

They may not enjoy the films, but they certainly know what's going on.

Explosions of cheering greeted the victory of the American fleet, and after a splendid cartoon, again American, the kids were chased out of the cinema. The fact that they go every week regardless of what's on must mean that the atmosphere is what matters, that they care about being with their friends, in the dark, with no adults yet on adult turf, and that they can shout and show off as much as they like. Maybe there are undercurrents of sinister gang warfare, maybe the strong bully the weak, maybe the poor rob the rich, but parents may rest assured, none of *that* kind of thing gets on the screen.

As I was leaving, the manager pointed to the last kid to go, my tiny toothless friend. 'You want to watch that one,' he told me. 'He doesn't look like much, but he's a real terror.'

BAD BOOK GUIDE

T. E. B. Clarke

All this free advice to collectors has made it difficult these days to spot a book bargain on a market stall. A chum and I, frustrated in our browsing, decided to upend the common aim with a wager on which of us could find the book least worth 5p. His choice: *Does Hitler Mean War?*. Mine: *Horses to Follow in 1948*.

His feeble effort to maintain that the performances of my horses could provide pointers to their contemporary descendants was countered on my part by a revival of a rumour current at the time they were running: namely, that Hitler lived on and could yet be in South America planning vengeance. After all, not every old man is mellowed at 91. In the absence of an umpire to cool us down we called it a draw and settled for a replay in the near future.

Talent spotting forays around the market barrows have brought me some invaluable—or should it be valueless?— resources for our next encounter. My best find is a Mudie's Library catalogue of 1918. At 20p it was too expensive and far too beguiling to be entered for the contest, but its 1,152 pages are an incomparable guide for non-bargain hunters. It needs but one old-timer to have cheated the Great Pulper and I am on to a sure winner.

Who today, for instance, would curl up with *Her Majesty the Flapper* or *Lady Ermyntrude and the Plumber*? I doubt whether the smartest agent could do a hype job with *Dumps, a Plain Girl*— whose author, L. T. Meade, was responsible for no fewer than 205 titles, ranging in repellence from *Daddy's Boy* to *The Maid with the Goggles*.

Their possible appeal to those with political aspirations must rule out *The Socialism of Lady Jim*, *The Beloved Premier* and *A Lovely Little Radical*. The kind of lip-moving reader who took *Romance of the Hebrides* to be about he brides might also fall for *Queer Lady Judas* or *The Wooing of a Fairy*; and there's a risk of one with a weakness for the hard stuff recognising a kindred spirit in *The Lady on the Drawing-Room Floor*.

Incidentally, I learn from my treasured catalogue that there really was a book entitled *Purple Passion*. It was by Gertie De S. Wentworth James, who also wrote *Pink Purity* and *Violet Virtue*. All of these I have in mind for the substitutes' bench along with *Little Miss Prim*, *Dolly the Romp*, *Kitty the Rag* and *Mollie the Handful*.

Fiction however is dicey for the chaff gatherer: it can on occasion produce the unlikeliest bounty. The screenwriter Michael Pertwee picked up for a few pence an obscure Victorian novel called *Israel Rank* which caught his eye because he was working at the time for the Rank Organisation. Anti-Semitic and deadly serious, it told of mass murder by its eponymous villain to inherit a coveted peerage. Adapted for the screen, turned into a comedy and given a necessarily new title, it became *Kind Hearts and Coronets*.

So for the coming contest I shall pin my colours to a one-man compendium of useful information: *What's What* by Harry Quilter. This may sound an indisputable snip at 5p for more than a thousand pages, but it fails gloriously on two counts. What was what in 1902, the date of its publication, is very far removed from what is what today; and because its author understandably wilted under the strain of producing nearly a million words in just over one year, it is of minimal value as a work of reference beyond the letter M.

'The idea of *What's What*', writes Mr Quilter in a disarming foreword, 'was conceived at Mullion in Cornwall on Sunday, the 2nd of September 1900, and was due to a suggestion of my wife's. Preparation for the work commenced the same day.'

A moment worth recreating. The stroll along the seashore after the Sunday joint and forty winks. 'What a pretty shell, Harry.'

'The species known as Scotch Bonnet, my dear. Carried here no doubt from its native habitat in the Caribbean.'

'Oh, Harry, you are so knowledgeable! You really ought to write an encyclopaedia.'

The sudden halt, the fist slapped into the palm. 'By Jove, little woman, what a spiffing idea! Dash it, I will! Come on, come on—no time to lose . . .'

Back in haste to Mrs Penbuttock's lodgings. Vespers neglected for advice on hotels in Aachen—'The Nuellens best for bachelors, the Grande Monarque for families and great invalids.'

A quick supper followed by the course of the River Aar—'which you will be lucky to see through a valley defiled by vile smoke clouds from a hideous, puffing little Swiss engine.' Harry is getting rather tired and irritable after his opening burst; one soon comes to recognise the symptoms.

Things go pretty well however from A B (Abernethy Biscuits) to G R (Grape Cure), with high praise for the novels of Rhoda Broughton (*Red as a Rose is She*) and the poetry of Sydney Dobell. (Sydney *who?*)

First sign of second thoughts on the great venture is perceptible as early as Guitar, an instrument of limited range and peculiar twang, which is hard on the hands and makes *Home Sweet Home* sound absurd.

By H, Mrs Quilter feels impelled to register a mild protest. 'Isn't it a little rude, dear, to describe people who take the waters at Homburg as imbeciles?'

'Don't carp woman. Just remember this was your d—d silly idea.'

The last half of the alphabet receives but one-fifth of the total wordage, most of it in the same testy vein. Nice is not a place to take your wife to, Odessa has nothing of interest to the tourist, Lord Rosebery looks like an overgrown and slightly overfed schoolboy.

By passing over such as Ruskin, Tennyson and H.G. Wells the end comes at last within blessed sight and is celebrated with Whisky, Wine and Workhouse Diet. Then come two feeling pages on Writer's Cramp, which Mr Quilter sought to alleviate with a mechanical hand invented by a German doctor. It was not a success, and after experimenting with an elastic band round flagging fingers he concluded that the only solution was ambidexterity.

Writing with both hands he finished up on Zero, which took

him from roulette to the cost of a day's hunting in Monte Carlo, and recklessly promised a new edition of *What's What* the following year. My one lingering fear is that my opponent may be lucky enough to unearth it.

'Straight on be quicker, but t'other be prettier.'

MY NEXT HUSBAND . . .

Dorothy Drake

My present husband is too good for me; my next one will be wicked. At the moment I am continually being urged to behave myself and not to do this or that in public. What I need is someone who will egg me on, someone very bad indeed. He will drink too much and smoke too much and gamble. We will have terrific rows because he won't be at all reasonable, and neither am I. He will shout at me and I will be able to scream and spit back at him without feeling mean about it. Whenever I want to annoy him I shall talk about my first husband and say what a pet he was and how reasonable. ('Not like you,' I shall say.)

Other women will chase him. He will be irresistible to them because of his charm and good looks. He will be cruel to them, though—leading them on for amusement, then, quickly becoming bored with them, hurrying back to me. His discarded women will weep and be sad, and I shall be kind to them and comfort them—but only a little.

On the other hand, no man will dare to make a pass at me because if he does my second husband will fight him—publicly too—yes!—even in a restaurant.

He will be lazy, just like me. The garden will become wild and overgrown. We will toss up to see who must go out to buy more gin, and I will cheat so that he has to go every time. Every morning we will stay in bed late and I won't feel at all guilty. Then we'll get up and quarrel about who makes the lunch and in the end we'll go out to a pub and buy sandwiches.

I shall run away from him occasionally. He will come after me, though, and force me to go back to him. If ever he doesn't come after me I shall tear back in a furious temper to find out why.

I am not sure how he will earn his living but he will be quite rich. We will go abroad very often and when we come back we will smuggle things into the country. This I have always wanted to do and husband number one watches me like a hawk and feels nervous in case I have got heroin in my powder compact. Husband number two will only be cross if I am found out.

All my relatives who now feel sorry for my present husband will sympathise with me when I get my new one. But also, especially if they are women, they will wonder why such a handsome, attractive, exciting man has chosen to marry me.

I shall say nothing, but I shall smile as enigmatically as I can, and fervently hope that they never find out about his wife.

'And I sort of hope that, in time, she will become your friend, too.'

JUMBLE

Joanna Lumley

It started with swapping: my set of jacks, one missing, for a tennis ball which was still impressively hairy but bounced like an apple; three crayons in yellow, pink and a reluctant burnt umber for a little wooden donkey on a pedestal, whose base, when depressed, caused the donkey's legs to give way, only some of the elastic had perished; a bra, all cotton, size 32A, for *Bamalama Bamaloo* by Little Richard (hellish hard, that last one, but the bra was a status symbol I couldn't be without).

Particularly strapped for cash one summer term, Mary Steele and I emptied out our desks and top drawers and arranged the— well, frankly—the detritus, the gubbins on to a tray, priced it, and trotted round the corridors selling the stuff. We displayed half-eaten erasers, broken pencils, lids off lost jars, bottles with no tops, Italian stamps, elastic bands, three sheets of crumpled airmail paper—nothing was too shabby or dingy for our sales push. In an hour we had sold every last gew-gaw and were the richer by £1 0s. 2d. As our whole term's pocket money was one pound, we were in a frenzy of wealth and excitement. We particularly congratulated ourselves on the sale of half a pair of scissors, which we told a junior girl 'would be useful for something' (she was a jumble addict if ever I've seen one). From my share, I paid 2/6d. for a Parian ware figure of a boy picking something out of his toe at the school fête, but that takes me down a different track of serious collecting which doesn't concern us here. However, I have never forgotten the feeling of mild disappointment at the end of the tray sale: we had money, certainly, but our desks gaped too tidily, our blazer pockets were strangely uncluttered. I never want to know again that kind of gnawing emptiness (and indeed I never have). I decided to change sides: vendor into emptor.

I should like to introduce my parents at this stage. As with many married couples, one is a Normal and one a Jumblie. Brought up to see into both camps, my sister and I have worked out a kind of compromise: throw away regularly the real rubbish we have accumulated to make room for the next influx of life-enhancing bargains. It would not be untrue to say that the Jumblie in us has been handed down through the female side. Indeed, my mother has developed a spectacular new approach which involves 'feeling sorry' for things and 'giving them a kind home'. This theme has emerged since the 'bound to come in useful' or 'almost the same colour' myth has been exploded. We now know, from her untiring example, that the jumble cup matcheth not any saucer neither shall the button ye purchase for a snip ever find a fellow. She plays a kind of cosmic Kim's Game, trawling in destitute knick-knacks, and no item is too large to escape her friendly compassion. Thus we have managed to train our own families to recognise the delights of differently patterned plates and the unparalleled thrill of wearing second-hand clothes. What is a whole Rockingham tea-set compared with one exquisite Rockingham milk-jug? Simply this: the second is easier to store, easier to admire (excess can glaze the eyes of appreciation; think of a roomful of Mona Lisas and you get the picture) and very much easier to buy.

My first chance for self-expression came when four of us shared a flat in Earl's Court in the first half of the Sixties. Since I was salaried at £8 a week before tax, there was not much boodle over to make the home Ideal. I shared with three other open-handed clutter addicts, however, and in no time we had chambers fascinating enough to rival the British Museum. Our skilfully exhibited possessions included an ostrich egg, tin advertising signs, an old-fashioned camera, peacock feathers, long patterned pieces of cloth and a set of brass scales.

Readers growing restless will want to know our contacts, our sources. Nothing fell off the back of a lorry, although some things looked as though they had, and as though the lorry had been travelling at some speed when they did. We visited junk shops and street markets, of course, but the sight to raise blood pressure (be still, my beating heart) was a hand-drawn notice reading 'Jumble Sale Church Room Today'.

You see, in a street market the laser-eyed dealers are about; they will have snapped up the aces before you have stumbled from your bed, and re-priced them and put them into ritzy curio boutiques (but I once won a Tiffany lampshade in oyster-coloured glass, some beads missing, for £4 in Brick Lane). In a jumble sale you have only the organisers to outwit; if they don't know their onions they will sell them to you for peanuts.

Example given: a straining grey November afternoon near Chelmsford, a charity jumble sale, jolly few people about; my fingers sifting in the old cardboard box full of broken jewellery; suddenly I am holding a dirty pink and black brooch marked 3p ('It's only plastic, dear'); my eyelids slam down over my eyes in case she sees the pound sign pinging up like a cash register; I give her 10p (it *is* a charity) and I own a perfect eighty-year-old cameo, palest cream and shell pink, set in solid silver. In the same sale, an excellent dinner jacket and trousers for £2. It was only when I got them home that I saw that they must have belonged to Fat Daniel Lambert, as they would have hung loosely on Cyril Smith. So it's swings and roundabouts and which gambler could resist it?

At a good jumble sale, there will be a trestle table groaning with home-made cakes and pots of elderberry and rhubarb jelly, cheese straws and shortcake and stoneground, husk-whiskered, underfelt biscuits. There will usually be a fruit cake of immense proportions whose leaden weight you are invited to guess. This stall empties the quickest, so many people visit it first. Then there is a Soft counter selling peg-bags, small cushions, shoe-bags, cloth dolls, knitting-bags, aprons and bags. These, as they are all clean and new, are good Christmas presents as they can be received, kept in a drawer and sent off to another sale next year. Some bags have been doing the rounds for many years and have forgotten their original purpose. There is a Bottle stall where you will fix your eyes on a bottle of whisky and win some tomato ketchup or a dandruff shampoo. There is a Tombola, where you will win nothing. Then, on table after table, rack upon rail, the jumble itself.

There are several views on how it should be displayed. Some feel happiest when it is all thrown together, like a Russian salad: I prefer books here, records there, bric-à-brac further along, but I have a suspicion that if it is too well-sorted laser-vision will have had a look-in. Taken from their natural surroundings, each object assumes an incandescent desirability. Decide swiftly: don't ponder and wander on, for it will be gone when you return. Have as many arms as the goddess Kali and remember that the good-natured punters are in fact grasping fanatics, as untrustworthy as a short spit. Only when the fever is dying and the pocket is empty can you afford to be magnanimous ('Oh, that's lovely, well done, what a find, pity about the stain'). Drained, you take a cup of tea in a thick china mug. Such a feeling of achievement swarms over as you have never felt before (since the last time). Later, you will pore and gloat over your booty, polishing and washing and boasting.

I am sometimes asked to officiate at charity jumble sales or fêtes, or Fayres as they're occasionally called. I warn them with quiet insistence that I will not be making a speech, no, cannot be persuaded. Two reasons (which I do not give) are these: first, I am awful at public speaking; and second, and far more important, once when I did attempt a few words ('Great pleasure . . . worthy cause . . . blah . . . do spend . . .'), I saw at the far end of the hall a stout, tweed-coated woman had jumped the gun and was negotiating in whispers over the price of a Coalport tureen. So now, barely pausing by the microphone to shout, 'Good afternoon it's open,' I hurl myself, elbows out, into the crowd of human locusts.

'Of course we must face facts. It's going to mean waiting.'

LITTLE LEWIS AND BIG BURGESS

Roger Lewis

Since I became, at the instigation of Malcolm Bradbury in 1983 (and not at the instigation of Anthony Burgess), Anthony Burgess's Recording Angel, I have met my quarry thrice.

The first confrontation was masterminded by Richard Ellmann, biographer of James Joyce and Oscar Wilde. Over in Britain for the publication of *The Kingdom of the Wicked*—an apostolic completion of the Bible's cinematic re-writing, filmed as *A.D. Anno Domini*; Burt Lancaster's *Moses the Lawgiver* and Robert Powell's *Jesus of Nazareth* forming earlier portions of the triptych—Burgess had agreed to take the train to Oxford, accompanied by his wife.

Ellmann and I had a long wait at the railway station. The InterCity from Paddington was delayed. We amused ourselves spotting dons depart for metropolitan weekends—John Wain, for example. 'I've just finished lunch at Brasenose,' said the quondam Professor of Poetry, 'and I've now to go and give a lecture I've not yet written in London. I'll scribble something between here and Reading.' We told him our mission: to await Anthony Burgess. 'Well,' replied John, 'I'd rather be doing what I'm doing than what you're doing.' He rattled his bicycle through the turnstile, snaking the machine with difficulty past an oncoming mob.

The oncoming mob consisted of passengers from London. A clatter and confusion of ticket punching and portmanteaus knocked against shins.

I was trepidatious. I'd read every word Burgess had published that I could find. That's thousands of articles and essays; dozens of books (novels, critical appreciations, translations); hundreds of forewords and afterwords and prefaces. I was a hierophant—but had mitigated my enthusiasm, now and again, with the odd high-handed undergraduate sneer in an occasional review. Salutary moderation. Would Burgess take offence? He accepts praise without demur, but censure makes him bridle.

But of Burgess there was no sign. We thought he'd forgotten about the trip, or had decided to travel later, or had come by another route. Then, up the steps, like a Mancunian Orpheus from the underworld tunnel beneath the tracks, came the man of letters, followed by a diminutive bundle in bombasine black, Burgess's Eurydice, the contessa Liliana Macellari, known as Liana.

It was Liana who did the talking, in a heavily accented English, a fiery torrent, or creole, of her own devising, darting in and out of French and Italian when the local word escaped her. She fizzed with admiration about her husband's *The End of the World News*, which she was currently translating; she fizzed with venom for an agent, or was it a publisher, who'd robbed her husband blind; she fizzed with enthusiasm for a book on Merlin she'd lately read, which would aid her husband's current composition—a novel about King Arthur called *The Sovereignty of the Sword*.

Meantime, Burgess was talking about a book on D. H. Lawrence he'd knocked off for Heinemann: 'Heinemann finally woke up to the fact that it was Lawrence's centenary, so I said, you'd better celebrate it duly, so I've written them a short book.' That was *Flame into Being*—a lively account of the Nottingham miner's son, which tells us as much about Burgess himself as about Lawrence. Both had indigent childhoods and were brought up hard; both were scoffed at for literary ambitions; both married foreign aristocrats; both became self-exiles. The first chapter is called 'Lawrence and Myself When Young'.

Ellmann directed us towards New College, whither he'd recently retired as Goldsmith Professor. 'This reminds me', said Liana, 'of the opening scene in Antonio's Shakespeare film. A beautiful, beautiful script I recently found in Bracciano. The film was never made, but it imagined Will meeting the philosopher Vico in Oxford.'

I heard about the Shakespeare film. It was meant to star Maggie Smith as Ann Hathaway and Peter Ustinov as Ben Jonson. 'Few of my scripts have ever been made,' said Burgess. 'The executive producers are fired, and projects are dropped.'

Ellmann pointed out statuary and gargoyles. Burgess looked at memorial tablets. He calculated ages of the deceased, and was shaken to espy names of contemporaries. 'All of us of that generation born just after the First World War are getting very old. We're dying off.'

We next went to Ellmann's house in St Giles's for gin. I noticed an onomastic proliferation. Liana called Burgess *Antonio*; Ellmann called him *John*—from John Wilson, the baptismal name; an ursine American academic, in for pre-prandials, called him *Mr Burgess*; Mary Ellmann, sceptical of the man's merit and smarting from an anti-feminist remark Burgess had made years previously, didn't call him anything; and I, too, avoided all monickers. I'd read all his books, remember. How do you address a stranger you think you know intimately?

I left the proceedings when Antonio, or John, or Mr Burgess, started to recite Thackeray by the yard. It had transpired that the ursine American academic was a Thackeray bibliographer named Gordon Ray. '*The Rose and the Ring* is one of my favourite books,' said Burgess, and off he went. Gordon Ray, now deceased, returned to New York to ask, 'Who the hell was that novelist with the Italian wife who knew the works of Thackeray by heart?'

My second meeting with Burgess was hardly that. We happened to be placed at the same table at a *Punch* lunch—a hebdomadal gathering of London media monkeys. Alan Coren was careful to separate us, fearing fisticuffs. He did not know we'd met. Ellmann was also present, listening to Irma Kurtz tell him about Laurence Sterne. I was next to Cyril Ray, wine's wittiest historian, and Dick Price, who is older than God and twice as knowledgeable; the only man I've met who can follow a Congreve plot.

Before the food, during drinks, I watched Burgess huffing and puffing on cigarillos, on display, baritonal and anecdotal during the boozy hours of obligatory wit. A critic, who'd best remain nameless, praised 'your wonderful latest novel'. Ten minutes previously, that nameless critic had asked me for a fast summary 'of the old bugger's new raving'.

Burgess and I later jostled on the stairs, both making egress, me rather drunk, my pockets full of cigars placed there by Michael ffolkes the cartoonist. 'What', I asked Burgess, who was searching for a plastic bag, 'do you have in that plastic bag?'

'Language tapes,' he responded. 'I'm teaching myself Russian.'

Or it may have been Welsh, I don't rightly recall.

My third encounter was at the Apollo Theatre, Oxford, in late 1985. Burgess had tailored a new libretto, called *Oberon Old and New*, for Scottish Opera's production of Carl Maria von Weber's *Oberon* (1826). I'd received a telemessage summoning my wife and me to the vestibule, 6.45.

Burgess was accompanied by Leslie and Gabriele Pantucci, his literary agents and close friends. We were introduced, and Leslie is now my literary agent. Liana had stayed home in Monaco or Lugano or Rome or Malta or Callian. Very sensibly, any half-decent publisher's advance, or film producer's fee, is banged direct into property. The Callian cottage was once generously offered as a holiday address for myself plus spouse. Then, with comic business almost hard to believe, the key couldn't be found. A big rusty medieval clanking job impossible to duplicate. So we were offered a studio flat in Monte Carlo— but by this time we'd flown to Greece.

At the Apollo Theatre, Burgess was utterly generous, utterly a modest man of letters, shy when recognised and insisting on brief chats with votaries requesting an autograph. He was clad in green and wore 'my Brancusi James Joyce tie'. Burgess is colour-blind. Not knowing this at the time, I thought homage to the Emerald Isle was the point.

'I've read', he said, 'Ellmann's *James Joyce* about twenty times.' What, I wondered, did he make of my anatomising of himself for a big literary biographical study, called *The Paper Man*? 'Shouldn't you wait until I'm dead? I do, though, and who wouldn't, enjoy being written about. Great fun. But I don't want actively to be involved or influence you in any way. I offer you this, and you mustn't make anything of it: Joyce told Gorman he could do a biography, but he, Joyce, had to come over as a saint whose life was one long martyrdom.'

We all laughed at this, and went in to enjoy the opera—a sur-realistic production, set, for some reason, in a decrepit 1930s cinema. The librettist was alarmed. 'Was that a boo?' he asked loudly at the conclusion. 'I hope so. Rossini was booed!'

'You! Go back to the Economy Section!'

UN BON HOMME IN UN QUANDARY

William Boyd

I should have been more suspicious, I suppose. Quite suddenly, my editor in Paris—Françoise—started speaking to me in French when hitherto she'd employed her extremely fluent English. Just testing, she said, for the *table ronde*. The *table ronde* was an event that had been organised by the British Council in Paris. In return for my air fare and two nights in a hotel I had agreed to participate in an informal discussion about my first novel, *A Good Man in Africa*, which had just been published in France (*Un Anglais sous Les Tropiques*). It seemed a reasonable quid pro quo: a few questions, a few answers, the odd carefully rehearsed anecdote—even my rusty French (product of a year-long sojourn on the Côte d'Azur in 1971) should be able to cope.

I flew to Paris, arriving in the mid afternoon. The *table ronde* had been scheduled for 6 p.m. that day. I had time to check into my hotel, meet at the British Council for a drink with my publishers, and then into the *table ronde*. It had struck me that I wasn't leaving much time for acclimatisation. I had meant to mug up a little on my irregular verbs, check out a few difficult words, but somehow had never got round to it. Not that it matters much, I told myself as I was driven to the hotel, abstract nouns are the same in French as in English. Keep it simple, throw in the odd *franchement* or *en principe*, a shrug or two, and you're laughing. The lady from the British Council assured me that everyone was very excited about the *table ronde*. Why's that? I enquired. It's unusual to conduct proceedings in French, she said; most British authors insist on talking English. Oh, I said, do they? Yes, but when we advertise that the *table ronde* will be in French we get a much bigger audience—and we've got a very distinguished panel. My mouth was getting strangely dry. She mentioned their names. No bells ringing. Tell me about them I said. Well, there was Georges Conchon, Goncourt prize-winning novelist, Catherine Rihoit, lecturer at the Sorbonne, famous for her rather raunchy feminist novels, and a celebrated Congolese writer Tchicaya U' Tam'si. Pronounced tremors had started up in both hands. I tried to translate this nightmare into English terms—it was like being invited to share a panel with Salman Rushdie, Germaine Greer and Wole Soyinka. Imagine some French novelist with semi-efficient English trying to hold his own with these luminaries . . .

In my hotel room I wiped the vomit from my lips and tried to memorise some vocabulary. What was the French for post-structuralist? How did one translate 'unreliable narrator'. My *Harraps New Shorter French and English Dictionary* was a legacy of my sixth form French (grade D at A-level) and was not over-burdened with the new literary jargon. I recalled my rule of thumb: all English nouns ending -*tion* are the same in French; all abstract nouns with a Latin root are the same in French—think of the English word, say it with a French accent, no problem. That was my first mistake.

Luckily by the time I arrived at the British Council I was on autopilot. This is a state that descends on me whenever a crisis state reaches panic proportions. Certain segments of my brain— the imagination, those nerve circuits that allow one to think in the future tense, the embarrassment glands, or whatever—are shut down. One enters a sort of solipsistic reverie—the world is a dream, nothing matters. The symptoms are a glazed smile, a dead look in the eyes and conversation pitched at a level of the commonplace and banal.

It was a state that was seldom to leave me during my two days in Paris, but it served me well during the *table ronde* and the din-ner with the panel afterwards (nobody told me about the dinner). I remember a huge room, and about a hundred people sitting down facing a dais upon which the panel sat. I was intro-duced and my decision to speak French was admired and generously applauded. The smile became more glazed. As for the discussion itself, my strategy was to keep my role to an absolute minimum. This turned out to be easily effected because everyone else had huge amounts to say. I remember stuttering to a halt during a lame defence of realism (*le réalisme*, I hoped). Tchicaya U' Tam'si, gamely undertaking the role of spokesman for Black Africa, upbraided me for neglecting to tackle *le racisme* ('*Mais, c'est un roman comique*' was my response) and then got into a 15-minute wrangle with my translator—who was in the audience—over her translation of 'French Letter'. The term she had used was *capot d'Anglais*. Tchicaya resented this for some reason and, I think, saw it as neo-colonialist. I was as vague as the rest of the audience about the precise nature of his objection, but that didn't stop anyone from talking about it.

Indeed the whole discussion—and this is what I see as typically French—was carried on in the higher altitudes of intellectual debate: the concrete, the empiric, were shunned absolutely—the book disappeared into a fug of abstract nouns. To which, apparently, I added some new ones. My rule of thumb let me down badly, and after the talk several broadly smiling people admired my way with neologisms. 'I do like your new words,' one lady said to me. 'They sound so much nicer than the old ones.'

Problems with words continued the next day. After lunch with a journalist, who mercifully spoke English, I was to be interviewed on French radio. Sadder and wiser I made sure that the publishers had conveyed to the interviewer that I possessed only rudimentary French. It made no difference, and I can only put the interviewer's intransigence and hostility down to rampant Anglophobia. He spoke French with a velocity that in any other circumstances would have been highly impressive. Although we faced each other across a table we might have been separated by thousands of miles of faulty telephone cable. Through the fizz, crackle and interference of his rapid fire I could only make out the occasional word. '*Politique*' was one. '*Plutôt à gauche*,' I said. He looked very puzzled. Soon I started asking him to redefine words in an effort to slow him down. We carried on in this way for ten minutes. 'How did it go?' I asked the subdued publicity person afterwards. 'It was . . . interesting,' she said.

That night, the plan was for me to go to a launching party. Not of my book, but of some French author. It seemed that key figures in the French literary world would be present, and it would be greatly advantageous to meet them. Brain death seemed imminent, but I thought I would give it one more try.

My editor, Françoise, drove me out to a small and fashionable bookshop in a fashionable arrondissement. The book being celebrated was a slim monograph on the Paris commune. The small bookshop was very crowded and very smoky. The 'look' for French intellectuals and literary folk, for those interested in fashion notes, hasn't changed since the sixties. Key props are a cigarette, a leather jacket, unstructured greasy hair and massive pretension. I was led through the crowd to meet the literary editrix of a major newspaper. She was pale, large, freckled and with a lot of lank ginger hair. 'I'm afraid she doesn't like Western literature,' Françoise whispered as we approached. 'But I don't write Westerns,' I said, vastly relieved. 'No, no,' Françoise said. The editrix reserved her admiration for works from beyond the Iron Curtain, preferably written by Jewish dissidents. 'How do you do?' I said. 'I've just been reading Penrose's book on English Surrealism,' were her first words to me, in French to boot. We did not find much common ground.

Perhaps as an oblique comment on my small talk, she swiftly introduced me to a translator who wanted to practise his English. Translators are a curious, generally seriously impoverished breed. Encounters with them can be deeply unsettling. At a party in London I was once introduced to a man who said, 'Hello, I your Polish translator are.' My Swedish translator wrote inviting me to 'crash in his pad in Stockholm' if I wanted to 'save some bread'. Quite apart from provoking anguish over what's happening to your books, you wonder what strange demon drove them to take up the career in the first place. This particular French translator was a suitably tall, dark, starved looking man. I asked him whom he was translating. Flann O'Brien he said. *At Swim-Two-Birds*. But, I said tactfully after a shocked pause, can it be done? Oh yes, he assured me, he'd been working on it for eight years. Deeply saddened, I was glad to be interrupted by Françoise who said she had to go. She was leaving me in the hands of François-Xavier, another editor, who would take me back to my hotel. I liked François-Xavier, and not just because he spoke very good English, and so was not in the least disappointed when he interrupted me trying not to give the French translator my address in London and said we had to go.

Outside, it was clear that François-Xavier was in something of a hurry. As we climbed into his Volkswagen he told me why. His mother, who was nearly eighty, was a very celebrated French actress who was currently appearing at the Comédie Française. It was his job to deliver her to the stage door each night. I asked when the play started. Eight o'clock. We had just under an hour, I couldn't see what the problem was. François-Xavier explained. His mother, apparently, liked to arrive at the theatre half an hour before her call so she could do her *friction*. Friction? Yes, she rubbed herself all over with a pumice stone. It made her all tingly and hot and was a crucial prerequisite to her nightly performance. If she couldn't do her *friction* all hell broke loose and tonight we were running a bit late.

François-Xavier suggested we pick up his mother before he dropped me off. I agreed, trying to imagine what it must be like to rub yourself all over with a pumice stone. We set off for her flat, we got caught in a traffic jam, we raced up side streets trying to get there more quickly.

As we approached, François-Xavier could see his mother pacing up and down on the pavement outside her apartment block.

I jumped into the back of the car as François-Xavier tried to mollify the near hysterical old actress. Introductions were scant. The conversation went, approximately, like this:

'You're so late! My *friction*, what about my *friction*!!'

'Darling, you look absolutely ravishing.'

'But it's ten to eight!'

'Plenty of time, my little cabbage, plenty of time.'

'But my *friction*.'

'You do too much of that *friction*, try just five minutes tonight.'

'It's a disaster, a disaster!'

'Nonsense, nonsense. You're so beautiful, so wonderful. Everybody loves you.'

MADAME, TO ME. 'I have, how you say, pumice? I rub myself. *Friction*. Before the show.'

ME. 'Ah. Yes.'

TO FRANÇOIS-XAVIER. 'You silly stupid boy. You promised not to be late.'

'Oh, darling, don't make such a fuss. We have hours of time. Hours. You will be magnificent.'

We stopped at a traffic light. François-Xavier kissed his mother's hand. 'Keep calm, my lovely, that's the main thing.'

I opened the door. 'I can walk from here.' I faintly said goodbye and thank you. I'm not sure they heard. I watched them drive off. I was on the Boulevard Montparnasse. There had to be a bar around here somewhere. I wandered off. This fiction *friction*, I thought, it can really get to you. I needed a drink very badly indeed: brain death had arrived.

' "Please excuse Arthur from all sports as he has a very bad cold." You know that this sort of attitude cuts absolutely no ice with me, don't you, Potterton?'

DEATH ON THE ROAD

George Melly

'Webster', wrote T. S. Eliot with prim relish, 'was much possessed by death,' and so, increasingly, am I. At 58 I am aware not only that my life is probably at least twenty years nearer the tomb than the womb, but that the Great Reaper may swing his scythe at any moment; 7.25 this evening for instance. Until I was about forty, death was almost an abstraction. It happened either to old people, or because of an accident, or an unlucky wager on the terminal roulette wheel. Then the number of my near contemporaries who had died would scarcely have made up a respectable tea party. Now it's a large cocktail party with gatecrashers showing up by the minute. Soon I'd need to hire the Albert Hall.

The intimations of my personal mortality are, as yet, modest: two teeth capped, reading glasses and a hearing aid, thickening toenails, a painful stiffening of the thighs after a mile walk. I'm beginning to feel like an old car, perfectly serviceable but a bit hard to start on cold mornings, heavy on petrol and a gear box with a knack to it. Years of life in it still, of course, and yet it's sobering to remember those old cars. There's one in the lane in Wales. Someone drove it down from London without much trouble but then, two days later, it just wouldn't start again.

Yet, rather to my surprise, none of this makes me feel gloomy. On the contrary, my reaction to a memento mori—the abandoned car in the lane, a dead hornet in an empty bath, the meaningless generalities of the crematorium clergyman over someone he didn't know—is a kind of euphoria. Death, I believe, is the apt punchline to the meandering joke of life. How we struggle to make good, to know everything about computers or the life cycle of the black ant, to play the bassoon better than anyone else in the world, to make millions through the skilful movement of currency from country to country. Then, in a single moment, it's all over. Sir James Goldsmith is no richer than the cheerful old black tramp, hung with pots and pans, clattering about the environs of Paddington. Arthur Scargill and Ian MacGregor will find themselves in total agreement. There will be no difference between the future work of Philip Larkin and E. J. Thribb (17).

I feel I might be less sanguine if I were not a convinced atheist. Belief in personal immortality would, I imagine, be far more worrying. As it is, the idea of non-being is no more disturbing than the thought of a dreamless if endless night.

None of this applies, of course, to the deaths of others. Here, if I was fond of them, I feel a probably selfish deprivation. Even the death of an enemy, while not exactly upsetting, unravels the edges of one's own life. After a funeral I find myself resenting the inability of the person I've just seen burnt or buried to experience not the rare great joys or griefs, but the humdrum and banal activities I can observe through the windows of the post-funeral car: slipping into a public house, waiting for the green man to light up at a traffic light, collecting a suit with a note pinned to it apologising that a stain couldn't be removed 'without serious risk to the material'. On the other hand, I find the unscheduled but ever closer approach of one's own death intensifies the pleasure of everything—banishes boredom. To hook a trout, to catch a certain effect of light on distant hills, to swallow the first oyster on September 1st, to make love—all these have become again as marvellous as the earliest remembered experiences of childhood. Then things were marvellous because they were without precedent. Now it's because it might always be the last time.

These thoughts, fairly commonplace I dare say, are much less concentrated than this piece might suggest. Only now and then am I aware, like Eliot's Webster, of 'the skull beneath the skin'. Nevertheless, as Auden advocated in relation to poets (why not plumbers and taxidermists? Come to that, why not jazz singers?), it's useful to think of one's death at least once a day. Recently, several deaths have ensured that I do: a much-loved interior decorator of genius, dead of a stroke at 63, his witty tongue and repertoire of facial mannerisms still widely if unconsciously reproduced by a large circle of friends; Alberta Hunter, the great blues *chanteuse* and the composer of the first blues

Bessie Smith ever recorded, dead in her eighties after a remarkable late renaissance in New York.

Also, I feel obliged to add, I had a nasty shock myself recently. I got up one Sunday morning and was crippled by an excruciating pain across my back, the only relief to pace the floor like a caged tiger, grey with anguish and bathed in cold sweat. It was only a kidney stone and, after twenty-four hours in a cheerful public ward floating on pethidine, it 'passed'. Before my injection though, the agony was what my mother called 'exquisite'. I can do without that at my end. I can do without angry senility too; biting the nurses and totally incontinent. Federico Garcia Lorca asked for a quiet death 'in clean sheets'. In the event he was shot, probably by the Falangists, during the Spanish Civil War. Better that, though, than the fate of his childhood friend Dali, senile, burnt and anorexic at 83. If there is to be pain I hope they'll turn me into an instant junkie.

Sometimes, after a fast number with a lot of prancing about, I imitate someone in the audience turning to a friend.

'If he goes on like that at his age,' I say, 'he'll drop dead!'

They usually laugh, but I mean it.

HOW JAZZ CAME TO ORANGE COUNTY STATE FAIR

*PAUL DESMOND, alto saxophonist with Dave
Brubeck and winner of countless polls, has been promising for
years to write the history of the Brubeck Quartet. This instalment is the first he has ever been persuaded to write*

Dawn. A station-wagon pulls up to the office of an obscure
motel in New Jersey. Three men enter—pasty-faced, grim-eyed,
silent (for those are their names). Perfect opening shot, before
credits, for a really lousy bank-robbery movie? Wrong. The
Dave Brubeck Quartet, some years ago, starting our day's work.

Today we have a contract (an offer we should have refused)
for two concerts at the Orange County State Fair in Middletown. 2 p.m. and 8 p.m. Brubeck likes to get to the job early.

So we pull up behind this hay truck around noon, finally locating the guy who had signed the contract. Stout, red-necked, gruff
and harried (from the old New Jersey law firm of the same
name), and clearly more comfortable judging cattle than book-
ing jazz groups. He peers into the station-wagon, which contains
four musicians, bass, drums, and assorted baggage, and for the
first and only time in our seventeen years of wandering about the
world, we get this question: 'Where's the piano?'

So, leaving Brubeck to cope with the situation, we head into
town for sandwiches and browsing. Since the sandwiches take
more time than the browsing, I pick up a copy of the *Middletown
Record* and things become a bit more clear. TEENAGERS' DAY
AT THE ORANGE COUNTY STATE FAIR, says the headline
across the two centre pages (*heavy* move, in that the paper only
has four pages). Those poor folk, especially the cattle-judge type
(who was probably lumbered into heading the entertainment
committee), thought we were this red-hot teenage attraction,

which Lord knows we've never been. Our basic audience begins with creaking elderly types of twenty-three and above.

Nevertheless, here we are, splashed all over this ad, along with the other attractions of the day—judo exhibition, fire-fighting demonstration, wild west show, and Animalorama (which may have been merely misspelled). And right at the top, first two columns on the left, is this picture of Brubeck's teeth and much of his face, along with the following text, which I'm paraphrasing only slightly. Hear the music teenagers everywhere thrill to [it begins]. Hear the music that rocked Newport Rhode Island [an unfortunate reference in that only a few weeks earlier the Newport Jazz Festival had undergone its first riot]. Hear Dave Brubeck sing and play his famous hits, including 'Jazz goes to college', 'Jazz in Europe', and 'Tangerine'.

So, now realising—in Brubeck's piquant ranch phrase—which way the hole slopes, we head back to the fairgrounds where the scene is roughly as follows: there is a smallish, almost transistorised, oval race track. (I'm not exactly sure how long a furlong is, but it seems not too many of them are actually present.) On one side of the oval is the grandstand, built to accommodate 2,000 or so, occupied at the moment by eight or nine elderly folk who clearly paid their money to sit in the shade and fan themselves, as opposed to any burning desire to hear the music their teenage grandchildren everywhere thrill to.

Directly across the track from them is our bandstand—a wooden platform, about ten feet high and immense. Evidently no piano has been locatable in Orange County, since the only props on-stage are a vintage electric organ and one mike. Behind us is a fair-sized tent containing about two hundred people, in which a horse show for young teenagers is currently in progress—scheduled, we soon discover, to continue throughout our concert. This is hazardous mainly because their sound system is vastly superior to ours.

So we begin our desperation opener, 'St Louis Blues'. Brubeck, who has never spent more than ten minutes of his life at an electric organ, much less the one he is now at, is producing sounds like an early Atwater-Kent Synthesiser. (Later he makes a few major breakthroughs, like locating the volume control pedal and figuring out how to wiggle his right hand, achieving a tremolo effect similar to Jimmy Smith with a terminal hangover, but it doesn't help much.) Eugene Wright, our noble bass player, and me take turns schlepping the mike back and forth between us and playing grouchy, doomed choruses, but the only sound we can hear comes from our friendly neighbourhood horse show.

'Lope,' it roars. 'Canter . . . trot . . . and the winner in the twelve-year-old class is . . . Jacqueline Higgs!'

As always in difficult situations such as these, we turn to our main man, primo virtuoso of the group, the Maria Callas of the drums, Joe Morello, who has rescued us from disaster from Grand Forks to Rajkot, India.

'You got it,' we said, 'stretch out,' which ordinarily is like issuing an air travel card to a hijacker. And, to his eternal credit, Morello outdoes himself. All cymbals sizzling, all feet working. (Morello has several. Not many people know this.) Now he's into the triplets around the tom-toms, which has shifted foundations from the Odeon Hammersmith to Free Trade Hall and turned Buddy Rich greener than usual with envy.

The horse show is suddenly silent. Fanning in the stands has subsided slightly.

Suddenly a figure emerges from the horse tent, hurtles to the side of the stage, and yells at Brubeck. 'For Chrissakes, could you tell the drummer not to play so loud? He's terrifying the horses.'

Never a group to accept defeat gracelessly, we play a sort of Muzak for a suitable period and split.

When we return at eight, all is different. A piano has been found, the stands are packed with our geriatric following of twenty-five and above, and we play a fairly respectable concert.

Even so, we're upstaged by the grand finale of the fair—the fire-fighting demonstration. A group of local residents has been bandaged and made up to appear as if they've just leapt from the Hindenburg and their last rites are imminent. But instead of remaining discreetly behind the scenes until their big moment, they mingle casually with friends and neighbours in the audience during the evening, sipping beer, munching popcorn, casting an eerie, Fellini-like quality over the gathering, and considerably diminishing the impact of their ultimate appearance.

After their pageant come the main events of the fair, which have clearly been planned for months: a flaming auto wreck, followed by a flaming plane wreck, each to be dealt with instantly and efficiently by the Middletown Fire Dept. At one end of the oval is a precariously balanced car; at the other end, a truly impressive skeletal mock-up of a single-engine plane, tail up. Midway, at ground zero, is the Middletown Fire Truck, bristling with ladders and hoses and overflowing with volunteers.

A hush falls over the stands. At a signal given by the fire chief, the car is ignited. The truck reaches it in two or three seconds, by which time the fire is roughly equivalent to that created by dropping a cigarette on the back seat for two or three seconds. It is extinguished by many men with several hoses.

A murmur falls over the stands. The fire chief, painfully aware that his moment of the year is at hand, signals for the plane to be ignited, also instructing the truck to take it easy, so that the fire should be blazing briskly when it arrives. The truck starts, at about the pace of a cab looking for a fare. The plane goes whoosh!, like a flashbulb, and by the time the leisurely truck arrives, has shrunk to a lovely camp-fire, just large enough for roasting marshmallows.

Later, four pasty-faced, grim-eyed men pile into a station-wagon and drive away. It may not be bank-robbery, but it's a living.

'I'm still hungry.'

BARGEPOLE

Michael Bywater

A chap wrote me a nice letter saying 'You are wonderful' which is the sort of thing one likes. Probably you don't get that sort of letter. Probably you get letters saying 'Henceforth you are no son of mine' and 'We are therefore commencing proceedings without further notice' and 'I don't know how to tell you this but I got the result and it's positive' but we all have our troubles and an excess of adulation is my cross.

This particular chap was on about films. I rang him up on the telephone and he said, 'Why don't we meet in the Groucho Club?' and I fiddled around on my desk looking for my Filofax and then I screamed and fell over. Good God in Heaven, I have become a media person, insouciantly making assignations with chaps about films in the Groucho Club and writing them down in a Filofax. What can be nastier or more alien to everything I hold beneath reproach?

I think all this Filofax balls has got to stop. One of the nice things about music is that it can only be addressed in its own terms, being a totally self-referential logical form. Herein lies a rich seam of bullshit crying out to be mined and I for one am happy to oblige. Hans Keller said it wasn't necessarily so, but look what happened to him. Fell down dead.

The Filofax generation never got to him, lucky old sod, but I think he'd have recognised it as something else to get his analytical teeth into. What are we talking about, for God's sake, but a bloody loose-leaf notebook? Yet the thing has become a cult object and now its makers are going for a quote on the USM. It's perfect. It's everything one would like to take a machine-gun to, creeping up in the dark on rubber-soled shoes with a few clips of soft-nosed shells close at hand. The Yuppy dream reaches fruition and is massacred in a flurry of upwardly-mobile blood and expensive bridgework. Kabooom! BMW paintwork flies about the desirable neighbourhood as tanned necks are ripped away from their stinking mid-Atlantic button-down collars. Why can't the bastards invent a button-down lip?

I had my first Filofax in 1968. It belonged to my grandfather. It was unpretentious. You put the pages in and wrote stuff on them. I rather liked it. It said N&H FILOFAX on it and nothing else. Research indicated that N&H stood for Norman & Hill and you had to track the buggers down and write to them for new pages. They had all sorts of arcana directed at doctors, officers and the clergy. I still have some old forms with a naïve drawing of the human frame *mirabiliter condidisti et mirabilius reformasti* on which Dr Snoddies could draw warts and lumps. (These pages are useful still, to me; I draw Yuppies infected with boils and protuberances on them. Some I afflict with trunks, some with great fin-like limbs or hypertrophied genitalia, and then pore over this ad-hoc bestiary in the privacy of my own home, murmuring gently *Nema; malo a nos libera et, tentationem in inducas nos ne* and so forth.)

How this is representative of my poor life. Not, I mean, the incantations and bile, but the dreadful fate of being doomed to be first, of finding unpretentious utility in simple things only to see them taken up as cult objects by hideous, grinning graphic designers in flat-top haircuts and Ray-Bans (I was wearing Ray-Ban Wayfarers in 1971). Every second-rate snotty prune in Covent Garden now carries a Filofax and Doesn't Know What He'd Do Without It. I am told it has even penetrated to something called *EastEnders*. Now they want lots of money so that the Filofax people can buy BMWs and cheese plants and eat at the Groucho Club.

To hell with the lot of them. I am no longer able to use mine. I have transferred to a nicer thing called Lefax which is much more stylish, but I expect that will become a cult object in due course. My repertoire is diminishing by the moment. Bereft of my hats, my Ray-Bans, my single gold ear-rings, my Trumpers shaving cream, my Penhaligon's scent, my yellow Argyle socks, my tortoiseshell specs, my trouser turnups, my bow ties, my braces and my spotted handkerchiefs, I suspect that soon I shall lose my Top-Siders, my walking sticks, my Leica, my snuff-box, my dip-pen and my Nellie Lutcher records to the relentless trendies. Anything that's any good at all, the buggers will take over.

I suppose the only way out of this conundrum is to adopt as essential elements of personal style only those things which are unacceptable or ruinously expensive. Henceforth I shall confine myself to bespoke shoes and Spam sandwiches. I shall pick my nose in public and eschew normal romance, instead, when the urges call, making a nice goat my own, preferably in Jermyn Street. I shall cultivate boils and nostril hair, and suck Sherbet Fountains at Demis Roussos concerts. I shall throw away my Filofax and hire a White Russian princess to act as amanuensis, transcribing my utterances on vellum with a platinum pen, a Transylvanian dwarf to hold my ink-pot. My bathroom will boast no pink Andrex but sheets of chamois, with an ancient Tibetan mute to measure you up; I shall wash, not in soap but in cheese, and will dine on mushy peas and virgins' blood. Doubtless the trendies will catch on before too long, but think what appalling bloody fools they'll look, and how I'll laugh up my iguana-skin sleeve (with integral phlegm-bag).

'It's The Wild again.'

AS I WENT DOWN LABURNUM WALK

Patrick Barrington

As I went down Laburnum Walk
    That's near to Potter's Bar,
I heard a Mrs Brinsley Yorke
    A-singing to her char—

A-singing to her loud and clear
    An anxious song and high
That percolated to my ear
    As I was passing by.

'Oh, char you under every door
    And char in every crack;
And char for me the kitchen floor
    And char the two-pair back;

'Char diligently every key
    And brightly every lock,
And char the pantry sink for me
    And char the cuckoo-clock;

'But char you not the potted plant
    That came for me last Yule,
For that's a present from my aunt,
    A Lady Nettlepool.

'Oh, char you not the potted plant
    That came last Yule for me,
For that's a present from my aunt
    And must not broken be.'

The char she charred the kitchen floor,
　　She charred it hard and well,
And long she charred the furniture
　　And loud the front-door bell.

She charred in every nook and chink
　　And under every chair;
She charred for her the pantry sink,
　　She charred the frigidaire;

But when she saw the potted plant
　　So homely and refined,
All recollections of the aunt
　　Went clean out of her mind.

And when she saw it where it stood
　　And nodded like a toque,
A madness came into her blood,
　　She charred it—and it broke.

Then up rose Mrs Brinsley Y.,
　　And loudly wailéd She,
And loud she cursed the charlady
　　With curses fifty-three.

She cursed her with unnumbered woes;
　　But e'er she cursed her fill
'Twas up the charlady arose
　　And wailéd louder still.

'Such language from a lady true,'
　　She cried in grief sincere,
'Such language from the likes of you
　　I never thought to hear.

'To hear such language in my house
　　I hope I never may.
Oh, hence I'll creep me like a mouse
　　And hide myself away.

'To hear such language as you sing
    I'm not accustoméd,
For I was once a tender thing
    And delicately bred;

'A delicately-nurtured thing
    And many men's desire,
The daughter of a Cotton King
    That ruled in Lancashire.'

'Oh, if and that it's truth you talk,
    O rude and naughty char,
How comes it', answered Mrs Yorke,
    'That you are what you are?

'Oh, if that really your papa
    A Cotton King has been,
How comes it that you are a char
    And not a Cotton Queen?'

'A Cotton King my father was,'
    The char she did reply,
'And of the wherefore and because
    I'll tell you how and why.

'A Cotton King my father was
    In Lancashire so fair,
And of the wherefore and because
    I'll tell you if you care.

'Of Cotton Kings he was the best
    That ever I did spy;
But Economical Unrest
    It done 'im in the eye.

' 'Twas Economical Unrest
    That knocked 'im off 'is perch;
And now the poor old top's gone West
    And left us in the lurch.

'The slump has fairly knocked us queer.
    Well, beat it if you can.
Poor Bob, that was a hengineer,
    Is now a handy-man;

'Young Brenda's on the comic stage,
    And Jane is high and dry,
And Hilda, she's a gossip-page,
    And me a charlady.'

Then Mrs Yorke she rent her gown
    And loud lamented she;
'Oh, step you up and sit you down
    And help yourself to tea.

'More loth were I to risk a breach
    With you than with my aunt.
Forget, forget my hasty speech
    And I'll forget the plant.

'Oh, help yourself to lemon curds,
    To cakes and crumpets hot;
Forget, forget my hasty words
    And I'll forget the pot.'

So down the charlady did sit
    And helped herself to jam,
And talked with dignity and wit
    About her diaphragm.

And up rose Mrs Brinsley Yorke
    And called up all her kin,
And all about the town did walk
    To fetch the neighbours in.

And wide the casement did she fling
    That all the world might see
The daughter of a Cotton King
    To be her charlady.

GETTING TO KNOW MY MED.

Jo Packer

In Paris our hostess seemed quite normal until Jean and I mentioned that we intended to hitch-hike to the Riviera. Then she became as excitable as a manic-depressive on the up-beat. Thrusting the *Paris Soir* at us, she commanded us to 'look at the hundreds of cases'. On French highways, it appeared, male behaviour hit a new low. 'They will take you to an hotel,' she predicted, 'and put something in your drink to make you sleep. When you wake up you will be in South America.' She had not spent her youth reading Phillips Oppenheim for nothing.

'You think you are smart, but let me tell you,' she called after us as we waved goodbye, 'they know it all, these men!' Certainly the Englishman who obliged with a lift over the French Alps admitted that he knew some of it. 'Oh, yes, I know my Med.,' he said complacently, and proceeded to put us to sleep with an account of his travels. We hoped he knew his Route Soleil, too, lest our blood should stain the saxifrage as we swerved down the helter-skelter highway. Fortunately the only things we hit were our ears, glugging madly in the high altitude like bath-pipes.

L'Idéal Camp at Nice, every tent a brilliant orange, looked like a sun-worshippers' convention. We knew at once that there were no British there, for abroad we are labelled by our green tents. Jean and I lacked even these national symbols. We crept into a corner of the field and unrolled our Army and Navy Surplus sleeping-bags.

The camp was thick with palms, but the beauty of the scene was spoilt by warning notices, signed by the proprietor, nailed to each trunk. He admonished us in three languages plus a cartoon for those unable to read. 'Do Not Let Your Dog Loose and Cause an Inconvenience to the Tents', we read on the palm in our small corner.

On our third day at the camp Jean announced that she had met a German in the wash-basins and had promised to go to a fiesta with him. So I rolled up my belongings in the sleeping-bag and set off for Monaco, arranging to meet Jean there later. Nice stopped following me after an hour's walk along the coast road. The highway grew tiresome, weaving among villas and bougain-villaeas, Capes and grapes. Soon I was creeping like a vine myself, what with the heat and the luggage. At last a car slowed down. By the time it had stopped I was sitting inside.

The middle-aged Frenchman behind the wheel, dressed in what I believe are called carefully casual clothes, had a pro-nounced military bearing. He told me in good English that he lived in Nice and promptly invited me to join him for a bath nearby. I wondered what my Paris hostess would have said about this technique, but when the car stopped near the sea I realised that 'bathe' was the word he should have used, and that I had actually taken part in what would have been a good joke in an early British film.

My swimsuit was wrapped in the sleeping-bag. As I grabbed the whole bundle my companion looked momentarily agitated; obviously we were going to a very classy place. It was a small, exclusive beach where one had to pay to gain admittance and again to use the changing huts. People, lying on foam rubber under Neapolitan parasols, littered the stretch of sand. My patron had his second shock when I announced that I could not swim. 'I thought all English girls were *très sportive!*' he cried.

Cementing the entente my host insisted on driving me to a camp on Cap Ferrat, which he said was the last until I got to Monaco. I had not the heart to tell him that five o'clock in the afternoon was too soon to get bedded down, or he would have insisted on driving me on to Monaco. So with thanks in school-girl French I left him at the camp entrance, waited until he was out of sight on his way back to Nice, and then pressed on.

Beyond Beaulieu a dark, handsome youth on a motor-scooter pulled up and introduced himself as Amanry. He had a radiantly simple aura and spoke a strange glibble, so I placed him as a primitive Italian peasant, knowing we were not far from the border. We tore along the coast road, leaning over professionally at all the bends, and shouting hopefully to each other in basic French. On learning that I intended to stay at a camp he yelled into the wind: '*Voulez-vous rester à moi?*' No doubt my Paris hostess would have advised me to jump off the pillion even at that speed, but thinking I might be taken into the bosom of his family, always a favourite scene of mine on the films, I said yes.

A mountain road off the main route took us higher and higher until Monaco was hundreds of feet below. Amanry stopped where the Alp rose almost sheer from the roadside, and parked his scooter under a bush. We started to scale the mountain. There was no proper path, only a few strategic rocks and some clumps of grass to grab. I grimped up after him, thankful that my gym shoes, though non-sexy, were also non-slip. Eventually we reached a vegetable plot which, as the geography primers say, had been scratched out of the bare hillside. Beyond it was a small house.

I was looking forward to meeting Amanry's family: the philosophic grandfather who tried to lure everybody into playing a game of draughts with him, the wastrel uncle who grabbed his shotgun whenever he fell into a rage, the mother with fat forearms who did nothing but carry steaming platters of food to the table. 'Will your parents be glad to see me?' I asked. He gave me a blank look. 'What parents?' he said. 'I live here with my cousin Zozo. That's all.'

The inside of the house was in darkness, or so it appeared from the outside, for all the shutters were closed and padlocked. In the kitchen cousin Zozo sat under a yellow paraffin-lamp. Was it the light, I wondered, or was every single thing in the room really coated in black? Then the smell hit me, the kind of smell that goes with things coated in black smuts.

Eventually the first course, spaghetti boiled in a saucepan with chopped onion, found its way to the newspaper-covered table. The water was not drained off but served as gravy. Spoons and forks looked as though they had just been washed up from a shipwreck. I ate the offering hoping the next would not be so watery; it wasn't, it was oily. Chopped hard-boiled eggs with tomatoes squelching in oil. Then shredded lettuce similarly treated. I ate plenty of bread to act as an internal blotter. Grapes, black coffee and cream biscuits followed.

After such a blow-out I felt like bed. I said I would sleep in the garden, but this was not seriously considered and I was taken to the only bedroom in the house, which contained a double and a single bed. I bagged the single with such obvious haste that my hosts assured me there was no need to worry; they were going to meet a certain garçon in a bistro. Amanry went to a mouldy cupboard, took out a bottle of perfume and shook it with great abandon all over the room.

I settled down under the coverlet, wondering how the two of them would negotiate the mountain in the darkness. I listened for shrieks which would hang in the air as they fell to their doom over the precipice, but all I could hear was the faint playing of a band in Monaco. Then the invasion of The Things began.

They came from beneath the bedclothes, quickly reached skin level in spite of the fact that I was wearing all my clothes, and crawled all over me. They tickled and itched and irritated. I leapt up, scratched wildly for ten seconds, sprang into my sleeping-bag and lay down again. All was quiet for a few minutes, then, after sizing up the situation, they attacked again, making a joke of the thick sleeping-bag and a maniac of me. I was about to rush demented into the garden when Zozo returned.

I lay perfectly still. After wandering about the room a bit he crawled on to my bed and started whispering things in Italian in an effort to wake me up. Under my eyelashes I could see his *retroussé* nose quite close; it was like looking into the muzzle of a double-barrelled shotgun. I gave an excellent imitation of one in profound sleep and he grew discouraged. Eventually he went to his own bed and slept. Amanry did not come back that night.

I lay awake all night, and when dawn came rose stealthily and sneaked out of the room. I descended the concrete stairs with elaborate silence lest Zozo should hear me, follow, and try to persuade me to see the light. The only light I wanted to see was that outside the back door.

But having parted from Zozo I fell foul of another of his breed in Monaco, a pedestrian who followed me around and got close enough on two occasions to pinch me in the place where they pinch pretty girls in Paris. I had no idea until then that the custom had spread so far south. The second time his pincers nipped me I swung my fist into his chest. It actually landed there and he actually went away.

Jean and I made our separate ways back to Paris. She did it in four lifts, but I took more than twenty. I noticed very soon that my drivers began to fidget uncomfortably after a few miles. Then they would stop and say that was as far as they were going. I got out with relief, for it's not very ladylike to scratch oneself in a strange car. And it proved to me quite clearly that bugs are the answer to the white slave traffic. Phillips Oppenheim never thought of that.

'It'll be the first time these boring Dashtons have been known to pass up an invitation.'

CALL OF THE RUNNING TIDE

Alexander Frater

The SS *Martha G. Duckworth*, 5,000 tons deadweight and bound from Tahiti to Port Brisbane, rolled sluggishly in the Pacific swell. We passengers sat in the lounge, portholes closed tightly against the reek of pork and old biscuits, and celebrated Christmas. The bulkheads were hung with army surplus holly wreaths and two grey sausage balloons stood rampant above the door. The Fijian claret was bitter on the tongue. Mrs Emily Pinkfoot, drunk, kept dropping her bottle which forced Mr Parshottam, the Indian gentleman, to get up continually and replace it on the table. Mr Parshottam was a Christian. After a while he started crying and recalling his baptism in the Hooghly at the hands of a motherly old Scots missionary whose name he had forgotten. We told him to shut up and get on with his toping; time was running out. 'Jingle bells,' said Mr Blaumstein ironically as he tore a cork out with his teeth. 'They jingle for *thee*, friends,' and we all felt heavy and oppressed at the ghastly injustice of it all.

The door opened and the captain walked in. 'It is now eleven o'clock in the morning,' he informed us. 'Christmas Day will end in precisely seven minutes.' His eyes were bloodshot and infinitely sad. 'Kindly return your false noses and party hats to the steward. Once again, I am sorry for this, but aboard this ship we stringently observe the International Date Line. I shall sound the siren when we cross it and the bar will be closed forthwith. On behalf of the owners,' he said, 'may I wish you all a happy Boxing Day.' He stepped out on to the deck while we sat silent, fighting the gushers of resentment welling up inside. Mrs Pinkfoot woke up and blew her squeaker, but no one praised her. We hated the sea and this rotten ship and, as the siren moaned and the steward plucked the wreaths from the walls and locked the bar cupboard, we hissed and filed out on to the heaving deck.

Mr Blaumstein joined me at the rail and we stared at the water. 'Where is this lousy Date Line?' he said.

'I don't know,' I said. 'A few hundred yards back, I suppose.'

He nodded. 'Know something?' he said. 'Somebody ought to work on it. Some promoter, or somebody like that. They ought to tart the damn thing up a bit.'

'I don't understand.' A mile away a sperm whale burped and a jet of spume rose high into the sky.

'Like they did to the Equator,' he said. 'The Date Line needs a bit of oomph see? A bit of zip. It needs the sort of image the public will go for. Why can't they have King Neptune come aboard at the Date Line? Or Admiral Tirpitz? Or Drake's Drum? They could have a short ceremony and hand out illuminated manuscripts.'

In the stern a man shouted and Mr Blaumstein, lighting a fag, laughed.

'What did he say?' I asked.

'Who?'

'That man in the stern.'

'He said Dog Overboard,' said Mr Blaumstein. 'Why?'

'Which dog?' cried the captain from the bridge, waving at the man in the stern. 'Now hear this: which dog?'

'Your dog, sah,' he shouted. 'I left him to go below and when I come up just now he was gone. No trace of him except for one or two old hambones.'

The captain sobbed and leapt for the engine-room telegraph; it jangled, the wheel spun and the ship, heeling like a rubber duck, turned at speed. The decks trembled and the blunt bows butted goat-like through the rollers as we retraced our course.

'I didn't know the skipper had a dog,' I said.

'An old peke,' said Mr Blaumstein. 'It was always snapping at albatrosses. I guess that was its undoing. I guess it gave one final mighty snap and fell into the sea. A noble way to go,' he observed, with a rare showing of sentiment.

We turned as Mrs Pinkfoot came staggering up the deck. 'Hey, my beauties,' she said. 'I've just realised something.'

'Yes?' we murmured.

'Well,' she said, absently hiking up her skirt and tightening the bow on her suspenders, 'if this ship continues on its present course for a few more minutes, we shall be crossing back into Christmas Day.'

'Blow me,' chuckled Mr Blaumstein. 'I never thought of that. It takes a woman, eh?'

'It certainly does,' I muttered, sprinting for the bridge. But Mr Parshottam, the Christian, had beaten us to it. He stood by the gimbals in his dhoti, crying 'If you are taking us back to Christmas, you must give us back our booze.'

'Damn right,' said Mrs Pinkfoot.

'That is reasonable,' said the harassed captain. We stood happy, winking at each other and relishing the wind in our faces; water suddenly seemed a friendly, reasonable element. Mr Parshottam said: 'I have some crackers and whistles in my cabin. Shall I fetch them?'

'At the double, Ghengis Khan,' said Mr Blaumstein and we all laughed. But it petered out as the masthead lookout called and the captain turned the ship yet again; we were now moving at right angles to our previous course. We stared at the captain. 'Where are you taking us?' we asked.

'Up the Date Line,' he said. 'The crow's nest has reported something in the sea a couple of miles ahead.'

'*Up* the Date Line?' we said.

He nodded absently as he focused his binoculars and raked the waters. 'I've had him since he was a pup,' he said. 'Since he was a little blind ball of fur.'

'What do you mean, *up* the Date Line?' barked Mrs Pinkfoot.

'It now runs', said the captain, 'straight through the middle of the ship. From stem to stern. That's what I mean.'

'Well, where the hell's Christmas?' we snapped.

'On the starboard side,' he said. 'But I regret', he added, as we spun and descended the stairs five at a time, 'that the bar is in Boxing Day.'

He had us by the short hairs, the fink, and not for an instant would he deviate a fraction of a degree to let us back to those bottles. Mind you, we tried. Mrs Pinkfoot did a sensual hoochi coochi strip for the benefit of the Tonkinese helmsman but he, not liking white women, only yawned. Mr Blaumstein was all for using force but Mr Parshottam spoke of the dreadful consequences of piracy and we headed moodily back to our cabins and tuned in on the Queen's broadcast. The reception was bad and we spent the rest of the day sucking peppermints and planning a New Year's orgy on the mainland.

They found the dog all right, a few minutes later, swimming strongly for Valparaiso.

WHEN A YOUNG MAN'S FANCY . . .

Diana Childe

My son fell in love again last month. This happens two or three times a year. He usually says This Time it is Different. He has gone a step further and says This Time it is the Real Thing.

We like him being in love. It means we hardly see him. He is quiet at breakfast, goes off to his studies all day, returns for a quick tea, bath and change, and is off to meet Her forthwith. We seldom see him again before we retire. It also means he baths and shaves every day without being asked, cajoled, shouted at, implored, or as a last resort, ordered to do these small things.

We do not have to listen to his musical choice for evenings on end. This is either r. 'n' r. (lessening in its popularity, thank goodness, as his twenties approach) or solid harpsichord long play, which sounds a little tinny to our ears during the third hour.

Housekeeping accounts show a good credit for once. We can afford to entertain more during these periods. When the current love is brought home she never eats a hearty meal. She toys with morsels, the while she gazes at my male offspring, obviously longing to get away from the rest of us.

I remember my first words on seeing him nearly twenty years ago. I said, 'He's just like a pug.' The rugged, pug-faced lad appears to be more handsome than we thought. Indeed, my daughter, after careful study to discover what They see in her brother, has reported that by candlelight he is quite glam.

Alas! The path of love, true or otherwise, never runs smooth.

The first, or Introductory-Probation Phase, is the best for all concerned. It is then we have the eagerness to please, the urge for outer cleanliness, the pressing (by himself) of suitings, Bedfords, jackets, ties, scarves. The charm is practised on us at home, to ensure perfection in action. No more the surly grunts, the voracious animal rushing through dinner with revolting noise, tearing off when the last mouthful is downed, unless it is a dreaded evening in, with music. The precious motor-bike can rust. Only urgent repairs are carried out, so that oily rags, filthy tools, tyres, what-have-yous are not brought into his room for overhaul.

This phase is too short for us, even if it is prolonged for eight weeks.

Phase Two is soon with us. This lasts the longest. It is the seeing every day, staying up late, talking or dancing or dining every night time. Too tired every morning, sleepy, grumpy, late up, late for breakfast, late leaving home. He has to be called half a dozen times at least before he even hears.

This might be termed the Panic Phase, for the rest of the family. We all begin to think it might be serious. We worry. But presently the first ominous sign appears. There is a request one Thursday 'Could you lend me five bob, please?' The next week it is a request for £1 on the Tuesday. He is getting broke. The testing time has come.

No sensible, normal young man in his late teens likes to be penniless. The battle, Woman versus Solvency, is on. Phase Three is here. The Painless Disposal.

There are long and earnest talks with each of us. He examines the situation from every angle. It is foolish in the extreme to marry young, while one is still studying. He announces what we all knew. He has been seeing too much of her. He is not 'at home' when she phones. We refuse to lie to the poor, unhappy nearly ex-love, so he dashes out of the front door like a frightened stag when he hears the telephone. As we receive a lot of calls during an average evening, he may do this five or six times before the expected call arrives. My husband, who has often waited fifteen minutes or longer for the heir to our overdrafts when they are going out together, is always amazed at his speed.

Doubt, certainty, contrition and other emotions hold sway for a few days each. At last Phase Three is over. My son breathes a great sigh of relief, rings up all his male friends and goes out on parties unencumbered by women. He says what we all know 'It's wonderful to be free.'

But is it?

DOWN AND OUT IN PARIS, ILLINOIS

Stanley Reynolds

Travelling across America, by car or bus or train, is one of the genuine pleasures left in the world. It is, indeed, the thing all Americans do themselves or at least dream of doing, but when they decide to head West or go back East or up North or down South they do not get the really fine treatment that a foreigner gets. The reason for this is simple. The South still hates the Yankees because of the Civil War, which the Southerners refuse even to call the Civil War, calling it the War Between the States instead. And Westerners think the United States ends at the Hudson River and Easterners, such as myself, think they are all hicks out there west of the Hudson. New Yorkers, who don't really go anywhere ever, are the worst offenders. They think anything north of New York is Bridgeport. Bridgeport, Connecticut, is the Watford Gap of America.

Untainted by any of this regional squabbling, the foreign tourist is very welcome and the British traveller most of all because he speaks English real good, for a foreigner. The new low-cost flights have brought a bumper crop of British tourists to America and I reckon they will go on receiving the A treatment until that unhappy day when Scotland or West Ham play in California and their massed supporters march down Route 66.

I have some little experience of the way a visiting foreigner is grasped to the American bosom for I once drove West in a Volkswagen with Rhode Island number plates. Now, Rhode Island is the smallest state in the Union and is often overlooked when people sit around bars and try to name all the 50 states for a bet—when the bars are opened all day, time sometimes hangs heavy. Still, Rhode Island is a part of the United States, in fact it is the first state because it declared itself free of the British Yoke on May 4, 1776, two months before the rest, but I didn't seem able to convince the Western hayseeds of this. VWs were also a rare sight then and that might have helped their ignorance along.

'You speak real good,' one of them said to me after he noticed the Rhode Island plates. 'Let me buy you a drink.'

I let him buy me several. And I got myself into one of those embarrassing situations where I couldn't suddenly tell him he was very ignorant and that I was clearly not some kind of a Greek but one of his own. He would have thought I was a city slicker from back East working a con on him. It might prove dangerous. But it was wondrous listening to him and seeing how proud he was of the twelve miles of paved road in his home town and how natural he thought it was for me to come out all the way from Greece to see the marvel of it for myself. His father was named Homer and he had an older brother named Homer too and everybody knew Homer had been some kind of a famous goddamn old-time Greek and, well, put it there and have another.

Well, maybe that is cliché America. But there is a hidden America out there that is vanishing a little bit more each year and is well worth seeing before it is lost forever. Of course most British TV viewers think they know all about America because they've seen *Dallas* and *Charlie's Angels* but it isn't like that at all. Certainly there is skyscraper America and there are beaches full of silver sand and beaches with golden sand and suburbs with tree-shaded streets so cosy you'd think you were in an old Fred McMurray movie. And all very nice it is, and yet there is this other and swiftly vanishing America out there as well, but the travel writers never seem to tell us about it.

It is Jack Kerouac America, Carl Sandburg America, Sinclair Lewis America, Jack London America, Walt Whitman America and, I suppose, to carry out the literary lineage, Sam Clemens America too. It is the America of the open road, of the hitch-hiker and the hopper of freight trains. I had quite thought they were lost for ever until a year ago when I found myself in Iowa. It was some woebegone town, plain as coffee grounds, a city of hardware stores and lunch-counters with steamy plate-glass windows, men in lumberjack shirts standing talking on street corners, talking in big, deep but quiet voices, voices redolent of pioneer days before someone decided everybody in America should talk through their noses. There was, as in all these towns, the old-fashioned hotel and I knew just what it would be like in that hotel's lobby; full of ghosts it would be, the shades of old-time travelling salesmen, drummers, swapping lies under the ornate chandeliers. No doubt the hotel would have the old brass spittoons stored away somewhere.

The brochures will tell you all about all the *nice* places you can get to very cheaply nowadays, but they don't do travel posters and guided tours of the tacky lunch-counters or the now (practically) defunct hobo jungles down by the railroad tracks with the broken bottles in the long grass.

Well, who'd want to do the Woody Guthrie Hobo Tour or the Jack Kerouac Wino Back-Alley Package Holiday, anyway? I would. And all my friends. Because this is the myth-making part of America. And, too, there is time enough to sit in the grand hotel when you are old and grey and grateful for the five-star service. To go to New York and not see Harlem, to go to Philadelphia and not spend a night in one of those seedy dim-lighted, heavy with menace bars full of hookers and pimps in the City of Brotherly Love, to ignore downtown St Louis, pool-room Denver, Burke's Hotel in Marquette, Iowa, St Mary's Street in San Antonio, Baltimore Street in Baltimore, Blackburn Avenue in Portland, Oregon, or a sailor's Saturday night out in San Diego . . . why it's like going to Brazil and never seeing the jungle!

This is not Ma and Pa America and it's not Mum and Dad's notion of a trip to America. But I love those comfortable old hotels, like the Palmer House in Chicago, on Wabash Avenue and State Street, now the forgotten part of modern Chicago, but the hotel where the robber barons sat up all night chewing on big black cigars and chewing up the map of the United States, parcelling out the country to one another just like they owned it, which, of course, they did. And up the street, at the corner of State and Lake, with Lake Michigan howling up the street, where the wind gets so bad in the wintertime that they have sometimes to stretch a length of rope across the street so you can hang on and not get blown away, there is a marvellous, brown-stained, old-fashioned greasy spoon and bar and grill, with a good-looking waitress, chewing gum and looking as I-Seen-It-All-But-I-Ain't-Broken-Not-Yet-At-Least as Ann Sheridan, taking your order saying, 'Listen, fella, where'd you pick up that accent?'

'London, England.'

'Listen,' says a John Garfield sort of fellow standing at the bar, 'I was stationed right outside of London, England, during the war. Sure I was,' he says, 'Wigan, right outside Liverpool, right outside London, England. Listen,' he says, 'what'll you have?'

That was last year. Maybe I should book right away, right now, before I get any older and have to stay at the Hilton.

*'Must be expecting trouble tonight, they've got the old
balsa-wood furniture out again . . .'*

THERE'S AN EAR IN MY MARTINI . . .

. . . and it belongs to relief barman ANDREW BARROW

BOBBY, THE HEAD BARMAN. You've put far too much gin in that Manhattan. Where's my profit margin going to go with you working for me?

CHAUFFEUR [*in staff canteen*]. I'm driving Lord Summerhill to Exeter but my car's playing up.

MAN [*talking to girl in restaurant*]. I'm well aware of the problems of life, my sweet, and I've thought about them a great deal.

BOBBY. Go down to the stores with this chit and get me a tin of black boot polish and a bottle of fruity sauce.

MAN [*at bar*]. I'm afraid I'd like another large dry martini.

BOBBY [*to junior barman*]. Haven't you brought a change of shirt along? Because that one's filthy.

BANQUETING MANAGER [*reminiscing*]. One o'clock in the morning. What a time to run out of lettuce.

WOMAN GUEST [*talking to doorman*]. Lovely day, William. I feel quite different somehow.

BOBBY. Every time I go and buy a packet of those miniature cigars I think 'That's another bloody fifty pence down the drain'.

DOORMAN [*replying to woman guest*]. We all do, madam.

MAN [*trying to get waiter's attention in restaurant*]. It's no good clapping your hands here. They only think you're applauding the food.

BOBBY. I think we may get through a lot of Dubonnet tonight—so put a dozen extra on the trolley. If there's any left over we can always use it for Major Hursley's party tomorrow night.

WOMAN [*talking to man in bar*]. You're an awful snob, you know, George. I never realised before what an awful snob you are.

CHAUFFEUR [*discussing Ascot*]. Parking is the bastard thing.

BOBBY. This ice is much too big. I wanted it marble-size. Who chopped it?

HALL PORTER [*watching party arrive for dinner at 10.45 p.m.*]. Swaying slightly.

BOBBY. That bloody woman has come in every day this week. She's got millions. To do with the autos.

CHAUFFEUR. I've got some crumpet waiting for me. I've got to get back.

MAN [*in restaurant as orchestra strikes up*]. I love this tune. It's five years old. Makes me think of a really hot day in June 1966.

HEAD WAITER [*to trainee waiter*]. Go and get a carving knife for the turkey on table twenty-four.

BOBBY. Alfred got very pissed last night. We had to put him under the shower.

HALL PORTER [*to guest*]. If I may say so, your ladyship is looking not a day older than when you first stayed here forty years ago.

BOBBY [*to junior barman*]. You came in at half past two yesterday. Then you come in today and say it's your day off. That's ridiculous. You only get days off when you've been working.

WOMAN [*in restaurant in a loud voice*]. You can always tell a man's sexual habits by the way he eats.

BOBBY [*seeing a copy of* Modern Man in Search of a Soul *sticking out of my pocket*]. I expect you'll be going down to the kitchen in a moment—looking for a sole!

BANQUETING MANAGER [*on telephone*]. Everything to be in pink. Beginning with pink lobster bisque and finishing with pink Chartreuse. Much to be prepared, I fear.

BOBBY [*pouring out a glass of whisky for a friend*]. Large, or very large?

ONE OF THE MANAGERS [*talking to a kitchen porter*]. Now, Mullah, you know you leave us tomorrow.

BOBBY. You know you can always get a drink at the Coach and Horses all afternoon, providing you're on spirits—because that's when they make their real money.

BUSINESSMAN [*when a Brussels sprout hops off his plate in restaurant*]. Look at that! See how it goes.

BOBBY [*continuing about the Coach and Horses*]. You just knock on

249

the door. Annie goes to the window. If it's the police, she doesn't let them in. If it's you or me or Alf, she lets us in.

FOOTMAN [*explaining cakes to small child*]. What's that? That's apple.

DOORMAN [*politely refusing to admit couple in hippy clothes*]. Monsieur, madame, I'm afraid . . .

HEAD WAITER [*to trainee waiter*]. Cotta, you haven't done cheese service before, have you? Maxwell, will you show Cotta how we do cheese service for one person?

WOMAN GUEST [*as she gets into taxi*]. I think you did the right thing, William.

BOBBY [*to customer who has been talking about the good old days*]. I remember it vividly, sir.

HOSTESS [*as famous multi-millionaire arrives at small private reception*]. Here comes John. A little late as usual.

BOBBY. Keep six pale ales for me. In the far fridge.

MULTI-MILLIONAIRE [*when dinner is announced*]. What happens now? Do I take somebody's arm?

BOBBY [*organising duties for the next week*]. Alfred will be on nights, midnight to dawn.

CHAUFFEUR. Believe me, it takes at least five hours to polish a Rolls properly.

BOBBY [*to junior barman*]. You're absolutely useless.

MAN [*in bar*]. I'd far sooner shoot ten cock pheasants coming over my head than footle around in a hotel in London.

BOBBY [*reminiscing*]. I remember after the Rose Ball last year Alf went into one of the banqueting kitchens and found a couple in there with no clothes on.

CHAUFFEUR [*killing time*]. He'll be out of the restaurant by half three, I hope.

BOBBY. You don't say go and get the soda waters. You say 'Go and get the bloody soda waters.' If you don't say bloody, they won't get them.

MAN [*in the restaurant*]. England is completely flaked out.

BANQUETING MANAGER [*on telephone*]. *Oeufs pochés benedictines*, if possible made with Flanders spinach.

SENIOR WAITER [*after having his £60 pay packet stolen*]. We live and learn.

MAN [*in bar*]. God, I hate the middle classes.

BOBBY. We may be finishing very late tonight—so you'll all get taxi money.

DRUNK MAN [*climbing into driver's seat of Bentley*]. This should be all right providing everybody keeps out of the way.

BOBBY [*finding that my repertoire of cocktails is limited*]. I reckon any barman who doesn't know how to make a Gimlet can't class himself a proper West End barman.

'And . . . you get first choice of a berth in the new yacht marina when the place is flooded.'

A MIDSUMMER DAY'S DREAM

Sue Arnold

Flaming June already and not a holiday brochure in the house. The knife falls from my hands. I forget the *poussin citronné aux fines herbes* I have been preparing for the children's lunch-boxes and I dream. I see a cobbled piazza bordered on three sides by a crumbling, sun-dappled palazzo and on the fourth by a blue, blue lake. I am sitting at a table on the terrace of the Hotel Gorgonzola sipping chilled Frascati. I am wearing white, all white and a wide-brimmed picture hat. Anita Brookner's latest emaciated volume lies open on the table in front of me unheeded, for I am gazing out at the picturesque harbour, with its flotilla of gaily coloured fishing boats bobbing up and down in the water like children's bath toys, where Giuseppe, faithful old Giuseppe, is teaching my small son to mend fishing-nets. On the steps of the quaint medieval church of San Altobelli, with its famous frescos depicting the childhood of Sophia Loren, my daughters laugh together with the local children as they play that popular old peasant game Pass the Pastasciuta and yes, here comes Angela, white Norland cuffs still crisp despite the heat, wheeling baby James into the courtyard ready for lunch.

What shall we do this afternoon? Maybe I shall ask Giulio, marvellous old Giulio, the local ferryman and brother of faithful old Giuseppe, to row me across to the island so that I can take tea with the contessa again. Although we met only three days ago at the launderette, Contessa Olivetti di Scalopini and I have become firm friends. Her family are descended from the Medici. They have an abbey in Amalfi, a penthouse off the Villa Borghese and a shoe factory in Turin, but we have a lot in common. 'Ah Suzannah, cara, tell me about life in England,' she says, snipping her thread with silver tapestry scissors that once belonged to a mistress of Lorenzo the Magnificent, 'How I loved my time in England when I was a student at the Loughborough College.'

So I tell her. I describe the extraordinary difference the M25 has made to peripheral traffic going east and the large selection of fresh fish to be found at the new Sainsbury's in Cromwell Road. The shadows lengthen. I can hear my children frolicking harmoniously with the little Scalopini, Bertorelli, Botticelli and Baby Buffo (no doubt they are playing that favourite Italian nursery game Hunt the Osso Bucco) and before we know it, it is time to row back to the mainland for dinner.

I stop dreaming, chuck the *poussin* devoid of *citron* and *fines herbes* into the lunch-boxes with packets of crisps and hurry to Hogg Robinson travel agent to stock up with bedside reading. 'Sorry, we've run out of Blue Sky,' says the girl behind the desk, 'and I'm pretty sure the last Horizon went this morning. Hang on, I think we've still got some Cosmos. Joyce, have you seen the Cosmos anywhere?' Joyce is persuading a senior citizen, with two Tesco carriers and a red beret, that the Tropical Garden Hotel in Torremolinos would suit her down to the ground. 'The brochures tend to be confusing,' Joyce is saying. 'I know it says only ten minutes' climb from the beach but I happen to know it's a very gentle slope.' 'But what's this about being near a bus-stop that provides regular services into the town?' asks the senior citizen, still holding the Tesco carriers, 'Does that mean we are a long way out?'

'Not really,' says Joyce. She lowers her voice. 'Between you and me, downtown Torremolinos can get a bit noisy what with all that flamenco and bullfighting and such. You're much better off away from it all.'

'What sort of holiday did you have in mind?' says the girl behind the desk. 'Somewhere in Italy,' I say, mindful of faithful old Giuseppe and his nets, 'a small family hotel in a square by a lake perhaps.' Five minutes and fifteen brochures later we have established, Sandra and I, that hotels in piazzas with or without cobbles anywhere within 100 kilometres of any Italian lake are well beyond our means. The same applies to *gîtes* in the Dordogne, villas in the Algarve, self-catering apartments in Majorca.

Even *demi pension* in a picturesque chalet on the high pastures of the Tyrol, which roughly translated means bed, breakfast and Sauerkraut in a field with cowbells, is beyond our means. 'How about one of the big new resort centres in Holland?' wonders Sandra, producing a brochure with what looks like an aerial view of military manoeuvres on Salisbury Plain on the cover. 'The self-catering bungalows are extremely reasonable.' 'No,' I say, 'not Holland.' A friend of mine took his family to one of the new Dutch all-purpose holiday resorts last year. 'How was it?' I asked when he got back looking shell-shocked. 'It was like a concentration camp with ponies,' he said.

Sandra has abandoned the racks full of glossy coloured brochures the size of telephone directories and is now examining a sheaf of flimsy leaflets, many in black and white. 'Have you ever considered camping in Wales?' she says. 'There are some really lovely spots in Pembrokeshire.' The picture on the cover of the leaflet she is reading shows a man with a ginger beard, a red T-shirt, green shorts, yellow socks and sandals frying sausages over a Primus stove. Beside him a woman in an anorak is pegging more yellow socks on to a washing-line strung between two trees. The hood of her anorak is up. Three children in gumboots appear to be torturing a lamb behind a tent. The most unnerving aspect of the whole scene is that everyone is smiling except the lamb. Why is everyone so happy? What's so funny about hanging out socks in an anorak with the hood up? Do sausages taste that much better when cooked by a man with a ginger beard and sandals? All these questions will no doubt be answered by Dai Davis, faithful old Dai Davis the shepherd, as he shows the children how to play that popular Welsh valleys' game, Pin the Tail on the Newborn Lamb. 'Give me all your brochures on camping holidays in Wales,' I tell Sandra.

I shall buy an anorak on my way home.

SEASON'S GRATINGS

Quentin Crisp

'Hateful is the dark blue sky, vaulted o'er the dark blue sea.' Thus moaned Mr Tennyson's lotus-eaters. They were the first tax evaders and what a miserable bunch they were!

Their cry has occasionally been taken up by their descendants, those British expatriates who sit all the year round by swimming pools in the West Indies and yawn and yearn for a November fog. I cannot seriously believe that these sybarites long to bring upon themselves the miseries of bronchitis. It seems more likely that what is found unbearable in places where the weather is never remarkable is the silence that falls from the lips of salesmen as they parcel up the various purchases.

I have no idea whether the noun 'season' is related to the verb of the same name but it is certainly true that for most English people the arrival and departure of the four quarters of the year adds the only spice to their lives that they are ever likely to receive. We who have decided not to leave this blessed plot but instead to brazen out the lies we have written on our income tax returns, tend, if we think of ourselves as intellectuals, to inveigh in secret against the more unwelcome changes in our climate and to disparage those who talk about them in public.

We do wrong.

Remarks about the unexpected warmth or coldness of the day are intended as the first tentative steps in a Platonic courtship. They are less open to misunderstanding than a feeble smile and less likely to be regarded as a sinister—even consumptive—manifestation than a clearing of the throat. To great talkers mention of the weather fulfils the function of a loud rap with a baton on the top of the music stand.

In any case the man who complains of the subject matter of a conversation is a lost soul. The purpose of speech should never be to impart information. Anyone who thinks it is, is merely liable to tell us what we already know, which is tedious, or what we do not, which is humiliating. The enjoyment to be derived from all verbal exchanges lies in the ideas that are introduced to illustrate it and the ingenuity with which these notions are expressed. As a fuse for pyrotechnical display the weather is the ideal topic. Just as great actresses such as Miss Garbo were at their best in trashy movies about hopeless love, so the more general the theme under discussion, the wider the range of opportunities for wit. The first man to describe a rainy afternoon as nice weather for ducks probably won the Nobel Prize for that year.

The season which occupies our thoughts most obsessively and on which we lavish the greatest number of words is spring. This is partly because it is the receptacle of our most fervent hopes but also in some measure because it is the time when the weather is at its most wayward. Every year, though the meteorological wizards of television never offer an explanation, at the end of February we are treated to a false spring. Dreams of a better life are wafted into our skulls on the mild breezes; even the flowering trees are taken in; they blossom. At the end of March we are plunged back into darkest winter; the blossoms die and our residual pessimism returns.

April is the cruellest month, breeding quarterly bills out of the dead land, mixing influenza with desire.

I personally take very little notice of the seasons. To maintain this aloofness is probably easier for me than for many people. I consider the sea to be one of nature's biggest mistakes; I never wish to sit on the prom eating a box of chocs during the hols. I also never have the slightest desire to travel inland. As far as I am concerned the countryside is one vast wasp's nest overhanging a ubiquitous antheap. I am allergic to almost everything and, as a city dweller, eagerly look forward to the day when England will be a slab of concrete from the Channel to the Cheviots. I do not think I have long to wait.

During the various seasonal festivities, such as Christmas, I try to go on as though nothing unpleasant had happened. Those of us who are usually happy have no need of jollification. My indifference to sudden changes in climatic conditions is not entirely due to my stoical nature; it is also an expression of my meanness. Women welcome the revolution of the year. Each season is a pretext for buying something new to wear. They rush from fur to wool to cotton with squeaks of delight. I resist this temptation partly in deference to my theories of the persistent public image but also because of the severe limitations of my wardrobe. On 1 April I exchange my overcoat for a mackintosh. This I shed on 1 July and resume in October. When my raincoat wears out I shall simply delete from my vocabulary the words 'spring' and 'autumn'. This will be cheaper than buying a new garment. What I shall do when finally my overcoat falls from my shoulders in rags, I have not yet made up my mind.

In spite of my reluctance to give way to the seasons of the year, I am aware of the uses to which capricious changes in the weather can be put. If there were none, not only would all conversation between strangers lapse into embarrassed silence but half the poetry in the English language would soon become as unintelligible as Chaucer. In particular we would become dead to the delight of the following . . .

> *Ha'g the Spri'g, hateful thi'g,*
> *bost idclebent tibe.*
> *All through you, I've got flu.*
> *Fide adother scribe.*

If I could remember the author of this gem (which appeared some fifty years ago in a paper entitled *London Calling*), I would gladly name her.

Of course I do not wish to imply that all meteorological poems are worthy of remembrance. A line I would love to delete from our anthologies is, 'If winter comes, can spring be far behind?'

The question is fatuous and the answer is 'Yes.'

DESKTOP PUBLISH AND BE DAMNED!

Keith Waterhouse

Plans are now highly advanced for writing this article by a revolutionary 'single-stroke' method using the latest in new technology and cutting out the cumbersome old three-stage process of pencil-stub draft, rough typescript and clean copy typed up by Tracy or Sharon from the temps agency.

When 'Exercise Desktop', as the new 'daisy-wheel' operation has been code-named, is 100 per cent functional, this article should be more saleable, funnier, easier to read, translatable into ten languages at the touch of a 'memory key' and free of the superfluous apostrophes which Tracy scatters over any typescript like raisins in a pudding mix.

A dictionary program 'input module' aims to eliminate Sharon's spelling mistakes entirely, although it does not itself seem to be any too certain how to spell 'programme'; while a 'storage system' or it may be a 'retrieval system' ensures that the article contains no used jokes. Being cheaper and quicker to produce than the old labour-intensive model, the article can be twice or even ten times the usual length without inducing writer's cramp, a flexibility feature not available with the conventional pencil. Should there be no space to publish the article this week, it may be stored, or lost in the system, or rerouted to *Horse & Hound*, or even converted into a cartoon.

However, owing to teething troubles, it has not yet proved possible to produce the whole of this article by the new high-tech process. Readers may experience most of it being typed on an old Adler, with occasional blank spaces where the switchover to the new word processor has not gone smoothly. These hiccups are being ironed out as quickly as possible, and as soon as the writer has acquired one of those adaptor affairs enabling the word processor and his desk lamp to be plugged into the only available socket, the way will be cleared for writing entire articles in green letters on a kind of television screen, then, simply by consulting a textbook, transmitting the finished product direct to somewhere else. The writer is not yet entirely clear where exactly — he was given to understand that his text could be fed straight into the page you are reading now, but does that mean bypassing the Editor? If so, presumably the computer knows how to set the type round the cartoon, if there is one, though it does not seem to have the nous not to split up words so that the t- of the appears at the end of one line and the -he at the beginning of the next; but what the writer wants to know is supposing the article is a few words too long for the page, will the article just carry on into the margin, or will the last paragraph be lopped off or rerouted to one of the back pages, or what?

'Exercise Desktop', or 'Exercise Tabletop' as it should be more accurately called at the moment, since this article is being composed in the dining-room where there are plugs available both for a reading lamp and the word processor, has been effected in three stages.

Initially, the old-fashioned mode of correcting the article by xxxxing out mistakes was phased out, and Tipp-Ex phased in, preparing the way for a smooth changeover to correction tape as soon as the writer acquired an electronic typewriter. Stage two was obviating carbon-paper and getting photocopies run off at the local chemist's — a dry run for when 'Exercise Desktop' is fully opera-tional and as many copies of an article as the

writer requires may be produced at the touch of a
button, or key rather, though what he is supposed
to do with them he doesn't quite know. File them,
he supposes.

Stage three was supposed to be the acquisition of
the electronic typewriter, but serious technical
difficulties were encountered when an experimental
attempt to write a portion of this article by this
method was made on a demonstration model in Ryman's.
Though it had the conventional QWERTY arrangement
of keys, the keyboard felt funny to the writer,
somewhat like one of those pressed-out plastic
trays you get in a box of chocolates, and he was
unable to type more than two words without making
a mistake. This disappointing result highlighted
one of the perils of the new technology — namely,
producing an article full of spelling mistakes
which the reader would assume were inserted for
cheap laughs, like some mock school essay ostensibly written by Smith Mi of the Lower Third. It
was decided, therefore, to leapfrog the interim
electronic typewriter stage and opt for a crash
course on operating a word processor, which would
clear the decks for a total desktop publishing
operation involving being able to understand
expressions like 'word-processed text', 'computer-
generated images' and 'on-screen representation',
as well as why all these bloody machines seem to be
named after fruit.

With the acquisition of the word processor, however, and over and above the difficulty in plugging
the thing in, it was discovered that owing to his
still not having got the hang of the keyboard, the
writer was still making mistakes and there was a
real danger that this article would go into production with the reader imagining that 'word
processor' transcribed as 'rowd precurser' was
supposed to be a joke. It was therefore decided
that in the initial stages of the switchover to
high tech, the word processor would be manned by

Sharon. This article is still waiting for her to arrive. She should have been here half an hour ago.

The writer apologises for any blank space that may appear in this article at this juncture, due to the changeover from the old Adler up in the study to the word processor down here in the dining-room. Sharon has now turned up, having had to wait forty minutes for a No. 27 whereupon three came at once, and is now taking down this article from dictation. An 'in-Sharon mode' has thus been achieved, whereby an 'on-screen representation' is made simply by the writer pacing up and down and feeding Sharon the material he would like positioning 'in-article'.

It is possible that in reading the first section of this article to be composed entirely by new technology, some readers may not be experiencing the sensation that it is getting any funnier. This is due to technical difficulties, i.e., the writer's acute awareness that the merest stroke of a key with one manicured finger could produce one of two terribly obvious jokes—either wiping out this article completely as these machines are said to be apt to do if you don't know how to use them properly, though what the Editor would have to say when confronted with a blank page and told it is the first total new technology joke is anybody's guess; or showing off the machine's versatility by juggling paragraphs around in whimsical juxtaposition—or, even worse, inserting a recipe for carrot cake copied by Sharon on to a 'floppy disc' or something. Or both. Or, and this has only just occurred to the writer, there could be the one where Sharon automatically converts into 'article input' everything that is said to her regardless of whether it was supposed to be 'in-article' material or not, for instance can't you type any faster, darling, I could have written the whole bloody article in the time it's taken you to peck out two paragraphs, I thought you people were supposed to be trained?

Readers in some areas may experience difficulty in reading the rest of this article due to its being written in ballpoint. The writer apologises for any inconvenience caused. This purely temporary setback has been caused by a massive simultaneous breakdown of all the factors involved in the new technology, starting with Sharon

262

who took the above references to herself at face value and flounced off, the stupid little bitch. Secondly, in attempting to take over the manning of the word processor himself, the writer experienced difficulty in 'calling up' whatever it is that switches on the electricity, damn and blast the bloody thing. Thirdly, no sooner had the writer transferred this article to the Adler which is kept for use in emergencies, than the elastic band thing which swings back the carriage snapped, rendering it inoperable. Fourthly, the point on the writer's pencil stub is worn down and he cannot find his pencil-sharpener. Normal service will be resumed as soon as possible.

THE POPE AND I

H. F. Ellis

Every time the Pope comes out on his balcony and gives his *urbi et orbi* blessing I am reminded of the time when that included me. It was the year of the Comet—the year the epoch-making, ill-fated Comet 1 came into service—and one of these beautiful machines, on a crew-training flight to Entebbe or some such place, kindly dropped me off in Rome. So I walked across the Tiber to see St Peter's, that being a must in any guidebook. A number of other people seemed to be taking the same route, and it suddenly came over me as I shuffled along the Via della Conciliazone that this was no polytechnic tour I had got myself involved with but pretty well the whole of Rome intent on a blessing. In short, it was Easter Sunday: a point that the excitement of flying at five hundred miles an hour had temporarily put out of my mind.

It was ten years and a month before I was in Rome again. Easter being well past and the day being in any case a Wednesday, it occurred to me to have another go at St Peter's. I wanted a closer look than is possible when half a million Italians, clapping and crying out 'Papa! Papa!', stand between oneself and Maderno's noble façade. I wanted to see the portico, described as 'splendid and sumptuous', and of course the interior, of which my guidebook remarked (a little ambiguously) 'The sense of a gigantic mass impresses the visitor.' The details of the basilica, I had also read, 'form a whole of insuperable beauty'; and that was something I certainly did not intend to miss.

I got in all right, and was at once impressed by the sense of a gigantic mass. All those Italians who, ten years ago, had filled the Piazza so near to bursting point that Bernini's splendid, and indeed sumptuous, colonnade appeared to be in danger of collapse were now inside the basilica. There was clapping and cries of 'Papa! Papa!' and there, borne aloft amidst the throng on his *sedia*, was the Pope again. Not the same Pope, because by this time John XXIII had succeeded Pius XII, but the Pope: enthroned, huzza'd, including me once more, I liked to think, among his freely bestowed blessings. The details that I had come to see were again obscured, not merely by the population of Italy but, at a higher level, by vast tiers of seats on scaffolding. But what of that? I came away, after this second visit, with the strong conviction that any time I cared to look in at St Peter's, there the Pope would be to greet me.

Coming now to the Archbishop of Canterbury, I have to ask myself how often I have found myself in *his* presence, and the answer that I get is a surprisingly nil return. I hardly know what to make of this. I have been to Canterbury Cathedral; I have mooched about among the tombs in Westminster Abbey; often and often I have stood beneath the cupola of St Paul's—more often anyway than I have stood beneath that of St Peter's—and never a glimpse. Never a blessing, never a gentle rotation of the raised hands in my direction, not a chance for me to cry 'Cantuar! Cantuar!' Where has he *been*? Kindly men in black gowns with whorls on their façades have spoken to me about Thomas à Becket and led me to the shrine of Edward the Confessor, but it is not the same. If I can have summit meetings at will in Rome, why am I denied similar courtesies in my own capital and in my own church?

So I picked the wrong day for my visits here at home? Very well, then, which was the right day? Certainly there are well-advertised occasions on which the Archbishop is billed to appear in all his glory at this cathedral or at that. I have seen him there, on TV, I have also seen the congregations and noted the unlikelihood of there being a place for me. The seats are numbered. Admirals are there, and ministers, and earls, and enough ranking clergy to make a show; rich men furnished with ability, and a sprinkling of such as have found out musical tunes or recited verses in writing—though these are mostly in Poets' Corner, taking small room. I should think that nine times out of ten, when the Archbishop turns round from the altar, he knows his whole congregation by name and only pauses to wonder where the President of the Board of Trade has got to and why the Master-General of the Ordnance has moved up one place at the expense of the Queen's Proctor. Small chance for a stray visitor to get himself included in an *urbi et orbi* at one of those affairs.

Am I then to hang about outside with the multitude until the Archbishop makes his appearance on the Golden Gallery above the dome and wafts me his benevolence? That would be a vigil.

To every Church its own ethos, its code, its protocol. It would never do to have the head of the Church of England borne aloft through applauding crowds of other ranks on a kind of open sedan chair, making himself beloved, scattering blessings abroad like confetti. I quite see that. No devoted Protestants need come clamouring round my doors with 'No Popery!' cries. I am no more attuned to clapping in church than they are; even an unintentional sneeze brings an automatic tightening of my thoroughly unRoman lips. All the same, the statistics are as stated:

	Visits to Capital	*Seen*	*Blessed*
Pope	2	2	2
Archbishop	30 years	nil	nil

I don't, as I said before, know what to make of this.

'Anyway, it's "fresh woods and pastures new."'

SEX À LA CARTE

Fay Maschler

On television the other night there was a programme about maleness and femaleness. It kicked off with a film about a family on an island in the Caribbean where two or three of the children, having started off life as girls, at puberty, much to the pride and joy of their parents, turned into boys. Though it was perfectly obvious (details were *generously* displayed) that they had changed sex, the doctor interviewing the mother asked questions like 'And what did the latterday boys play with when they were little?'

Having elicited the answer 'dolls', he seemed satisfied that here was the incontrovertible truth that these kids had indeed begun life as girls. He was also gratified to discover that they had not baulked at washing clothes or fetching water. Later on in the programme, an Englishwoman who apparently has testicles (somewhere) was shown doing the washing-up. This was another piece of scientific evidence that she was in fact living her life as a woman.

Speculation as to where our gender stems from led to the question of whether there is a difference in male and female brains. Experiments in America on rats, and in Germany even more indefensible tests on some, understandably, depressed-looking homosexual man, seemed to prove that there might be something in it. Slides were shown with the section of male brain looking complicated and dense, like a mass of vermicelli, and the female brain less elaborately entwined, more like linguine. None of the experiments, which included dressing boy babies up in pink frilly dresses and handing them to goofy strangers who had to choose a toy with which to amuse him be it squeaking rubber hammer or cuddly dolly (guess which one the pseudo girl was handed? 'She' bawled, of course, having just been plonked on the lap of a stranger, but proved to the tester, I suppose, that 'her' boyish brain was offended), concerned themselves with preferences for food.

I felt there were two ways I could help these eminent doctors. One was to remind them of the truth that every child in my old school knew: that if you touch your elbows behind your back you will change sex. The other was to study the eating habits of men and women and then in the case of confusion between the two, a simple menu test could help decide which sex the doubtful case might be encouraged to choose.

Waiters will tell you that women like things wrapped in pancakes. Perhaps it reminds them of their mothering role. Perhaps it is because, as a dish, it is soft and yielding and pale skinned, like themselves, they think. Anyway, men do not go for chicken in bechamel sauce enclosed in a pancake. On the whole they don't go for chicken at all. This guideline has become unreliable since chickens nowadays taste so dreary that no one in their right mind orders chicken in a restaurant. So, it is a more useful test of faculties than gender.

Women eat more fish. A TWA airline steward, who had to load his plane with the various main course dishes that were offered to all passengers, but couldn't take on board enough of each item to supply everyone, told me that, consulting the passenger list, he was usually able to get the balance right. Certain names were obviously not going to choose pork, men would have steak, Fridays and women would up the numbers for fish.

Men do like eating steak and an ethologist would no doubt say that this was due to their repressed hunting instincts. By the same token they go for game, the rarer the better, and for raw meat as in steak tartare. Steak tartare also involves a dialogue with the waiter who must hover in attendance, adding a little more Tabasco, weeding out an over-abundance of capers, grinding on more grinds of the pepper mill, proffering a little taste of the mixture and then going back to mash in maybe another anchovy. It reminds the man of how his mother used to wait on him and stand aside watching his reaction to the first mouthful and be fulfilled or cast down accordingly.

Of course, men like anything their mothers used to make and this usually includes things like Eccles cakes and matzoh balls that no one else will ever get quite right. Despite the fact that a man on a permanent diet will be infuriated if offered fattening meals, he will eat his Mum's suet stodge and reproachfully let it be known that no one else ever bothers to make it for him. Women are not similarly hung-up on the food of their past. On the contrary, for that reason they might avoid obvious English cooking or items reminiscent of school dinners. Women, though, also like to be seen to be on a diet and restaurateurs, realising this, have developed some ghastly dishes they know the would-be-thin women will order. They are mostly composed of cottage cheese, lettuce leaves, radishes and tinned pineapple. They often are garnished with one Maraschino cherry.

Afterwards these same canny restaurateurs will make sure there are plenty of creamy pastries on hand, for the women, having slimmed for most of the lunch, will reward themselves with a *mille feuille* or two. Men are not attracted to gâteaux or patisserie, but they do like a pudding or a sweet. Steamed puddings are always welcome, but best of all is home-made custard. I recently offered a man some *Iles Flottantes*, which has a base of custard. He loved it. He ate all that was there and finally simply sank his face into the bowl to get at the edges. Men like chocolate mousse, but according to Francis Crick a liking for chocolate is genetic. It is hardly necessary for survival yet everyone appreciates it and wants it. You don't have to trick children into eating their chocolate.

Vegetables are a less clear-cut test of sexual standing. I think men are a bit wary of peas and rarely order cauliflower. They are inordinately pleased to be offered broad beans which women don't seem to like or want to cook. They like asparagus but the obvious phallic explanation was upset for me by some wife at one of my dinners who protectively announced that her husband would not bother with the first course of leeks vinaigrette. Had I seen the *Horizon* programme at that point I would have known him to be in possession of a female brain. Instead I was indignant.

WITH THIS PINT, I THEE WED

Michael Parkinson

The first thing to understand about north country weddings is that they are the same as north country funerals, the only difference being that at a funeral only one person is being buried. That apart, the cars are the same, they use the same church hall for the 'do', they hire the same teapot, and the same women who laid Grandad to rest are the ones who made the wedding cake. Sometimes you hear the same dialogue.

When Grandad died, we all went back to his house where Auntie Ada said to my old man:

'Has tha' found his bank book then?' Father nodded.

'How much did he leave then?' she asked eagerly.

'Threepence ha'penny and six Craven A,' said my old man.

'Pity you don't smoke,' he added.

It was the same cast of characters in the same room eighteen months later when our Jessie got married. We were having a few after the wedding when Auntie Ada asked Jessie:

'Has tha' seen his bank book then?'

Jessie looked at her for a moment, then said:

'He doesn't believe in banks, he keeps it buried in a steel box in t'allotment.'

I don't know if Auntie Ada believed her or not, although I have a cousin who swears he once saw her heading for the allotment carrying a shovel.

I don't much go for weddings of any kind, but if it were obligatory that everyone went to at least one a year then I would want it to be a north country wedding. North country weddings, at least the sort I went to, do not entail a visit to Moss Bros nor polite chit-chat over the top of a champagne glass. They are occasions on which one gets roaring daft drunk on whatever you fancy (excepting champagne).

When I got married we accommodated overnight fifty people in a three-bedroomed council house. This miracle of hospitality was achieved by letting people lay where they fell. The position was eased by the fact that some chose to sleep in the garden! Next morning the lawn looked like a field in Flanders after a dawn attack.

On the question of dress, the convention was that everyone should look as smart as possible, but no one raises an eyebrow at the odd eccentricity. For instance, one uncle of mine attended my wedding wearing his best suit, white shirt and silk scarf knotted round his neck—the scarf he wore when he went whippet racing. It wasn't that he didn't own a tie, he just wanted me to know that he liked me as much as he liked his whippets. And I still have a photograph of the wedding which shows my Auntie Florrie looking a million dollars in a smart dress, big hat and posh gloves. The effect is somewhat spoiled if you look at her feet, which are encased in a large and battered pair of carpet slippers.

I became an expert on north country weddings soon after I left school and started work as a reporter on a local newspaper. Like most local newspapers, it based its circulation effort on the amount of wedding reports, funeral details and beetle drive winners it could carry in any one issue. It was during this period that I first became aware of the aforementioned similarity between north country funerals and marriages. For one thing, when I called at a house which was going to have either a wedding or a funeral, there was always the same ritual to go through. The wedding dialogue would go:

'Come in, love. Would you like to see the wedding dress?' And you'd be led into the best room where they kept the piano and never lit the fire, to inspect a wedding dress knitted by some mad aunt in Barnsley.

'Lovely,' you'd say, and they'd thank you for your kindness and give you a tot of rum. If, on the other hand, it was a funeral they were expecting, you would again be shown into the best room, where the deceased would be laid out by the local Co-op with a frill round his face. You would be invited to inspect the undertaker's art by peering at the dead face, as smooth and unlined as a balloon.

'He does look peaceful,' you'd say, and they'd thank you for your kindness and give you a tot of rum.

Simple though it may seem, there were hazards to this kind of reporting, particularly at Easter and Christmas time. These were the periods when most people got married, and when my working day was one long round of inspecting wedding dresses and collecting reports. In those days, being just a raw sprog reporter and having seen too many American movies, I fancied myself strongly as Humphrey Bogart. The fact that I was sixteen years old, didn't smoke or drink and spent my time cycling round my area on a drop-handled Raleigh in no way dissuaded me from my fantasy. I even went to the extent of buying myself a snap brim trilby such as Bogart wore. The difficulties of keeping a trilby on my head while travelling downhill at 30 m.p.h. with a following wind need no explaining, and I overcame them by attaching an elastic chinstrap to my hat, thus inventing a new fashion in headwear.

This particular Easter, celebrated by my new bonnet, I called on twelve people and collected my wedding reports. At each house I accepted a drink because I thought Bogy would not have refused. The consequence was that I became drunk for the first time in my life, went to sleep in a bus shelter near Barnsley, and when I awoke was minus my trilby and my bike. The end of this saga of misfortune came at the end of the week when, scanning the paper for signs of my handiwork, I came across this line in one of my reports:

'As a wedding gift the bride presented the bridegroom with an electric cock.'

Like I said, north country weddings are different.